GLOBALISATION, EDUCATION AND CULTURE SHOCK

Monitoring Change in Education

Series Editor:
Cedric Cullingford
University of Huddersfield, UK

Change is a key characteristic of the worlds of business, education and industry and the rapidity of change underlines an urgent need to analyze, evaluate and, where appropriate, correct its direction. The series is aimed at contributing to this analysis. Its unique contribution consists of making sense of changes in education and in offering a timely and considered response to new challenges; the series, therefore, focuses on contemporary issues and does so with academic rigour.

Other titles in the series

Risk, Education and Culture
Edited by
Andrew Hope and Paul Oliver
ISBN 0 7546 4172 4

Literacy and Schooling
Towards Renewal in Primary Education Policy
Kathy Hall
ISBN 0 7546 4179 1

Race and Ethnicity in Education
Ranjit Arora
ISBN 0 7546 1441 7

Globalisation, Education and Culture Shock

Edited by

CEDRIC CULLINGFORD AND STAN GUNN
University of Huddersfield, UK

ASHGATE

Published by
Ashgate Publishing Limited
Gower House
Croft Road
Aldershot
Hants GU11 3HR
England

Ashgate Publishing Company
Suite 420
101 Cherry Street
Burlington, VT 05401-4405
USA

Ashgate website: http://www.ashgate.com

British Library Cataloguing in Publication Data
Globalisation, education and culture shock. - (Monitoring
    change in education)
    1. Multicultural education 2. Culture shock 3. Globalization -
    Social aspects
    I. Cullingford, Cedric II. Gunn, Stan
    370.1'17

Library of Congress Cataloging-in-Publication Data
Globalisation, education and culture shock / Cedric Cullingford and Stan Gunn (eds.).
        p. cm. -- (Monitoring change in education)
    Includes bibliographical references and indexes.
    ISBN 0-7546-4201-1
    1. Education--Social aspects. 2. Education and globalization. 3. Multicultural education.
    I. Cullingford, Cedric. II. Gunn, Stan. III. Series.

LC191.G543 2004
302.43--dc22

2004046382

ISBN 0 7546 4201 1

Printed and bound by Athenaeum Press, Ltd.,
Gateshead, Tyne & Wear.

Contents

List of Figures and Tables

List of Contributors

Professor Tony Charlton and Charlie Panting are at the Centre for Behavioural Studies, University of Gloucestershire.

Professor Cedric Cullingford is at the University of Huddersfield.

Stan Gunn was at the University of Huddersfield for many years.

Dr Helen Jones is in the Department of Community and International Education at the University of Huddersfield.

Professor W. John Morgan is at the University of Nottingham.

Dale O'Neill is an ethnographer now working in market research.

Dr Paul Oliver is Principal Lecturer at the University of Huddersfield.

Dr Marion Shaw is at Oxford Brookes University.

Professor Les Tickle is at the University of East Anglia.

Dr Elwyn Thomas was at the Institute of Education, London, and is a visiting professor at the University of Singapore.

Dr Christine Twigg is at the University of Manchester in the former UMIST.

Preface

Cedric Cullingford

The phenomenon of what is usually termed globalisation is obvious, whether it is interpreted as benign or malign, or both. Examples of the international connections continue to grow, whether military invasions or the distribution of financial aid. The expansion of trade has all kinds of international implications, from the Diaspora of call centres to places like India to the scattering of cheap manufacturing. The most obvious sign of the phenomenon is in the communication of ideas and news, of awareness of other countries and images of them. That these pictures have an immediate impact on the young is made clear in chapter 3. We can never again assume the naïve innocence that depends on ignorance.

The most important aspect of globalisation, however, is also the most neglected; the impact it has on individuals. This book is not about policies or interpretations of monetary policies. There are many examples of that, including general accounts of educational policies and their homogenisation. This book is far more concerned with the way in which people react to and interpret those ideas and influences that come from elsewhere and therefore demand a fresh understanding.

It is also about the personal experience of entering into other cultures.

This raises issues that bind all the chapters together. All the authors question simplistic notions of effect, of the spread of one simple culture over others. All define "culture" as a far more complex issue and raise questions about the tendency to be complacently embedded in an unexamined set of assumptions of superiority. The book demonstrates that the reality is more varied and that it is multi-directional and not merely a matter of stimulus and response. Definitions of culture include a celebration of otherness.

Definitions that make one reconsider are difficult but necessary. The first chapter puts the overall concerns into context, including Toffler's original concept of Future Shock. This aspect of change in time is more important than ever since there are many examples of old and new ideas clashing, like the internet and a traditional religious way of life. There are also many examples of the clash between education systems geared to international skills and those deemed appropriate to the local conditions.

Chapter 2 questions the concepts involved showing the increasing sense of complexity. There is more stress laid on the erosion of assumed values than on cultural imperialism. Local communities can be transformed and strengthened in their own identity as well as being obliterated by external demands. The internationalisation of companies and agencies is not a smooth process. Both knowledge and educational systems can look like battlefields rather than a simple engagement with ideas. Some might argue that the notions are very "post-modern" but the case studies that follow demand the interrogation of any label.

The third chapter looks at the result of the globalisation of the media. They are the prime source of information on the forming of opinions of the very young; indeed on helping the young to create their own world view. Certain patterns and prejudices are inevitably formed, often with sophistication and often despite, not because of, the formal education system. One of the essential facts that children learn is of the unfairness of the world as a whole.

Chapter 4 develops the different levels of knowledge, contrasting the awareness of the local over time with illustrations of levels of awareness. Again, one is made to question the educational assumptions and implications. A sense of relativity of comparison of awareness of local context is heightened by knowledge of the whole world. Diversity and contrast supersedes homogeneity.

Chapter 5 continues the theme of questioning the spread of particular models of understanding. The evidence unpicks and questions notions of donor ship and gives examples of the crucial aspect of local ownership. Again, issues of language, context and varied perceptions are brought out in the place of simple beliefs in the spread of enlightenment.

This complexity, which underlines the juxtaposition of the local and the general, the individual in a new context, is illustrated in the following chapters. Chapter 6 explores the ways in which students learn in subtle and social ways from the experience of alternative cultures. The experience enhances self-awareness in contrast to imbibing simple and coherent new knowledge. Chapter 7 also demonstrates the overlapping of cultures in the experiences of overseas students coming to Great Britain, contrasting personal values with those of the contrasting culture. Chapter 8 explores further the perceptions of people who are faced with new cultural challenges. We discover the longing for the familiar, what has been left behind, the concerns for the universal practical awareness of how to cope and the sense of growing self-knowledge.

Chapter 9 analyses the reactions of people in a local community to a new flood of external information. Using the unique opportunity of the introduction of mass media to St. Helena, the chapter outlines the interesting and comfortingly complex and discriminating responses of the islanders, balancing awareness of international fashion with awareness of their own culture.

This awareness of the complexities of cultures is the essential starting point for chapter 10. Replacing the assumption of the superiority of western educational practice should be a greater sensitivity to cultural diversity, and this needs to be applied to teacher education in particular.

The celebration of differences and the respect for alternative modes of thought is also at the heart of chapter 11. Wisdoms both ancient and far afield can be applied to the nature of globalisation and challenge at a deeper level. The chapter demonstrates how cultural sensitivity can make us address deep issues that surround us everyday.

All the chapters therefore follow a theme that draws them together. Globalisation is a complex phenomenon and needs to be understood as well as experienced. Cultural understanding leads not just of relativism but a question of assumptions often taken for granted. The sense of "shock" is that of surprise of having understanding forced upon us painfully unless we embrace and anticipate it. The examples of the painfulness of cultural international misunderstandings are so many they make this book the more necessary.

Chapter 1

Introduction

Stan Gunn

The term globalisation is used in a variety of ways. These include the emergence of supranational institutions which threaten the powers of the nation state, the impact of economic change on a world wide scale and changes in technology and communication which impact on the culture of nation states. At a fundamental level globalisation is concerned with change. Increasingly individuals and their culture cannot be disconnected from the world in general. Changes in many cultural practices and beliefs have been induced by improved technologies and in the context of the world as a whole rather than within separate nation states that in the past enjoyed considerable autonomy. The changes created by the forces of globalisation impact on individuals and groups and can be assimilated, modified or rejected by them. The changes are not in one direction, for example from the West to the rest of the world, and they are not only concerned with the present but also the future. A clash of cultural values is inevitable where new ideas and values are introduced in some form whether it is at an organisational or institutional level or in the individual's own psyche. The changes may be induced by powerful groups who exercise control over large organisations or by individuals or groups who have some form of political power base even though they command limited resources. It is not that change is new but the extent and the speed of change which gives globalisation its distinguishing characteristics. Inevitably culture and therefore education is influenced. The processes of globalisation have produced a reconsideration of the aims of education, the content of education, the processes or methods by which it is delivered and the ways in which the outcomes are assessed.

Harrison (2002) in a political context analyses globalisation from an orthodox point of view. The process is seen to comprise of three main influences technology, global finance and the decline of the nations state's power. Technological innovation has made the transmission of information, people and goods very rapid. Global finance and the transfer of money and the trading in shares, currencies and futures can happen not only very quickly but 24 hours per day and can be instigated from anywhere in the world. The establishment of global free markets leads to improved efficiency in industry and an improvement in standards of living but the influence of national economies and governments has been undermined. Giddens (1990) pointed to the influence of globalisation on social relationships and suggested that globalisation was '....the intensification of world-wide social relationships which link distinct localities in such a way that local happenings are shaped by events, occurring miles and miles away and vice versa'. Robertson

(1992) contended that the process of globalisation is not necessarily complete in terms of producing a homogeneous world and that 'globalisation is ....best understood as indicating the problem of the form in terms of which the world becomes 'united' but by no means integrated'. Globalisation is seen by these authors as a series of long term processes which occur unevenly across the world, processes which affect and influence people's knowledge, thoughts, attitudes and actions and which also impact on the material conditions under which people live. Maguire (1999) recognises the emergence of a global economy but also points to a transnational cosmopolitan culture and international social movements which give rise to pressure for change. He along with Robertson avoids the prediction of whether this leads to homogeneity or heterogeneity within cultures. Alexander (2000) in a review of the concept of globalisation suggests that globalisation consists of two elements: global and economic independence and competitiveness and the limitless potential of informational and communications technology. He draws attention to the lack of 'acknowledgement of the human and social downside of these developments, especially for those – individuals, groups, nations, states, continents even – who will neither be beneficiaries not participants'. Held et al (2000) comment that 'there can be little doubt that one of the most directly perceived and experienced forms of globalisation is the cultural form' (p. 327). He argues that people, objects and ideas have always moved around the world and that cultures have always been modified or changed by these.

Changes in telecommunications are seen as one of the more dominant influences in the process of globalisation. It is argued (see for example, Held et al (2000) and Burbules and Torres (2000)) that there has been a qualitative and quantitative change in the intensity and scope of telecommunications in the last decades of the twentieth century and that this has produced considerable social change. Transmitting information has become cheaper and faster on a world wide scale than ever before. This has led, for example, to an increase in international business connections and an increase in the number of tourists and migrants but also and perhaps more importantly it has demanded shared language and linguistic competences. While some languages dominate in particular areas of the world e.g. the old colonial languages of English, French, Portuguese and Spanish, the dominant world language in communications is English. It has become dominant in business communications, politics, administration, academic communications, safety, technology and science and advertising. The effect of the media, in particular music, television and cinema, and tourism has been significant. Alongside the technological innovations in communications, global economic restructuring has occurred. This has led to the development of the economic integration of national economies, an international division of labour, increasing internationalization of trade and changes in labour and capital relationships and working practices. The ways in which products are produced and marketed has an effect on the culture of nation states.

It can be argued that the processes involved in globalisation are not new although Alexander (2000) in an educational context does not acknowledge this in his analysis and points to the very different contexts in which education has operated in the past. The differences between Held et al (2000) and Alexander

(2000) lie in the speed of change and the context rather than the process. Held et al (2000) propose three categories of argument about the nature and impact of globalisation: the hyperglobalisers who predict the homogenisation of the world under Western consumerism or American popular culture, transformationals who advocate the mixing of cultures to produce new cultural hybrids and those who are concerned with the impact of contemporary cultural globalisation on national communities. Held et al conclude that all three approaches are limited by the absence of a systematic framework to describe the flow of culture across and between societies, a lack of understanding of the impact of historical questions and the lack of distinction between changes in national cultural identity and values and the processes and context of their formation. It is argued that cultural globalisation is the changing context and means whereby national cultures are produced and reproduced. This occurs through the movements of objects, signs and people across regions and intercontinental space. Historically the movement of people was the most important and influential agent in cultural transmission and this was followed by the movement of objects e.g. books, written records and cultural artefacts and latterly the improvement in communications. The effects of cultural globalisation can be demonstrated through the extent, intensity and the velocity which the ideas and images can be transmitted.

To support this analysis Held et al (2000) examine in an historical context the influence of religion and empire. World religions, in particular Islam and Christianity, have been able to move from their place of origin and convert other religions and overthrow other cultures. They often achieved this by being in alliance with dominant states and political and economic elites. Christianity started to have a world wide influence with the colonial and military expansion of the European nations in the sixteenth and seventeenth centuries. This was aided by the development of writing and texts which assisted the transmission of values and ideas and the establishment of institutions and hierarchies which produced effective ways of influencing other cultures. Buddhism and Hinduism did not extend on a global scale in that they were limited to South and East Asia but they did establish similar frameworks which cut across cultural and linguistic boundaries. Give the contemporary theory whereby migration and the diffusion of values, doctrines and beliefs related to religious beliefs can be and are globally transmitted, the impact on and implications for education are significant.

In the case of empire new cultural ideas are imposed through the threat or use of force and political dominance. Held et al (2000) argue that this is a simplistic explanation which ignores the ways in which emulation and diffusion work alongside imposition. Cultural practices are often assimilated through repeated contact and adapted at a local level. These cultural practices require institutions which create, transmit, reproduce and receive cultural messages or practices which include modes of transportation as well as communication. The technologies involved in transportation and communication require social organisations. In education a minimal requirement is linguistic competence which is reflected in the establishment of colonial educational establishments but there is also the necessity of institutions to teach new competences, skills and knowledge to the indigenous population. A new form of stratification develops related to the new institutions and the technologies since these are not readily available to all. In this sense the process of globalisation is often incomplete in that not all are active participants in the process. Let us take the example of the Romans who generated and reproduced a trans-imperial ruling class which was a political community which had shared cultural values, beliefs and aesthetics and which persisted after the decline of the empire. The export and import of educational ideas and the establishment of institutions to transmit them is not new. The transmission of British ideas and cultural practices was transmitted through the development of the colonial educational systems and the content that they purveyed. These remain virtually unchanged in some of the former colonies where the children of local elites are educated in models of the English public school using English curriculum materials. These schools were and still are seen as places where the elites of tomorrow are cultivated. The control exerted by elites is one of the major criticisms of the process of globalisation as the majority of people are perceived to be passive receivers and consumers rather than critical appraisers and adaptors of that on offer and this applies not only to education but also to economic, religious and political elites. However, cultural power has also played a role in the development of empire and the ruling elites have been influenced by movements upwards rather than imposition downwards. Held et al (2000) cites the influence of the Christian church in the Roman Empire to support this point of view. Held et al (2000) go on to argue that 'Contemporary cultural globalisation is associated with several developments: global infrastructures of an unprecedented scale, generating an enormous capacity for cross-border penetration and a decline in the cost of their use; an increase in the intensity, volume and speed of cultural exchange and communication of all kinds; the rise of Western popular culture and inter business communication as the primary content of global cultural interaction; the dominance of culture multinationals in the creation and ownership of infrastuctures and organizations for the production and distribution of cultural goods; and a shift in the geography of global cultural interaction departing in some significant ways from the geography of the pre-Second World War global order.' (p. 341) Globalisation is seen as pervasive and all consuming.

The processes, concerns and fears and hopes associated with cultural change are not limited to the concept of globalisation. In the late 1960s and early 1970's futurology became an accepted academic discipline in some universities. The future and what it is possible to achieve, what will probably be achieved and what preferably will be achieved has been a constant source of speculation both in the past and present. Alvin Toffler (1970) in Future Shock put it this way:

> Every society faces not merely a succession of probable futures, but an array of possible futures, and a conflict over preferable futures. The management of change is the effort to convert certain possibles into probables, in pursuit of agreed-on preferables. Determining the probable calls for a science of futurism. Delineating the possible calls for an art of futurism. Defining the preferable calls for a politics of futurism. (p. 415).

Although the process of globalisation may not be directly determined by these in an overt way, the practice almost certainly is, even though these underlying assumptions may go untested and unchallenged. The concern for globalisation, education and culture shock is about who decides what is possible, what is probable and what is preferable. The political context cannot be ignored.

One of the defining characteristics of globalisation is the speed of change in a global context. Toffler (1970) examined the effects of the acceleration of change and what he termed 'future shock' in an American context. He referred to 'the shattering stress and disorientation that we induce in individuals by subjecting them to too much change in too short a time' (p. 12) and the lack of knowledge about 'adaptivity either by those who call for and create vast changes in society, or by those who supposedly prepare us to cope with those changes' (p. 12). The purpose of his text was to help people and American society in particular to cope more effectively with change and to increase the understanding of how man responds to it. A distinction is drawn between the rate of change and the direction of change. The rate of change is seen to be as important, and more important in some cases, than the direction of change. The more rapid the change the more disorienting it is for the individual. Allied to the idea of 'future shock' is the concept of 'culture shock'. 'Culture shock is the effect that the emersion in a strange culture has on the unprepared visitor...It is what happens when the familiar psychological cues that help an individual to function in society are suddenly withdrawn and replaced by new ones that are strange and incomprehensible' (p. 19). Culture shock for Toffler (1970) has two facets. It is not only the imposition of a new culture on an old one but also the shock experienced by the individual when placed in an unfamiliar culture when the original culture of the individual is no longer there and causes a breakdown in communication, a misreading of reality and an inability to cope. It is arguable that Toffler (1970) exaggerated the problems created by rapid change but nevertheless many of the processes he describes are pertinent and applicable to the effects of the process of globalisation and adaptation to change and their implications for education in a world wide context.

Toffler (1970) saw education as one of the means of ameliorating the problems created by future shock. Education can be considered to be the transmission of the values and accumulated knowledge of society. As societies become more and more complex, the nature of education and the means of transmission become more and more institutionalised and less related to daily life. Learning in formally established institutions allows the learner to learn far more about their culture than they are able to do through observation and imitation. As complexity within and between cultures increases and knowledge expands, the greater the importance placed on education by society. This is accompanied by a desire by society to exert greater control on education through the formulation of the overall aims and objectives of education, the content to be transmitted, the organisation and strategies involved in this transmission and the ways in which all these are seen to be accountable. This description of the nature of education is based on that given by the Encyclopaedia Britannica (2003). It depicts a series of stages through which the form of education changes and responsibility for education passes more and more from the parents, to the community, to the state. With increasing wealth there is increasing expenditure on education but also increasing accountability. This can be seen as a transient model since if wealth becomes global and there is ample expenditure on education for all, will education take on a less 'economic' based approach and a more 'liberal' form? The Britannica based definition describes the process involved in the development of educational systems but it fails to show the importance of whose or what values and content are transmitted. The United Nations in 1997 defined education as being '...fundamental to enhancing the quality of human life and ensuring social and economic progress' (United Nations, 1997). This definition equally emphasises the process, albeit stressing the quality of life for people, but ignores the challenge of whether there are, could be or should be a common set of values, ideas, attitudes and opinions which are transmitted or whether education is designed to produce cultural diversity or a mixture of the two. Both the Britannica and United Nations descriptions of the process of education allude to economic criteria. While it is acknowledged that economic wealth and the surplus it can create fund education, there is an implicit assumption that it is the economic system that drives the educational system without recognition of the values and methods of the economic system itself. Education in its 'primitive' sense, that is that provided by the family and community on an almost chance basis, is seen to have 'lesser' values than those expressed explicitly and implicitly by a sophisticated 'economic' based education system. Avis (1997) in a discussion of contemporary Post-Compulsory Education in Great Britain makes a similar point when he says '... a common sense surrounding the nature of the economy and education, resulting in the construction of a framework that we can all buy into, a set of ideas taken for granted unproblematically' (Avis, 1997). There is an implicit view that if economic success i.e. wealth is achieved then a social and educational utopia will be achieved automatically.

Earlier Toffler (1970) saw education in the United States in the following way, '... the whole idea of assembling masses of students (raw materials) to be processed by teachers (workers) in a centrally located school (factory) was a stroke of industrial genius. The whole administrative hierarchy of education, as it grew up, followed the model of industrial bureaucracy. The very organisation of knowledge into permanent disciplines was grounded on industrial assumptions.' Further on he comments 'The most criticised features of education today – the regimentation, lack of individualisation, the rigid systems of seating, grouping, grading and marking, the authoritarian role of the teacher – are precisely those that made mass public education so effective an instrument of adaptation for its place and time.' He sees the emphasis on education for industry and economic survival and the industrial models of managing schools, teachers and learning as creating the conditions which give rise to the pernicious aspects of future shock and failing to give the receivers of education in this form a means of avoiding it.

Many of the characteristics of educational practice outlined by Toffler are still present in educational thought and practice today along with some of the anticipated outcomes. His responses to the predicted rapidly changing society and technology change emphasise the need for education to produce people 'who can make critical judgements, who can weave their way through novel environments, who are quick to spot new relationships in the rapidly changing reality ...(and who) can adapt to continual change' (p. 364). The form of schooling would change for an increasing number of children of highly educated parents as the use of computer aided learning would enable the children of these parents to spend less time in the classroom and more time in the home. Schools would provide tuition in areas which students could not learn on their own or in the home. He forecasts lifelong learning and questions the administration of an education system which is based on industrial models of bureaucracy. He sees the need for a unifying system of skills but skills which require the student to learn to manipulate data rather than just retain it and learn how to learn. The curriculum would support this in terms of its diversity and creative view of content and would not be presented as if it were value free. Diversity in the curriculum is seen as insurance against our inability to predict the future in much the same way as genetic diversity ensures the preservation of the species. This model however is not without its dangers if there is a lack of balance between standardization and variety in the curriculum. Toffler points out that an extremely wide range of choice can lead to the individual losing a clear grasp of their own values. Too much choice in the educational market place can produce problems for the individual and society in general.

> Diversity carried to its extreme could produce a non-society in which the lack of common frames of reference would make communication between people even more difficult that it is today. (p. 372)

Perhaps most significantly of all is his emphasis on the 'human' aspects of education and in particular how to relate to others and to make and maintain human ties and the need for students to analyse their own values and the values of their teachers and peers. Toffler here is referring to the problems of human relationships created by rapid change within a culture and the same prediction can be made in the case of globalisation and culture clash.

One of the problems associated with the impact of cultural globalisation is actually determining what a particular culture consists of. What is for example, English, British, Western European, American culture? Within titles such as these there exist profound cultural differences in terms of gender, race, religion, region and class. There are some similarities to the problems of defining social class. While class can be defined in terms of a single variable, for example income or the relationship to the means of production, in more general usage it is refers to a whole range of attributes. It has many dimensions and it can be argued that it is the unique mix and interaction of these dimensions which determines a particular class. A similar problem is experienced in psychology in the study of personality and the ideographic/nomothetic distinction which draws attention to the generality of traits and their interaction to produce the unique individual. The same argument can be applied to the term culture which could be defined in terms of specific dimensions and also the aggregate and interaction of many dimensions. In global terms some of the dimensions in education which have been cited include the corporate takeover of education i.e. the influence of multinationals and a business approach in terms of the market and management practices, the cultivation of marketable skills and competencies i.e. the pupil who can confidently enter the labour market and succeed in a career and defining particular approaches to teaching and learning (see for example, Burbules and Torres 2000). Within many of these areas a single dimension has been measured or imposed with little regard to the impact on the individual or the local culture. Where a culture is influenced or changed by an innovation the problem arises in determining which dimensions are affected and what are the interaction effects. This is further complicated by changes and distortions over time. Thus when an innovation or change is instigated it is not only the initial impact which is of interest but also the ways in which the original ideas modify or are modified by the culture into which they are absorbed.

With the putative trend towards the diminution of the power of the nation state and the view that there is a global education system emerging, questions arise about the nature of the transfer of educational practices and models between nation states and different cultures. Alexander (2000) examines the issues of the transfer of the findings from comparative education studies by asking the question whether there can be a direct transfer of the models and practices used in education between countries and what are the rules for doing this in a systematic way. The comparing, importing and exporting of ideas is intrinsic to educational development and factors outside the educational system are as important, if not more so, than those within the schools. The culture and the political context which surrounds the system cannot be ignored if the evaluation of national systems in an international context is used as a guide for educational policy. There is a search for models and practices that can be used in a global sense and be seen to be useful in determining policy. The policy makers require a simple relationship between the policy and its effect. Even if fundamental practices and theories are developed, their application in a simplistic way, without any recognition of the cultural context and the interactions within this, will not guarantee change in the desired direction. The modifications of, or the ways in which the fundamental practices and theories are changed when they are applied in differing cultural contexts, are important not only in giving indications of what may or may not be appropriate policies and strategies in a particular cultural context but they can also serve to indicate a diversity of approaches to similar problems. Although Toffler was writing some 30 years ago his analysis still has relevance to the global context of today, in particular his emphasis on diversity in education, an understanding of the values and ideals held by others and an awareness by innovators and policy makers of the possible, probable and preferable when confronted with an uncertain future and a need for change.

References

Alexander, R. (2000), *Culture and Pedagogy*, Malden M.A, Blackwell.

Avis, J. (1997), 'Globalisation, the Learner and Post-Compulsory Education: Policy Fictions'. Research in Post-Compulsory Education, vol. 2(3).

Burbules, N. and Torres, C. (2000), *Globalisation and Education: Critical Perspectives*, London, Routledge.

Giddens, A. (1990), *The Consequences of Modernity*, Cambridge, Polity Press.

Harrison, A. (2002), 'Globalisation' in G. Blakeley and V. Bryson (eds), *Contemporary Political Concepts*, London, Pluto Press.

Held, D., McGrew, A., Goldblatt, D. and Perraton, J. (1999), *Global Transformations*, Cambridge, Polity.

Maguire, J. (1999), *Global Sport*, Cambridge, Polity Press.

Robertson, R. (1992), *Globalisation and Social Theory and Global Culture*, London, Sage.

Toffler, A. (1970), *Future Shock*, London, Pan.

Chapter 2

The Concepts of Globalisation and Culture

Paul Oliver

Discourse involving globalisation has become so pervasive in postmodern society that it easy to think of it as a disembodied process, somehow independent of the rapidly-developing society in which it evolved. To reify globalisation in this manner is to disengage it from the social processes which gave rise to the complex economic and cultural interactions which we see in contemporary life. For globalisation arose from within that particular mode of cultural organization which succeeded modernity. Moreover, the complex exchanges which are the distinctive feature of globalisation have generated new cultural variants, and continue to influence the development of cultures on a transnational basis. An important element of the thesis of this chapter is that it is less a case of globalisation influencing culture, or of cultural forms initiating innovative types of global interaction; but rather that globalisation and culture are in a symbiotic relationship. They are key elements in a dynamic equilibrium of societal transformation.

The transmisson of cultural forms across time and space is not a new phenomenon. The migration of peoples, political and economic hegemonies, and the impact of key individual thinkers, have all at times influenced the dissemination of culture. But this cultural dispersion has often been slow, and been limited by geographical and political boundaries. The significance of globalisation is that it has enabled cultural transmission to take place on a scale which would not be conceivable without contemporary technological infrastructures. The sheer extent of such cultural dispersion has encouraged the view of globalized culture not exclusively as idea or concept, but as commodity. The diversity of cultural modalities and forms are entities now to be traded in economic exchange, rather than to be considered cognitively or as a reflection upon the nature of existence.

The economization of culture has resulted in a form of cultural imperialism, less imposed by political power, but permeated and reinforced by economic power (see Friedman, 1995). The global marketing of artefacts is not simply an economic enterprise designed to maximize profit but, most importantly, a means of disseminating and reinforcing the cultural influence of an economic power. The products of a culture do not have an existence independent of that culture. They derive from that culture, and have the effect of sustaining the milieu from which they evolved. Even when cultural products are selected from other societies through the patronage of an economic power, the almost inevitable concomitant is that they come to mirror the values of the society which is supporting them.

Cultural dissemination is rarely neutral. Cultural products reflect the value systems inherent in the originating culture, and in the contemporary world such values are typically a variant of capitalist values. When a cultural artefact is conveyed from a donor culture to a recipient culture, then it is not a neutral transaction, but rather a statement is being made about the relative worth of the recipient and the donor culture. In accepting the artefact, the recipient is acknowledging something of the values of the donor. In purchasing the product, the recipient is helping to support the economic system of the donor. Whether the recipient culture is enriched through this process is a matter for debate, and different parties to the arrangement may hold divergent views.

The purpose of the dissemination of mass culture in a globalized society is at least partly to reinforce the prevailing economic system, but also partly to ensure the creation of a form of cultural dependence. Without such a dependence, there will be no impetus for globalisation to be sustained. It is here that can be viewed part of the shifting equilibrium which characterizes the global relationship. The acceptance by a recipient culture of the values of a donor culture helps to generate a form of commodity need in the recipient. This commodity need then fuels and supports an even greater level of global interaction. Culture, economic forces, and globalisation are connected in an ever-changing web of interaction.

The commodification of culture is seen at its most potent in the influence of the mass electronic media. When one accesses forms of electronic media one is subject to the particular cultural forms which are being perpetuated by that system. It is difficult to dissociate an analysis of the functioning of international media from that of the corporations of capitalism which support them. Media are not only an essential means of the marketing and distribution of cultural forms, but constitute *a fortiori* a mechanism for cultural production. The constituent elements of cultural forms are distributed electronically, and within the global marketplace are restructured into those forms which are viewed as of significance within the recipient society. A particular cultural commodity may become embedded in one society in one continent, while the same form may be rejected as irrelevant in another society. There may be no reliable means of predicting the extent to which a cultural product may be accepted or rejected. It is to this extent that we view the rather uncertain relationship between globalisation, capitalism, the media and culture. It is perhaps tempting to view the process of cultural dissemination as a linear, uni-directional process, whereby a particular facet of culture is distributed to a pre-determined and identified market, with the inexorable certainty that it will be accepted. In fact, the process may be far more complex. While linear cultural hegemony is a significant factor in global capitalism, there is also a much more amorphous process operating. Within this less-clearly delineated interaction, cultures are continually influencing each other in an unpredictable network of relationships. Nor does it necessarily follow that the cultural influence operates from the technologically-sophisticated countries to the less-developed world. Music and cinema are two art forms where there are significant flows of cultural products in the other direction. It would thus be over-simplistic to view globalisation as engendering a flow of homogeneous western culture to mass markets eager for the products of a technological society. The process is more sophisticated, and there are aspects of the process which may be less to the detriment of the developing world. Globalisation has thus, to some extent, encouraged a degree of cultural hybridity which would have been difficult to achieve without electronic communication.

It may be argued that one of the logical consequences of globalisation is the creation of a homogenous world culture, sustained by the dissemination of powerful images which cross the boundaries of existing cultures. While this may be a distinct trend, particularly in the spheres of consumer brands, cinema, music and television, the process depends for its success on both the ability and willingness of a host society to absorb the cultural products of another. This is far from being a certain process, and one might equally adopt the proposition that globalisation encourages a heterogenous mosaic of cultures, separate from each other in time and distance (see Beck, 2000). On such a cultural fragmentation model, individual cultures are selective in the forms which they absorb through the process of globalisation, and maintain their cultural individuality. Globalized cultural change may therefore not be seen as an inexorable process by which cultures are transformed by economic influence, but an interaction between globalisation and culture whereby globalisation itself is constrained and adapted by culture.

One alleged feature of the postmodern is the lessening significance of the sweeping, paradigmatic explanations of society known as metanarratives (see Lyotard, 1984). Such explanations and models were a significant feature of medieval and modern society. In a postmodern, globalized world, there does not appear to be the equivalent of Christianity or Marxism, in terms of a widely-accepted, interpretive framework. Such metanarratives appear to have been replaced by a proliferation of models and explanations which in some cases compete with each other, and in other cases coexist reasonably amicably. One might argue that capitalism itself comes closest to being a metanarrative, and indeed directly or indirectly appears to support a great deal of globalized activity.

At the other end of the continuum from metanarratives, globalisation has enabled minorities to communicate their ideas and ideals to audiences which could not previously have been contemplated. To that extent globalisation has sustained a diversity of culture and of ideas. Political groups, leisure groups and religious groups are all enabled and empowered to perpetuate their philosophies via the new electronic media. This has in many ways resulted in a democratization and relativization of knowledge. When so many diverse organizations can gain access to electronic communication via the internet, then it becomes difficult to attribute significantly more authority to one group than another. Power of all types is much more evenly dispersed. In epistemological terms it is also much more difficult to formulate comparisons in terms of the hypothesized validity of knowledge. It is difficult to argue that one organization, when compared with another, has unique epistemological insights. There is hence a tendency to a levelling-down of knowledge, and an assumption that varied truth claims are different but equal. In a relativized and globalized world, everyone is an expert at the same time. Knowledge belongs to everyone simultaneously. Although it remains true that economic power, and particularly the power which accompanies the means of communication, is arguably the most significant factor in a globalized world, nevertheless the democratization of knowledge enables small groups of world citizens to formulate challenges to that authority, and to hold it accountable. In a global environment, where everyone can communicate with everyone else, it requires only a dedicated and electronically-vociferous few, to mount a challenge to economic hegemonies. In this way, the global process is again subject to localized cultural forces.

A particularly interesting exemplar of this is the inception and influence of new social movements, which seek to address issues which are somewhat different from the traditional polarities of protest. Such movements are initially localized but through the possibilities of global technology are able to unify their actions and achieve an impact apparently out of proportion to their original size as an organization. They are typically concerned with issues which appear to influence the quality of life of individuals, such as the impact of environmental degeneration. Globalisation has enabled localized, direct action groups to at least engage with political issues on a world scale, even if their influence has been arguably marginal.

One of the important features of globalisation is that it has enabled localized social actors to be aware of events on a larger scale (see Tomlinson, 1999). Not only has it enabled them to be aware of events, but also to be conscious of the implications of those events for distant places and societies. The global society is seen as one in which risk has an inevitable presence. Local communities have become aware of the consequences for them of environmental disasters many miles away. Environmental degradation is no longer perceived as a phenomenon which may exist and influence events on an exclusively local scale. The inter-relationships within the global society are now seen as pre-eminently important, and local cultures recognize the impact which global risks may potentially hold for them. At a local level cultures may no longer be willing to accept the adverse influences of other societies and via global communications may make their claims for fairness and justice heard.

The localization of culture is important in the manner in which the meanings of cultural artefacts are interpreted. A cultural artefact may have one particular meaning in one culture while having a very different significance in a different culture. The process of signification indicates the manner in which a particular cultural artefact, acting as a single signifier, can result in a wide range of different meanings. That which is signified will depend very much upon the significance attributed by culture. Globally-transmitted products are very often important signifiers, whether they are fashion products, music products, or marketable individuals such as sports stars. Blue jeans, commencing as a signifier of simple, straightforward work, were transformed through a process of signification into a desirable fashion product. Even then, through global marketing they continued to embrace multiple meanings. For example, when marketed as an important element of the open-air lifestyle associated with the American West, they connoted ideas of freedom, individuality, and a rugged outdoor life. On the other hand they have been marketed in the context of a sophisticated urban lifestyle. Such meanings, and their associated variants, are amply represented in global marketing, yet an almost inevitable concomitant is that they are beyond the economic resources of many of those who are reached by the globalized message. But fashion garments as globally-marketed products have other connotations, usually involving a representation of the economically-developed West, and the capacity of individuals to pay relatively large amounts of money for expensive casual dress. It is difficult to imagine what must be signified in cultures where individuals have the greatest difficulty in affording the rudiments of clothes.

The process of signification however, highlights the manner in which the signifier is interpreted according to the cultural norms of an individual society. The meanings which are attached to newly generated global signifiers contribute to the development of culture. Through a process of cultural materialism, meanings are attached to cultural artefacts, and absorbed into a new culture, albeit being adapted in the process. Cultural materialism, as a concept, emphasises the process by which cultures are continually produced. Indeed, it is arguably a feature of a globalized society that cultures change more rapidly than during periods where there was less interaction between societies. Cultures can no longer insulate themselves against the influences of signifiers which, in a globalized environment, are ever-present and ever-influential.

The impact of global signifiers is one of the major influences upon the life of the individual social actor within contemporary social structures. There exists an important dialectic between the structures of contemporary global society and the individual social actor, as exemplified in structuration theory (see Giddens, 1984). Social structure places inevitable limitations upon the actions of the individual agent, which may be political, economic or social. Nevertheless, the individual actor retains considerable freedom of action, depending at least partly upon the culture and social context, and in so doing is able to exert some influence upon the societal structures. Large multinational companies may migrate productive activities around the global environment, in order to maximize economic returns. Such activities reduce labour opportunities in one country and enhance them in another. Such global capitalist ventures impose limitations upon industrial labour and hence upon the individual agent, but nevertheless, other individuals may influence such a system. The very communication of a global system, which enable the movement of production across the planet, also enable consumers on another continent to be aware of the working conditions of those manufacturing the goods which they purchase. Campaigns to highlight any undesirable practices in such working conditions may result in not only adverse publicity for the multinational companies concerned, but also in the individual agent withdrawing purchasing power from that product. Globalisation may thus be viewed as a complex interplay of social forces, engaging structure and social actors in a dynamic dialectic. While at times the system of global capitalism may appear to be able to employ the characteristics of globalisation for its own benefits, the distribution of power and influence is perhaps more diffuse within the global environment than may at first appear to be the case. The communicative networks of globalisation can enable the individual to exert an influence and to a degree, a system of checks and balances, over the apparently formidable social and economic forces at work.

Such developments have taken place within the broad parameters of the dissipation of capital within global society. Transnational companies have been able to move capital to locations from which a more beneficial economic return could be generated. Perhaps ironically, as capital has been transferred from the developed world, in which the large transnational company often had its origin, enormous changes have taken place in the distribution of work patterns and social culture. As manufacturing jobs pursued the transferred capital, the developed world tended largely to retain employment in those sectors which provided the support and infrastructure for manufacturing, rather than the productivity itself. The globalisation of labour and of manufacturing has resulted in dramatic social change in the West. Towns which relied during the period of modernity on heavy manufacturing industry, or on mining, have completely changed in character, being dependent now on finance, information technology and retail and distributive occupations. With this transformation in economic character has come a change in social structure and in culture. Communities with a strong sense of social solidarity, dependent for their livelihoods on a single manufacturing industry, have been replaced by a society with a much reduced sense of cohesion, yet at the same time, more outward-looking and aware of global potentialities and threats. Culture, in terms of social patterns, and of values and norms, is influenced to a not inconsiderable extent by the patterns of employment in that society. Both the developed and the less well developed countries of the world are progressing through an employment revolution, which is fuelled by the rapid flow of global capital, and by a range of marketing potential which is difficult to anticipate, and difficult to address. The movement of capital and the transformation of industrial development are both significant variables in the fluidity of culture around the world.

It is a feature of postmodern society that the centralization of capital is often disengaged from the location of mass production. Capital is moved around the global economy so effectively that it can be transferred to an optimal site for production, and then withdrawn almost as quickly if the economic situation should change (see Castells, 2000). Many of the most influential centres of capital are located in the major cities of western Europe and North America, although it is no longer necessary for aggregations of capital to coincide with aggregations of production. Nevertheless, although centres of transnational capital remain extremely powerful in both an economic and political sense, they are nevertheless subject to reflexive challenges from both individuals and organizations. The globalisation of knowledge has resulted in manufacturers, workers and consumers being far better informed of the advantages and limitations of life in the global environment, and far more able to critically analyse through a process of reflexivity, the consequences of global capitalist production.

The accessibility of knowledge, notably by means of the internet, has had other far-reaching effects in postmodern society. It is now much harder for individuals or small groups to attain a monopoly over knowledge, and hence to define certain types of knowledge as having more validity than others. In other words, absolutist conceptions of knowledge are much more difficult to sustain, because individuals have access to the expertise upon which they can base challenges to definitions of knowledge. It is hence much more difficult to argue that there are concepts of reality which have a wide general applicability in a global society. Individuals are much more likely to look to the norms and values of their own culture for interpretations of the validity of claims to understanding and knowledge. The problem with this analysis, however, is that it becomes very difficult to settle competing claims to truth. Each group is in theory capable of mounting a robust defence of their own analysis of reality. In short, it is possible to conceive of global society as a network of relativistic understandings each competing with each other for acceptance, and reinforced by the specific understandings and conventions of their own culture. It is not easy to conceive of the outcome of such a scenario, since we have become accustomed to relying upon broader claims to universal understanding, whether political, historical, scientific or philosophical. Although such narratives provide criteria by which people may judge their own lives, there is the ever-present danger that absolutist definitions may overwhelm individualist cultural claims to understanding. There does appear to be a trend, however, in postmodernity, to a level of uncertainty in the global environment, with which we are unfamiliar, and to which we may have to adjust. A relativistic world may have some advantages, but it is an uncertain world.

In a situation where there is a profusion of relativities, and no clearly defined strategy for determining the validity or otherwise of claims to knowledge, it is very easy for individuals to find themselves submerged in a large number of competing symbols and signs (see Bauman, 1992). In a confusion of competing images, social definitions and cultural forms, individuals may be forgiven for viewing the world as a very superficial form of existence. It is difficult any longer to attach significant meaning to a cultural image. All images appear to be of equal value and compete with each other for our attention. It is difficult any longer to separate 'the real' from the representation of the real. The world seems to be almost an exaggerated version of reality – a kind of hyperreality.

In a sense, art has always had the function of emphasizing some aspects of reality, and creating a form of hyperreality, but this has generally been achieved on a limited scale. For example, novels and film achieve their impact at least partly by being selective about the lives of characters. Usually authors concentrate on writing about very selective elements of lives, which combine to provide a theme and plot. Many of the routine elements of lives are omitted, because they are incidental to the story. In a sense, literature and film take us beyond reality, because they emphasize certain aspects at the expense of others. Art relies for its impact on a distortion of sorts. Generally speaking, natural existence as art may be less than interesting; it becomes interesting when the artist engages in a selective process.

In the case of postmodernity, this effect can become enhanced through the multiplicity of images of people's lives which are presented through the global media. This process is typified by the representation of 'ordinary' lives as 'extraordinary' when they are presented as social documentaries or non-participant observation, television ethnographies. When a person's normal working life is subjected to televised documentary scrutiny, then certain facets of that existence are selected for emphasis, and inevitably the individual life and its social context are distorted to some extent. This is not to take into account the additional impact of the film-maker in transforming reality. The viewer then has the task of seeking to interpret the film as reality. The temptation is to view the visual presentation as reality, when in fact it is a selective impression of some facets of the individual existence.

The effects are more complex when individuals are placed together in closed social groups, and their interactions observed and filmed over a period of time, and under a variety of varyingly demanding situations. It is easy to assume that the interactions of the 'artificial' social group represent reality, rather than their 'previous' lives. Nevertheless, one might argue that their present existence is, de facto, a form of reality. We are left wondering about the exact location and nature of reality.

There are apparently more and more opportunities for the individual to move from one stratum of public existence into a different stratum. A teenager may move by means of a television series from being a talented private singer, to being a celebrity with large potential earnings. It is partly the speed of the transition, but also the potentially large number of individuals who are able to transcend their given existence and social stratum, to emerge as a public persona. The variation in, and number of, such potential personas tend to contribute to a sense of hyperreality.

The impact of globalisation on culture is witnessed with particular clarity in its influence on ethnicity and ethnic groups. During modernity, although there were numerous examples of large-scale migrations and diasporas, there was often relatively little cultural exchange between the host ethnic community and the immigrant culture. When through political events or economic factors, a particular ethnic group migrated to a new society, there was often a broad pattern to the structure of the migration. It often involved male family members migrating initially, and finding employment and temporary accommodation. They would typically find employment in the same range of industries. As their economic base became more firmly established, and they were able to find more permanent accommodation, their families followed them. The immigrant community often sought accommodation in a clearly-defined geographical area, usually in an urban environment which provided sufficient employment. This localized environment enabled the immigrant community to adhere to its cultural norms and values and to sustain religious practices. Nevertheless, although there was interaction with the host community through, for example schools, both the immigrant and the host community were able to control, to some extent, the degree of social interaction between their two communities.

Immigrant communities were gradually able to establish their own places of worship, their own shops and businesses which provided some employment for their own community, and in some cases were also able to establish their own schools. Nevertheless, at this stage of the development of the community, one might generally argue that the culture and ethnicity of the community remained largely unchanged. A further dimension was that links were often carefully sustained with the country of origin, in order at least partly to sustain the cultural integrity of the community, and to act as a reference point for cultural norms and mores.

Globalisation, however, has had a dramatic influence upon this pattern of cultural development. First of all, with all communities, whether host or immigrant, receiving an enormous variety of cultural images from around the world, there has become little possibility of a single culture not absorbing other cultural forms. The absorption of cultural forms has generally taken place very rapidly, with the effect that the number of possible points of intersection between different cultures has been greatly enhanced. Not only that, but simultaneously with transition in the immigrant community, there have been parallel, if not greater, changes in the countries of origin. The forces of global communication have had consequences there, so that when individuals visited their country of origin, they often found that society there had evolved with even greater rapidity than their own. Far from finding a culture which could consolidate their own traditional values, people have found a culture in a very rapid state of transition, and one in which they perhaps felt themselves to be a stranger.

In modernity there was a sense in which the continuity of a specific culture was a possibility. There was the clear possibility that individual cultures could retain their distinctive features, even if that particular society was fragmented geographically. There were social mechanisms which to a greater or lesser extent, contributed to a degree of social and cultural cohesion and continuity. In postmodernity, however, these social mechanisms have almost become subservient to the larger-scale influence of globalisation. The number of different regions of interaction between cultures have become so great that it is increasingly difficult to predict the evolutionary path which an individual culture might take. Postmodern cultures are characterized, at least in part, by their rapidity of dissociation, and subsequent reassociation in new cultural forms. This is combined with an extensive and frequent absorption of forms and characteristics from other cultures.

These developments in globalized culture are potentially very important for education throughout the world, and particularly for the evolution of the curriculum. It is perhaps natural that in modernity, with limited opportunities for cultural interaction, the curriculum of a country should reflect a considerable proportion of national history and national interests, or at least the points of commonality with countries with similar cultural histories. This, in a sense, is partly the origin of such orientations as ethnocentrism and Eurocentrism, in that countries or groups of countries tended to view the world from a particular interpretive orientation which reflected their own value system and means of understanding. The increased globalisation of culture has not only created new cultural hybrids, but in educational terms has dramatically increased the potential for curricular diversity.

The historical economic, industrial and political power of North America and western Europe has tended to encourage a world view which accorded relatively little importance to the cultures of other ethnicities, and particularly to those societies deemed less well-developed technologically. There has been a tendency to associate lower levels of technological development with lower levels of cultural activity, and lower levels in terms of a sophistication of understanding the world. Globalisation is showing signs of reversing this tendency. The availability on the internet of detailed information in graphic form, of other belief systems, ideologies, world views, and ways of life, encourages students to reflect on the potential contribution of other cultures. In some cases there have been major contributions to world learning in the past, by other cultures, and yet this has tended not to be as well documented as contributions by those in the west. This would be so in the case of the contribution of Indian and Arabic cultures to mathematics and science. However, there are signs that the richness of world culture is now being recognized, and there are many examples of this, from the contribution of African musicians to popular music, and to the presence of writers from Africa and South America on literature course reading lists. Through the influence of globalisation, and tendencies to cultural hybridity, educational systems which were previously rather insular in curricular terms are now beginning to turn outwards, and embrace other cultural forms.

As has been discussed, one of the consequences of globalisation has been a tendency towards epistemological relativity. In a world where it is less easy to evaluate a multiplicity of competing claims to valid knowledge, one of the major difficulties for all educational systems is a lack of sense of direction. There appears to be a lack of general consensus concerning how one ought best to prepare young people for the future. Perhaps this is partly because the future is so difficult to divine. In the nineteenth century it was perceived as perfectly sensible to give someone a good grounding in the Greek and Roman classics, in order to equip them to administer large areas of a distant colonial dominion. In the twentieth century, with great technological advances, including space exploration, an education in science and technology was seen as being very relevant to society. However, in the postmodern world it is far from clear how educational systems ought to be preparing young people.

The plethora of succeeding initiatives which characterize the educational systems of contemporary times, may be seen as less the product of a lack of direction in individual politicians and educational thinkers, but rather of the fundamental uncertainty and imponderability of contemporary times. In a globalized world which is continually generating new cultural forms, there seems to be an impetus to create the new. It seems almost incongruous that an established idea or procedure could possibly be adequate in a world which is changing so rapidly. Thus, new initiatives are developed; and where previously an initiative might last for several years, it almost seems as if the currency of the new is becoming shorter and shorter.

However, the relativization of knowledge has also had another important consequence for education. In a world where everyone has access, via the internet, to unlimited knowledge, if not understanding, then the status of the transmitters of knowledge is inevitably undermined. Certainly in the nineteenth century, and to a large extent in the twentieth century, the public status and authority of the teacher rested upon subject expertise which was acquired through personal study, and which was not generally available to members of the general public. The advent of the internet has however made available that expertise to everyone, including students. It is thus much more difficult to make claims to expertise, and such claims in a globalized world, will perhaps need to be made on other grounds. It is arguably for such reasons, that one sees the rise of such roles as that of the facilitator, or one who organizes and manages learning experiences, rather than transmitting knowledge. Perhaps it is also why there is sometimes a tendency to focus upon learning rather than teaching. One might argue that in a globalized world the transmission of knowledge by specialist practitioners becomes much less important, and hence the increased focus upon the acquisition of knowledge and skills, rather than the process by which they are acquired.

Finally, globalisation is having a significant effect upon education through the changes in emphasis in forms of work and employment in both developed and developing countries. In a globalized world, transnational companies may export product manufacture to a developing country where labour costs and infrastructural investment costs are significantly lower. Such changes in the pattern of global industrial production have resulted in a significant movement towards the service and financial sectors of employment in the developed world, and a diversification of work in manufacturing industry in the developing world. A logical result of such changes will be a parallel transformation of the educational system to prepare young people for changes in employment patterns.

In conclusion, it appears that globalisation is having a significant effect upon both world cultures and upon the nature of employment patterns. These two factors together are influencing the educational system which, in its role of preparing young people for the future, will have an inevitable effect upon the nature of the global enterprise. This may appear to suggest a neat circular causal loop. In fact, the above discussion appears to suggest that although on the macro level there may be a series of apparent causal connections, it is arguably more accurate to view globalisation and culture, along with education and employment, as connected in a network of relationships of ever-increasing complexity.

References

Bauman, Z. (1992), *Intimations of Postmodernity*, London, Routledge.

Beck, U. (2000), 'Living Your Own Life in a Runaway World: Individualisation, Globalisation and Politics', in W. Hutton and A. Giddens (eds), *On the Edge: Living with Global Capitalism*, London, Jonathan Cape.

Castells, M. (2000), 'Information Technology and Global Capitalism', in W. Hutton and A. Giddens (eds), *On the Edge: Living with Global Capitalism*, London, Jonathan Cape.

Friedman, J. (1995), 'Global System, Globalisation and the Parameters of Modernity', in M. Featherstone, S. Lash and R. Robertson (eds), *Global Modernities*, London, Sage.

Giddens, A. (1984), *The Constitution of Society*, Cambridge, Polity.

Lyotard, J-F. (1984), *The Postmodern Condition: A Report on Knowledge*, Manchester, Manchester University Press.

Tomlinson, J. (1999), *Globalisation and Culture*, Cambridge, Polity.

Chapter 3

Globalisation as Education?
Images of Other Countries

Cedric Cullingford

The techniques of international communication are constantly evolving. The transmission of pictures and text, and the transportation of goods and ideas have opened up the world to cultural influences that are sometimes as unexpected as they are widespread, like the celebration of Christmas in China as a result of its producing the majority of seasonal artefacts. The development of the means of communication has long been celebrated, and many assumptions made about the result of it, since McLuhan's image of the 'global village' (McLuhan, 1964). Whilst the technical advances are rapid, it is just as clear that the means of communication have not led to greater international understanding. The conflicts along tribal or national boundaries abound. There are few signs of greater religious tolerance, or greater insights into other ways of living. And yet there is a continuous, indeed growing belief in the importance of ever faster and more efficient communication systems, as if change were brought about simply by the application of technology.

We tend to suffer from two unexamined assumptions. One is that we live in a time of profound change, with the inexorable threat or challenge of continually new contexts. Those who undergo key-note speeches will inevitably be reminded of the need to face new challenges, and to adapt to new situations. At one level, the changes, for instance to the internet and its uses, are obvious. Chat rooms, internet banking and world wide auctions all demonstrate access to other people and goods in a variety of ways, personal as well as commercial. What remains unexamined is the extent to which these facilities themselves have an effect on the thinking and the culture of those making use of them. Change is invoked as changes to systems and technique, rather than changes to the human psyche.

Change also becomes part of the second unexamined assumption, that all change presents wonderful new opportunities. The other typical key note lecture over the past thirty five years has consistently been about the fact that any day now the computer will (it is always 'will') utterly transform schools and schooling. Access to such reams of knowledge, the ability to communicate globally and the chance to speak to many thousands of people are all seen as enabling greater understandings, more individualised learning and the highest quality of material. The fact that we have been hearing these assertions for so long reminds us that change can also appear ephemeral, a constant fact in itself. Schooling remains very much what it always was, bound in the delivery, in classes, of a static traditional curriculum, whose relevance lies in its capacity to be tested.

We should therefore challenge some of the assertions that surround globalisation in its guise of communication. The problem is the tendency to mix up knowledge with understanding, to mistake technique for thought. The belief that communication systems will do something by themselves, without being used or exploited for particular purposes, is undermined by all the examples from research and from history which suggest a quite different and more subtle impact of knowledge and understanding.

International communication is not a new phenomenon. The techniques are simply much faster. They only slowly reach a wider audience. Communication systems also tend to be one way, and whilst we hope, whilst we lurch slowly towards civilisation, that most of the planet will be involved, the material that is being communicated is mostly commercial or trivial. Entertainment has a far bigger and more immediate impact than dialogue. Whilst there are some aspects that have changed, others have always been essentially there. We have had trade routes before, from the Silk Road to the Levant. We have had a lingua franca before, and it has merely changed from Latin to English. And most political systems remain un-evolved. Whilst the new Europe rather than the Holy Roman Empire ironically raises consciousness of cultural identity, the political systems of the world remain rooted in local and tribal traditions. When Lord McCartney made his first commercial excursion to China in the late 18th century, he was seen as a trivial outsider with as little relevance to the everyday life of the Country as any tourist or explorer is now in the far reaches of Sechuan (Peyrefitte, 1993).

This reality of parochialism which is as deeply ingrained in Texas as in Rwanda persists in the face of the changes in communication. The belief remains, however, that an awareness of the other countries, and a knowledge about other people, transmitted through television pictures and images rather than books, will in themselves create new understanding. European commissioners have long advocated the utility and importance of people, especially young people, travelling to other countries in the belief that the very experience of being in a different place, like a multiple grand tour, will easily transform the mode of thinking. Anyone who has seen crowds of foreign students, in scattered English coastal resorts, linked by their use of their own tongue, by their excitement in being free to pursue the first excitements of gender, and indifferent to the actuality of their surroundings (apart from the inadequate quality of the food) will doubt the efficacy of instant travel. Those who have not borne witness to this will nevertheless be aware of all those resorts on the coasts of Spain where, apart from the wonders of warm weather, the holiday makers relish the familiarities of their own television channels, the atmosphere of pubs and the availability of fish and chips. An alternative culture does not come into it.

Visiting a place as a tourist, like an excursion from a cruise ship, hardly guarantees greater understanding. A little more knowledge might be accrued but this is not the same thing. The distinction between the availability of knowledge and real understanding is not only an important one but always has been. Greater powers of communication, through trade and the technical resources to make it faster, or through information and the technical resources which make it cheaper, have always been seen to have two alternative consequences. Those who believe in the efficiency of communication have argued that the benefits will not only reach more people but elevate them. Those who worry about massification have conversely argued that more means worse, that, for example, the development of cheap paper and steam presses led not so much to the rise of public libraries as to the spread of vulgar and pornographic tastes (Altick, 1957).

International communication, or globalisation, can have contrasting effects. The potential of understanding is clear, but so is the possibility of cheap exploitation. Those Chinese workers becoming interested in the paraphernalia of Christmas, with the common artefacts and inexpensive decorations, are being seduced into the commercial merriment of the season and not its religious implications. The most obvious impact of the globalised culture of the 'West' is not music, opera or theatre, but the fast food 'outlets' of McDonalds and the availability of Coca-Cola. We have to remember that the effects of mass communication are complex, that change is not automatically for the good, and that the distinction between knowledge (or awareness) and understanding is profound.

In global information systems culture is no shock because it has little immediate impact. It is slowly and subtly imbibed, or ignored, a part of the background context that can remain ostensibly unnoticed. In this context of the different types of influence, this chapter explores the complexities of young people's understanding of, and attitude towards, other countries. The effects of knowledge on understanding are very complex and often inadvertent. Some of the material of the chapter has been reported elsewhere, and the methodology outlined (Cullingford, 2000) demonstrates, in the context of the book, the significance of the raw material of individual understanding. The kinds of knowledge of other countries that are taken in are many. They are a mixture of stereotypes and generalisations, of precise details and profound prejudice. Cultural antipathies and images are formed as rapidly and as effectively as a sense of mutual understanding and tolerance.

Perhaps the greatest underlying motive force behind this unexamined belief in the powers of international communication, the impact of the internet on education, and the inevitability of globalisation, is the atavistic hope that all this knowledge will lead to greater understanding, that the technologies will themselves transform society. There is a latent desire, as well as hope, for changes, in circumstances and atmosphere, for breakthroughs in the evolving cultures of international educational understanding. The problem is that without really analysing the effects, there is comparatively little to be learned from all the innovations, the interventions, the systems and the sophistications of new media. Knowledge is freely available to those who seek it. Understanding is a far harder matter.

Knowledge can come at a variety of levels and in a variety of forms. It can be presented as stereotypes, as well as greater insight. The constantly evoked belief in sustainable globalised informational change is as often a denial of the formation of prejudice as the evocation of understanding. Greater knowledge can be even more dangerous than little. The image of 'fuzzy-wuzzies', of 'slit eyes' as if their appearance were their minds, reminds us that the prejudices of race can be just as cheaply and instantly fostered by the media as any greater understanding.

This understanding begins young. When the first systematic research was carried out into the attitudes of people towards other countries certain patterns emerged, most of which reflected predictable prejudices, but which were surprising for being so deeply held. The pattern of the world is seen in terms of contrasts between those nations or groups of people or tribes which are favoured and those which are not. There are a number of clear divisions between those with whom young people feel an automatic affinity and those who conjure up immediate images of the alien (Tajfel, 1981). There are many instances of a north/south divide within countries such as Great Britain, Italy and Germany and in the world as a whole. The constant testing of broad public opinion as in the "Euro barometer" gives continuous evidence of prejudices and antipathies that are the residue of World War. Certain countries are deeply linked with consistent emotional traits, as Germany is with efficiency and Italy with emotion (Linssen, 1994). There are long standing rivalries and national hatreds that are not only carried on politically from year to year but imbued in the young like the continuing enmity, within the modern European orbit, of Greece and Turkey (Lister and Paida, 1994). Children's views of themselves and the country in which they live is dependant on the defining constraints with other people and other states (Cullingford, 1992) The patterns of national prejudice have long been understood (Piaget and Weil, 1951). What impact these attitudes have had has been less often explored.

Despite all the global information systems and increasing experience of travel, distinctions of culture, and therefore of attitude and understanding, remain. Knowledge does not necessarily lead to greater sympathy. Sometimes the opposite is the case. There are ways of travelling that remain essentially superficial, either by being incarcerated within familiar international luxury or by being enclosed in adventure where the activity is more significant than the environment. Despite the expressed intensions of some politicians, the old established notion of cultural geography, the knowledge of economies and climate as well as the capitals of all countries, are not a deeply engrained part of the modern curriculum. By the time formal approaches to political structures are made in the education system, young children's understanding and attitudes towards the world they live in are well established. They are created, sometimes inadvertently out of all the second hand information that is conveyed throughout the media, through news and through films. Whilst there might be some domestic dialogue about other countries and the occasional visit on holiday either to the homeland of ancestors or the fruits of curiosity or self indulgence, young children mostly fend intellectually for themselves and create an understanding of the world in which they live which always includes some simple contrasts, some consistent preferences about many attempts both to make sense of particular groups of people and their own place in the environment.

The first and crucial understanding of the world as a whole is that it is divided into the rich and the poor. This realisation of inequity affects children's understanding of the society in which they live and the way in which the world as a whole operates. The sense of contrast, even unfairness, abounds and the question is how children come to terms with this. If we consider the images that are presented on the television we will realise that the Oxfam image of Africa, of starving hopeless people, of constant war, is one that is easily generalised as well as shocking and that against this are the pictures of the very rich, the 'celebrities' with their private jets, their mansions and their designer wear and possessions. The age old sense of division not only of 'us' versus 'them' but more pointedly the desire to be 'us' rather than 'them', continues. Knowledge of other cultures, presented in such a way, fosters prejudice.

One positive result of the images of other countries presented by international communication is that there are certain ones which are seen not only to be eminently worth visiting but worth living in. To that extent the very possibility of living somewhere other than our own familiar surroundings gives us a different sense of mobility and of cultural adaptation. The proviso is of course, that the country is a rich one, inclusive of all modern conveniences and preferably using the same language. This outlook is certainly true of children in the United Kingdom and, the strictures of language apart, it is true of most of northern Europe. There is of course one country that stands for all that is positive and desirable. This is the United States which is constantly in the forefront of the news, which dominates the western film industry and which is clearly associated with wealth. Young people have easily imbibed the Auden categories of the U.S.A. as 'so large, so friendly and so rich' (Auden, 1963).

The image of the United States as rich and desirable puts young people's feelings about their own circumstances into a different context. Perhaps this is one result of globalisation, that there should be a far more relative view about ones personal position of the world. The children rarely assert the sense of their own geographical superiority, knowing that the weather, for instance, is better elsewhere. Nor do they assert a sense of chauvinism, as if they had an inalienable right to assert a monopoly of virtue or success. Those demonstrations of hooligan nationalism, of banal symbolism so clearly associated with sport; do not affect the children's understanding of their particular environment (Billig, 1995) They know it could be better elsewhere. Whilst they are fully appreciative of local knowledge and familiarity and content with what they have, they realise this is a matter of chance rather than some divine fate, as in the mood of children's literature one hundred years ago (Cullingford, 1998). They appreciate their friends and family, but they would have these wherever they are.

There is one strong association with the Unites States that is both immediately apparent and which gives the children a taste of what many a smaller country has had for generations, an awareness of inferiority. America is far richer.

'They're really rich and they can buy really good cars and stuff.' (Boy 8)

It's a richer country than this country. ''Cos it's big. They have loads of money and they buy things.' (Girl 8)

In the ethos of the time, with so many advertisements directed at young people, possessions count. There are so many levels of desire, from toys that would give immediate gratification to the symbols of future riches, like fast cars and large homes, as well as the consuming desire for more space. In the United States people possess things. They have 'good (bigger?) cars'. The ownership of money leads to the ability to have what one desires. Children do not see the contrasts that they see in the world as a whole as prevailing in the United States itself. They are imbued with the image of Manhattan rather than the Bronx with just one side of the unequally distributed riches of the United States which they assume affects everyone.

''Cos everyone's rich there and it's the same in New York. 'Cos everyone's got about three hundred million dollars.' (Boy 8)

There might be some confusion about the figures and the denotions of currencies, but there is no mistake about what being rich means.

This feeling about the riches of the United States is not a vague one. It is detailed in the precise outcomes of personal desire. Being a good place at one level means the ability to own the best and most expensive toys, an ability clearly denied many elsewhere.

'It's a good place and you get so many things. Skateboards are made there. Really good ones like mountain bikes and you know really good things. I've seen programmes.' (Boy 9)

Not only are there 'really good things' bought in the United States but made there. It is seen as the source, the centre of all largesse. The way the image is conveyed and nurtured is also clear. He has seen programmes which reiterate this association of the desirable with the gloss of coming from over the Atlantic. This strong perception of the United States is not only of a mechanical exploitation of money but of an image of extra desirability. The country is liked because it is fashionable.

'A lot more expensive clothes. 'Cos a lot of things like movies and new things come first in America, before Britain. So I can imagine American people wearing the latest fashion.' (Girl 9)

The advantages of the control of the public channels of communication are clear. Children are aware of the source of the products and of the movies. This supports the notion of globalisation as one way traffic, of the dominance not just of a particular way of life but of a particular nation. No one associates Canada with these riches or with power. The newest things like the latest fashions come from an American image clearly fostered by Hollywood. As well as more desirable possessions, the United States possesses fashion and a stronger hold on the future and on taste.

'They got dollars and I like dollars. They've got different cars on there and they have different all kinds of stuff there. They get really big pizzas about *that* size in Pizza Hut. And they have French Fries and Chicken MacNuggets.' (Boy 8)

This a typical example of all the different levels of association with the impact of that culture. The very sound of money gives a better frisson, as if dollars were themselves special, as indeed they are in countries with weak currencies. The pound or Euro or even Zen have no such effect. America is not only full of 'stuff' including bigger cars but is also the source of fashionable fast food. Not only are two particular brand names cited, but they are named in association with size, with the idea of greater generosity rather than greed, with largesse rather than waste. Even the most traditional of English food, chips, is transformed into an American concept, French fries.

The presentation of America is not only through films but through marketing.

Everyone knows where CocaCola comes from. But the underlying message is that the United States is the major source of what is desirable; being so rich we are merely enjoying its excess. Size and power are assumed to mean something better.

'It's good because there's lots of places. It's big. It's got big houses. Big cars. Better houses, because more of them are bigger and they've got different styles. There's better films that you can watch. There's bigger playgrounds. Lots of things to do.' (Boy 9)

Bigger clearly means better. Fashion, possessions and styles of living are all presented as preferable. Even the sense of personal space is provided for in the minds of children, to the extent that even the playgrounds are bigger. At the same time, as Auden notes, the charm of the United States lies in the idea that it is also friendly. It does not appear threatening to these young people. They clearly associate the country with "Have a nice day!", with cheerfulness, openness and approachability. And nothing could be more approachable than money.

The United States stands for one extreme in the divided world. If it is all that is desirable there is just as consistent an association with the developing world, Africa in particular. One of the results of globalisation is supposed to be a spread of the benefits of industrialisation and the availability of sophisticated goods and transport systems. Internationalism means the growth of airports and towns, the development of modern architecture and a recognisable homogenisation of places, with systems of banking and exchange available every where. Judging by the impressions given by the children, one would have thought that nothing had changed during the last one hundred years. Africa, is if it were a country, and despite cities from Nairobi to Cape Town, is associated with poverty. This association does not, however, trigger a sense of pity. The image of Africa is taken as inexorable, as constant, without hope. The people there are not only known to be suffering, but to be so without familiar possessions, that they are felt to be somehow fundamentally different. They are looked at with a mixture of pity and distaste.

Children know the essential contrasts.

'Some countries are poor and some rich like America. You get very rich some by oil and everything and they have a lot of money, and its completely the opposite in Ethiopia. By oil, and other things like, because they're big businesses.' (Girl 9)

Big business and the exploitation of natural resources are interpreted as the driving forces of riches, but the most striking awareness is the contrast – the 'complete opposite.' Whilst some countries, like Ethiopia, have been particularly associated with poverty, famine and disaster (as well as with terrible governments and cruel wars) it is Africa as a whole that is seen as being in this benighted state.

'The children, well they're brown and they're not well fed and they're small and they're skinny because they haven't got enough food and some die of, er, water and hunger because they haven't got any food to eat.' (Girl 9)

In Africa you 'only starve and die'. This is not a matter of the absence of possessions but the extremes of having nothing, no clothes, no proper housing and no hope. Many countries are seen like this.

'Countries which have no food and have no clothes. Africa. Some of them have no clothes and you can see some of the people they're shivering. Some don't have clothes and some just have rags and things like that.' (Girl 6)

The image of poverty is stark. People are seen as suffering in large numbers. The lack of clothes, the rags, appears to be part of the prevailing condition. Children have seen so many images of suffering that it has been a part of their awareness of the permanent world. International communication has brought with it a strong sense of comparison; of one's own country with the richer more attractive United States. It has also made clear that for many human beings life is nothing but suffering. In the past people could live in contented ignorance, with sudden crises, of war or plague a palpable if temporary threat but, like the weather, better times were also possible. Today children know that they could be far worse (as well as better) off. They know that for some people the way of living is abject They have seen many a television report on the suffering. They present what they have seen in detail.

'They were black. They had flies all round them. Some of them had wounds.' (Girl 9)

'Really, really hot and they don't have much water. They have to dig to get the water and then you get dirty water to drink and sometimes it's poisonous. They hardly have any rain, they put buckets and they dig holes. The places that are starving, they've only got like big sticks with cloth on the top and leaves.' (Boy 9)

The problem with such precise images is that they suggest that this is a permanent condition. It is not taken to be a sudden calamity, a disaster that can be dealt with, that, like a flood, will subside. This is the way part of the world is, so that the contrasts between the haves and the have nots is taken to be permanent. Beneath any cultural differences lies the great divide, a world seen not as spreading wealth and unifying understanding but as one of essential disparity and unfairness.

Images of poverty can have the opposite effect to those intended. Instead of provoking pity, they are so constant as to be interpreted as a condition not only permanent but the responsibility of those suffering them. When the children describe what they have learned, particularly in programmes like Blue Peter designed to inform them, they sometimes hint at exasperation and distaste.

'They had to carry their pills home in just tissues and they just disintegrated by the time they got home because of the heat. It's stupid.' (Boy 9)

That sense of difference, of not only living in difficult conditions but doing things in a way that does not make sense points up the feeling of loss of the familiar. These people do not posses the same accoutrements of civilised luxury. Whilst in the past such assumptions of superiority may have been expected and remained unexamined, today this feeling that 'normal' people live in a particular way suggests a lack of sympathetic appreciation, that the effects of Oxfam and other appeals create a sentimentally and equally unexamined reaction without true understanding. It is as if largesse, the occasional outpouring of aid were still enough. These children are not being taught to analyse or appreciate the wider world but to accept their part in it, and the inevitability of the status quo. Thus we find not only an appreciation of the greater possessions of the United States, but a prevailing attitude that civilisation, and all that is worthwhile in globalisation, is also a matter of familiar objects.

'Things like plants and three piece suites and things like that. And transistor radios and personal stereos and things. They've not got proper houses at all. Sticks and bits of material stuck together.' (Girl 9)

The poor of Africa are defined not just as suffering but of living a life without any of the familiar virtues of normality. Such a distancing is also expressed in the suspicions about food. Not only do the Africans have to do without food but what they eat is distasteful.

'They eat what things move, like beetles and snails and slugs.' (Girl 6)

The problem is that they are 'not like us'. They do not eat hamburgers.

'If they had burgers they would have nothing to cook them with. No cookers and don't have proper food to eat.' (Boy 9)

These well defined and widely shared attitudes towards the world depend not only on contrasts but of different levels of interpretation The existence of preferred or disliked nations can depend on small clichés and stereotypes or on deeply set suspicions. The influence of the images of the pictorial media and of gossip can be trivial or deep. Food is itself symbolic of the alien aspects of Africa; not only forced to do without, the people have neither the means nor the will to do things in the way the children would expect. Other more advanced countries exhibit equally peculiar traits, like Germans perceived as eating lots of sausages. The French are stereotyped as wearing particular clothes but also inexorably with culinary peculiarities.

'Snails shells and frogs legs .... they usually sell them in stores and sometimes in restaurants.' (Boy 7)

'They eat snails and I think they eat horse. And they eat French bread. 'Cos when we went there we went into this shop and I saw some snails and they eat octopuses.' (Girl 7)

The same two children mention berets and what they have picked out on television. There might be an antipathy to eating snails but there are fairly benign images. They are no threat.

Other parts of the world are presented in very different terms and have a marked effect on political attitudes. The vision of a divided world is itself political of course, but a pointed attitude is struck in seeing the reporting of violence mixed up with very clear images of costume and habit. The differences of the world are not just in possessions but in the immutable cultural habits, and these are not always assumed to be a benign multicultural token, like samosas, saris and chicken marsala.

'They're terrorists there. I think they're a bit like Arab people. I think their habits are different maybe, but I don't really know. They wear sort of long sheets wrapped around their heads to keep the heat off them. I'm afraid of the people there.' (Girl 9)

The imagery of dress is associated with fear and with violence. Long before the intricacies of cause and effect, of political points of view and tribal and religious allegiances are explained, some prevailing attitudes are felt and made personal. The raw presentation of fact and action leads to the forming of opinion and associations.

'On the television you see all smashed up homes and its quite hard to see what they are ... I've noticed the women wear dresses, like of, like white dresses and black shoes and black kind of scarf around the head and they're covered to their eyes. And some even have it round their eyes. If you like cover your face it wouldn't feel nice. You wouldn't feel right. You wouldn't feel free. I think because of their religion.' (Girl 9)

Globalisation is sometimes seen as a kind of sweeping understanding, a broadening of educational experience. It is at other times seen as the inexorable spread of western values in all their levels, as the march of capitalism and McDonald's across all borders. In terms of seeing the world from a very fixed point of view, these children demonstrate their experience of the media. Part of their education is to underscore the sense of their own personal values, including a particular way of life. They like those things that are as much like their own experience as possible. They appreciate those parts of the world that take this experience further and exaggerate it, but it is the familiar that matters. Insights into alternatives do not of themselves foster understanding. The more these children learn about the rest of the world the more, not less, alienating it becomes. Children learn a great deal, in an undeliberate way, about the different parts and countries of the world. This does not mean that they understand better or are more tolerant. Religion, dress codes and terror are easily associated with each other depending on your point of view. An American seen from an Iraqi point of view would exhibit the association of all three clearly enough. For young people in Great Britain the means by which they gain understanding is equally clear.

At the age of this sample there are few attempts to give any formal input into their understanding. The curriculum concentrates on core subjects and specific skills, and does not allow for much discussion on personal, social and global issues. The raw data that is seen by children inevitably colours their view of the world. They do their best with it. They have to construct a sense of the world at once general and clearly structured as well as true. They therefore see the great divisions of the world at a variety of levels. And much of what they see is disturbing.

As they grow older young people have to see the world in more complex terms. The ability at a young age to understand different points of view and to be tolerant is very marked but this very virtue is all too often stamped out of them. Instead the lessons have to be learned all over again for themselves. Visits to other countries beyond tourism and a curiosity about what they are really like needs to be a mixture of anticipation and experience. There will be expectations and assumptions made about other countries, and about the imagery with which they are presented. What then is the difference of the idea of a country and the reality?

This issue was explored with the cohort of students who came to England. (Billig, 1995) They knew what they wanted and went through all sorts of personal experience. Before they came they had been carefully primed as to what to expect. They had actually sought out knowledge of a practical kind and had been presented by the British Council with lectures on everyday life. Whilst their preparations both excited and perturbed then, they felt afterwards that this kind of cultural inoculation was inappropriate. They were appalled at the withholding of information. They were disappointed at the absence of practicalities. What they wanted, in fact, was not a series of cultural depictions with the associations of the traditional images of the old country but practical survival techniques. They received a dose of Queen, Horse Guards Parade, the Changing of the Guard and Tower Bridge. They realised afterwards that what they wanted was more down to earth. If they knew how to survive easily they could deal with cultural matters themselves.

The domestic realities that students saw they need contrast with the kind of generalised talks that they were given in their home countries. The preparation for the period overseas was seen in terms of general cultural orientation, making them sensitive to cultural differences and avoiding the kinds of confrontation which are anticipated. When students reconsidered what they were told in the light of their actual experience, they saw a distinct contrast between the myths and unhelpful generalities and the realities. Part of this mythology was to do with the very recognition of tribal or national stereotypes or characteristics. At the heart of this lies the projection of the English character, as cold and distant, formal and unfriendly. This was an issue constantly addressed by them when they challenged what they heard against what they experienced. They saw the presentation of what they were likely to encounter before they came as a perpetuation of the myth. They constantly asserted that the English are not as they are portrayed but on the contrary, friendly and welcoming ... quite normal, in fact. Any generalisation is a stereotype but the very treatment of the English character in the same terms as the weather created a picture which did not only apply to their personal experience but diverted attention from what could be useful to them.

Even in the heightened expression and hopes of going overseas to study, with all the heavy emotional investment this involves, students really want to know how to cope on a practical level. It is the information about how they carry with them their normal, personal and social connections and need to survive with as few strains and as little loss of dignity as possible. Instead they bring with them a mythology – perhaps an inevitable one – which is afterwards contrasted with their own private experiences.

> Coming here for a change, going to people's country, to know people, to learn their language, to learn about customs, its just like going to some place that you are, that you never dream of. Only seeing it, watching television and all that ...
> We have also learned about knowing the Queen, so we would like to come one day giving opportunity to see the Queen. That probably was a childish idea long time ago, that make us to feel like you know, interested coming here overseas to study.

'Childish' or not, the presentation of national imagery, whether seen on television or acquitted through hearsay, is very powerful. It both attracts and puts them off. The sense of the distinction of the place in its public accoutrements, like the Queen, makes it 'totally different'. Just as there are often deliberately crude contracts made between particular countries, developed at an early age (Hofstede, 1991) so the more distinct an image of a country the more significant is the emotional reaction in terms of power relationships.

Other countries, once they are recognised, are rarely seen as neutral. This concept mapping has a long history but the consistent point is the creation of distinctions between the rich and poor, between the familiar and unfamiliar, the welcoming and the unattractive (Cullingford, 1999). The more a country is described, as in being prepared for, the more powerful its image.

> he shares out his slides, showing about England and of course what we see is quite different from what we have at home. Things to come to know for instance about the weather.

The more the official talks the more the awareness of difference, even at the obvious level of the climate, is fostered. The lecturers might not anticipate that they create anything but further understanding but the very delineation of the curiosities suggests the possibilities of alienation. This causes something of a dilemma. One could argue that the greater the understanding of other countries the better. This is, after all, the aim of the European Union, or of any international body promoting good will and the overcoming of ethnic conflict. To discover that visitations can have the opposite effect, that images of other countries can be counterproductive, is hard for some to accept. The problem is that what people are seeking is greater understanding of people in society a general, including their own patterns of behaviour and dialogue that affects all. If a particular part of the world is singled out, there is a tendency to create stereotypes, sometimes quite dated (Cullingford and Husemann, 1995). What is certain is that the 'tokenism' of national characteristics does not foster the practical understanding that the students felt they needed.

If there was a surprise on entering the country it came about because the myths of impenetrable and arcane habits of the natives, purposely withheld from newcomers, turned out to be an untrue reflection on the immediate transactions (and problems) of everyday life. The myths that surrounded England had to be overcome, however powerful. The sense that the locals would feel a potential superiority was supposedly deeply held including academics. At one level of pre-visit presentations were the accepted patinas of description like the weather:

> I always think of the four seasons, you know, they're always nice, the four seasons ... the students think the four seasons here how it is like...

At another was the almost cultivated image of the historical weight, which could be introduced with awe:

> The thing I know about England, I know that it is you know compared with the United States, it is a historical place – it's not the place that you come to see, like to visit because you want to have fun. If it is you can go to the US and there you can look for the fun place. Basically from reading books, I was told that England you see castles and such things, it's history ...

All this gives a weighty and to some extent unattractive impression. After all, if you want 'fun' you go to the United States. The most crucial cultural impression is the tone. The people are associated with their historical monuments. There is an invoked, if accidental, assumption that the locals are unfriendly.

And one thing I heard before we came, that most likely, the English are very snobbish, you see, just beware they're very snobbish ...

It does not turn out to be quite like this – 'if you talk to them they are very nice.' But the expectation caused a number of difficulties.

The degree of the mythology with which the students had themselves presented was so unlike the realities that they subsequently resented this fact. If there had been any sense of 'culture shock', it was created before actually coming to the country. The actual experience was supposed to be difficult. It did not turn out that way in the manner that was envisaged. The problems turned out to be practical rather than personal. The stress on the need for ordinary down to earth advice rather than the generalised cultural descriptions comes about partly because it was just this practical help which was missing, whether from officials or returning students.

> It's very sad to say they have been very unhelpful. The people who came and went back and I don't see any reason why they had to act in this manner. Or maybe they felt they were one up than us they didn't want to say much ... they were not willing to tell us exactly, in spite of repeatedly asking them.

The sense that knowledge is power is difficult to resist. Those returning to their homeland can feel they have entered into and opened up what was a secret world and that it should remain mysterious for those who have not yet entered it. It is more spectacular to exaggerate the arcane, the mythological and the difficulties overcome that to outline the practical steps with which to enter other people's cultural hegemony.

What young people learn about other countries are often the most obvious and crude of cultural images, from the pomp of Great Britain, and the riches of the United States, to the poverty of Africa and the terror of the Middle East. The world is not seen as a place where people can understand each other. Certain parts are accepted, as long as they can be made familiar. Others become even more alien in the process of globalisation. The comforting fact is that there is also a yearning for the kind of everyday, practical understanding. This would ultimately do much more for communication and tolerance than any amount of excitatory images and celebrations of peculiarity and difference.

References

Altick, R. (1957), *The English Common Reader: A Social History of the Mass Reading Public*, Chicago University Press.

Auden, W.H. 'On the Circuit', *Collected Poems*, Faber & Faber, London.

Auden, W.H. (1976), *Collected Poems*, Faber & Faber, pp. 548.

Billig, M. (1995), *Banal Nationalism*, Sage, London.

Cullingford, C. (1998), *Children's Literature and Its Effects*, Cassell, London.

Cullingford, C. (1999), *The Human Experience: The Early Years*, Ashgate, Aldershot.

Cullingford, C. (2000), *Prejudice: From Individual Identity to Nationalism in Young People*,

Kogan Page, London.

Cullingford, C. and Husemann, H. (1995), *Anglo-German Attitudes*, Avebury. Aldershot.

Hofstede, G. (1991), *Culture and Organizations: Software of the Mind*, McGraw-Hill, London.

Linssen, H. and Hagendoorn, L. (1994), 'Social and geographical factors in the explanation of European nationality stereotypes', *British Journal of Social Psychology*, vol. 33(2), pp. 165–182.

Lister, I. and Paida, S. (1997), 'Young children's images of the evening: an explanation into mental mapping', *New Era in Education*, vol. 3, pp. 81–84.

McLuhan, M. (1964), *Understanding Media: The Extensions of Man*, McGraw-Hill, New York.

Peyrefitte, A. (1993), 'The collision of two civilisations', *The British Expedition to China 1792–4*, Harvill, London.

Piaget, J. and Weil, R. (1951), 'The development in children of the idea of the homeland and of relations with other countries', *International Social Science, Bulletin* No 3 pp. 561–578.

Tajfel, H. (1981), *Human Groups and Social Categories*, Cambridge University Press.

Chapter 4

Local Knowledge and Globalisation: Are they Compatible?

W. John Morgan

Introduction

In anthropology, the term *indigenous* refers to the original inhabitants of a specific geographical area, a land, which has been occupied subsequently by migrants or colonists. Such later occupations and territorial disputes have, historically, been accompanied by ethnic, cultural, religious and linguistic tensions. Indigenous peoples are thus synonymous with the terms *aboriginal* and *native*, to which it is now often preferred, where the two latter terms have acquired pejorative connotations. There are many historical examples and, more importantly for the purposes of this chapter, many examples that are still currently sources of dispute. These may be found in the Americas, in Africa and in Australia and New Zealand, the well known sites of European imperialism and colonial settlement in the final centuries of the last millennium. They may also be found in China, in Central Asia and also in both 'old' and 'new' Europe. They are, in both the historical and the contemporary senses, intimately bound up with the concept of *local knowledge* and its relationship with *globalisation*, which is the focus of this chapter. This is why the anthropological perspective is necessary to understanding the impact of globalisation on local cultures and systems of education. As Kate Crehan points out in a recent book on Gramsci and anthropology, it is 'an interesting vantage point from which to examine the hegemonic ... and taken-for-granted certainties of what is commonly referred to nowadays as our 'globalized' world. All too often the term globalisation seems to involve the assumption that capitalism and democracy, as these have developed in certain societies in the North, represent a *telos* to which every human society everywhere is (or should be) aspiring (Crehan, 2002, p. 4).

The concept of 'local knowledge' has its basis in the indigenous, in the traditional and the established. In archaeology, for instance, a *tradition* is a set of cultural elements or traits that are both inter-related and which persist over a relatively long time-span. In the sister discipline of anthropology, the word is used to describe patterns of belief, customs, wisdom which guides behaviour, and technical expertise or *knowledge*. These are handed down from generation to generation through a socialization process that is, or has been, confined to an identifiable and given population. This socialization process is often, even usually, coded so that it is restricted to the initiated. This may be interpreted by insiders as protective and sustaining and by outsiders as at best conservative and at worst discriminatory and reactionary. This reveals another source of misunderstanding and tension, that between so-called 'backward', 'primitive' peoples, usually without power, and the so-called 'modern', 'progressive' peoples, usually with it.

The term *local knowledge* has sometimes been used as a synonym for *culture*. This has been the case particularly in the discipline of ethnology, where the study of 'traditional everyday culture' or *folk culture* has been a dominant concern. This has led to a paradox in the post-colonial world. Ethnology was an important practice in the colonial world, with many resident officials, missionaries and even traders engaged in the collection, translation and interpretation of the oral traditions and material artifacts of local folk culture amongst the colonized peoples. Such activity was based theoretically on European folklore studies, particularly in Germany, which had there formed an intellectual basis for nationalism. These were based on the rural-urban and dialect-standard language dichotomies, considered usefully by Raymond Williams in *The Country and the City* (Williams, 1975). They were complicated in the colonial setting by inter-cultural, religious and multi-lingual factors, as well as by the presence of sophisticated indigenous scholars. In the post-colonial world, there have been and are serious efforts to de-construct and come to terms with this legacy of colonial cultural interpretation. These were led notably by K.M. Panniker in his seminal classic *Asia and Western Dominance* and, more recently by Edward Said in both *Orientalism* and in *Culture and Imperialism* (Panniker, 1953 and Said, 1995 and 1993). It has been argued, however, that historically such features of colonialism are also found within Europe also. The history of the Celtic peoples of the British Isles and of France provides a well-researched and documented example and one that revived as a site of economic, political and cultural tension in the final decades of the last century (Prebble, 1963, Hechter, 1975, Nairn, 1977). It was and is a product of the struggle between a centralizing and modernizing nation-state and indigenous and culturally separate local communities. The paradox is that both looked to consolidate their own ideological or 'imagined' versions of cultural space and of national identity through an emphasis on folklore, with often an accompanying 'invention of tradition' (Anderson, 1991, Guidance and Porter, 2001, Ranger and Hobsbawm, 1983, Hutchinson, 1987). The concept of local knowledge cannot be separated from this process.

Local Knowledge and the Little Tradition

However, modern anthropology has tended not to place so much emphasis on the centrality of tradition in analyzing or understanding contemporary communities. This is because they believe that such an approach does not allow for the essentially dynamic and adaptive nature of socio-cultural systems. The uncritical use of the concepts of folk culture and tradition may result, it is suggested, in a failure to examine the fundamental problem of the *relationship* between cultural persistence or continuity and acculturation and cultural change. As some of the studies mentioned above argue, this is a problem that is best approached not only in terms of the cultural elements themselves, but also as an historical process of social reproduction and social change in the peoples concerned. The paradoxes that they reveal require a more analytical and critical approach than that provided by the antiquarianism of the 19th century and early 20th century folklorists. It should be remembered, however, that ideological and political agendas continue to be contested.

Such an approach has not been confined to very recent commentators. This was emphasized by the Marxist cultural critic Georg Lukács in his appreciation of the Scottish novels of Sir Walter Scott (and of his novel *Ivanhoe* that also dealt with enforced cultural change) and also of the colonial American novels of James Fenimore Cooper. These writers are now often dismissed as descriptive, romantic and 'old-fashioned' by modern and certainly by post-modern critics. Yet in *The Historical Novel*, Lukács argues '...that Scott did not become a Romantic, a glorifier or elegist of past ages. And it was for this reason that he was able to portray objectively the ruination of past social formations, despite all his human sympathy for, and artistic sensitivity, to the splendid heroic qualities which they contained. Objectively, in a large historical and artistic sense: he saw at one and the same time their {the Highland Clans} outstanding qualities and the historical necessity of their decline' (Lukács, 1962, p. 55). In the same way, Lukács says, the novels of James Fenimore Cooper focus on the 'colonizing capitalism of France and England which destroys physically and morally the society of the indigenous Americans which had flourished almost unchanged for thousands of years. Cooper also portrays the: '...enormous historical tragedy of those early colonizers who emigrated from England {and elsewhere in Europe} in order to preserve their freedom, but who themselves destroy this freedom by their own deeds in America' (Lukács, 1962, pp. 64–65).

These are early historical and literary examples of the culture shock that modernization inflicts when it is experienced globally. This may be illustrated further through a brief consideration of the concept of the *Great and the Little Traditions*, terms coined by the American anthropologist Robert Redfield in his studies of peasant society and culture (Redfield, 1956). These included the Andaman Islanders, the Maori, the Maya, the Tiv, the Sudanese, communities in West Africa and in India, as well as examples of the traditions in Islamic and Catholic societies. Redfield considers social structure, not only as a system of relationships, of existing ties among people, but also as '... a system of norms and expectations ... as an ethical system' (Redfield, 1956, pp. 45–46). Most importantly, for the discussion here, Redfield drew a contrast between the formal literate tradition of an urban elite and the largely oral and informal tradition of the rural peasant community. An oral tradition is that part of a society's cultural knowledge or 'traditional culture' which is passed on by word of mouth rather than through a recorded form. Redfield also drew a distinction between what an ideal social structure says should be and what actually happens. This may occur if there are moral imperatives in competition or if the social structure breaks down. He refers to a case described by Professor Raymond Firth from the remote Pacific island of Tikopia. In that social structure it is required that the chief pass on his sacred knowledge to his eldest son: 'In this case the eldest son had deserted the father and gone to live in another district. The son thus failed to fulfil a demand made upon him by the moral dimension of the social structure, for he had an obligation to remain by his father' side. Angered by this desertion, the father told his younger son what he should have communicated to the elder and then died. Then as the social structure required, the elder son was made chief. But of course at that moment he lacked the esoteric knowledge necessary to a chief' (Redfield, 1956, p. 47). The result is a moral and a social dilemma of fundamental consequence. This example emphasizes the fundamental part played by local knowledge in the development of systems of law and of notions of justice. As Clifford Geertz points out in a comparative analysis of local knowledge, fact and law, works of legal anthropology using this approach, such as Malinowski's *Crime and Custom in Savage Society* (1926) and Llewellyn and Hoebel's *The Cheyenne Way* (1941): '... remain the classic analyses of social control in tribal societies ...' (Geertz, 1983, p. 169). The systems they analyze rest on the oral transmission of what is essentially local knowledge.

Such oral traditions are to be found throughout the world. An example in Western Europe is the Celtic bardic tradition of story telling. These complex tales were delivered orally and centuries passed before some of them were recorded in writing. As the translators of the ancient Welsh folk tales *The Mabinogion* commented: 'They had thus no fixed and inviolable form, but took shape and colour from a hundred minds, each with its human disposition to variance and mutability', while: The traditional material on which they had worked for many, many centuries, accreting, rejecting, explaining, forgetting, goes back to the earliest creative impulses of the Celtic world and far from its being surprising that great changes took place, the wonder would be had they not' (Jones and Jones, 1973, pp. xi–xiii). They are a type of local cultural ecology and form the continuous core of local knowledge that stand in implied opposition to the literate tradition that has dominated all attempts at economic and social modernization.

For instance, the anthropologist Fei Xiao Tong, celebrated for his studies of peasant life in China (Fei, 1939) has observed that: 'Rural people not only know each other intimately; they also get to know other aspects of rural life equally well. Knowledge acquired from familiarity is specific and is not deduced from abstract general principles. People who grow up in a familiar environment do not need such principles. They only need to know the specific relationship between means and ends within the scope of their activities. They do not seek universal truths' (Fei, 1992, p. 43). It is worth noting that in the period leading up to the Liberation of China in 1949, the Chinese Communist Party skilfully used folk-artists and especially traditional story tellers in propaganda and education among the rural masses. One example was the 'Story-telling Group of the Shaan-Gan-Ning (Shaanxi-Gansu-Ninxia) Border Region Cultural Association. This was an organization founded in early 1945. A key figure in this group was the blind storyteller Han Qixiang whose experience is analyzed in an interesting article by Chang-Tai Hung (1993). The article attempts to answer some key questions about how communists interpreted Chinese folk culture: what was the relationship between communist cadres and folk storytellers: did communists really 'learn from the masses' as instructed by Mao Zedong in his Yan'an Forum on Literature and Art? It is concluded that folk-artists such as Han Qixiang were fostered as symbols of the Party's claim to be the voice of the people. The medium was as important as the message. 'Such a concept of élite-folk co-operation, however, must be analyzed with care. It is an ambiguous idea with different, and sometimes conflicting, implications: collaboration between Communist intellectuals and folk artists, conformity of storytellers to the Party line and imposition of doctrine from above' (Hung, 1993, p. 419). It should also be remembered that for much of the 20th century communism presented itself as an alternative 'globalisation' that would start from the people's roots, with education and culture prime vehicles for the transmission of ideology (Morgan, 2003).

Fei's remarks in particular may be compared with those of the writer and naturalist W. H. Hudson and his attack on the 'one size fits all' system of national education in Edwardian England. An Anglo-Argentinian, of pioneering farming stock steeped in country ways, Hudson commented: 'One can only hope that the slow intellect of the country will wake to this question some day, that the countryman will say to the townsman: Go on making laws and systems of education for your own children, who will live as you do indoors; while I shall devise a different one for mine, one which will give them hard muscles and teach them to raise the mutton and pork and cultivate the potatoes and cabbages on which we all feed' (Hudson, 1936, pp. 6–7). That was written in 1910, a time when Hudson still hoped that authentic and organic rural communities such as those described in his classic *A Shepherd's Life*, might and should survive. That they have not is a consequence of industrialization and of the modernization of agriculture for a commercial mass market. Almost a century later, these trends have penetrated to all corners of the globe, making traditional ways of life vulnerable and perhaps obsolete.

J. A. Majasan, in his discussion of *Folklore as an Instrument of Education among the Yoruba* of Nigeria, recognizes these cultural dilemmas. After a survey of the continuing importance of myths, folktales, legends, riddles, proverbs, tongue-twisters, taboos, ballads, songs and folk dance in the ethno- genesis and cultural continuity of the Yoruba people, he concludes: 'It is obvious now that the content of Yoruba education by itself cannot satisfy the aspirations of the people today. But a re-organization of modern education in Yorubaland should include so much of functional Yoruba culture as will re-establish confidence in its growth and popularity among the rising generation. This will make then realize that the fundamental task of education is to foster and develop indigenous culture with all the necessary modifications for a new age' (Majasan, 1969, p. 59). By the first decade of the new millennium, the cultural dilemma has become urgent of resolution. Similarly, Kevin Maxwell, in his study of Bemba myth and ritual in east Africa, focuses on the differences between an oral society and a literate one. He points out that the Bemba are a formally oral, aural people. Hearing is their primary cognitive sense and the physical properties of sound affect the Bemba world-view significantly. This is evidenced in their charter myth, initiation rites, traditional authorities and tales of spirits. These make up a network of central religious metaphors and limit-symbols, each of which is signalized by its acoustic characteristics. Maxwell argues that literacy has re-structured Bemba consciousness and society, making vision the primary sense and written codes, not tribal personalities, the basis of government. As more Bemba convert to Christianity and interiorize writing technology, elements of their oral religion and ethnic sense of identity ironically become more dependent for survival on acculturation with these literate forces (Maxwell, 1983). This is a process that has continued with the intensity of a geometric progression, for the past twenty years, not only in Africa, but where ever local, traditional communities with an oral culture are still to be found (Postiglione, 1999).

Globalisation and Knowledge

Globalisation is not, of course, Karl Marx and Friedrich Engels in The Communist Manifesto of 1848 identified a recent phenomenon and its colonial and imperialist roots and cultural implications. As they pointed out in a graphic yet concise description of mid-19th century bourgeois globalisation: 'In place of the old local and national seclusion and self-sufficiency we have intercourse in every direction, universal interdependence of nations. And as in material, so also in intellectual production. The intellectual creations of individual nations become common property. National one-sidedness and narrow mindedness become more and more impossible and from the numerous national and local literatures there arises a world literature ... The bourgeoisie ... compels all nations, on pain of extinction, to adopt the bourgeois mode of production ... i.e. to become bourgeois themselves. In one word, it creates a world after its own image' (Marx and Engels, 1967, p. 84) Although they did not use the same terms, Marx and Engels were conscious of the tension between the Great and Little Traditions; and were convinced of the superiority of the former over the latter. In their opinion, it had '... rescued a considerable part of the population from the idiocy of rural life' just as it made '... barbarian and semi-barbarian countries dependent on the civilized ones ... the East on the West' (Marx and Engels, 84)

This is symptomatic of the progressive modernizer's basic contempt for local knowledge that has, with some exceptions, continued to the present day. Western modernization's claims to superiority, Dascal suggests, have been based on its global capacity, on its allegedly unlimited ability to achieve self-improvement in any domain, both for individual and for society. The possibility of non-invidious comparisons only arises, Dascal says, if it is possible to assign to other cultures a set of global abilities comparable in scope and quality. This is '... a set that characterizes a full-blooded form of life, complete with its self-evaluation and other evaluation standards and with its perfectibility potential. Holism seems to be then a necessary ingredient of unprejudiced cultural comparison' (Dascal, 1991, pp. 284–85). Putting it bluntly: 'Our science yields a systematic and profound knowledge of horses, camels and snow that gauchos, bedouins and eskimos, respectively, cannot dream of; our instruments can improve our capacity of orientation anywhere. Our medicine, unhindered by "superstitions and other peculiarities characteristic of the primitive mind" can explain and rationally use

Shuar pharmacology as well as Chinese acupuncture; and our taste may be refined so as to appreciate the best there is in other cultures' art' (Dascal, 1991, p. 284)

This raises the further questions of by what processes is knowledge generated, communicated, adapted, incorporated and transmitted and, crucially, who controls this? As Smith reminds us the development of scientific thought, the exploration and 'discovery' by Europeans of other world, the expansion of trade, the establishment of colonies and the systematic colonization of indigenous peoples in the 18th and 19th centuries are all part of the modernist project. A fundamental consequence was that: 'The production of knowledge, new knowledge and transformed 'old knowledge, ideas about the nature of knowledge and the validity of specific forms of knowledge, became as much commodities of colonial expansion as other natural resources' (Smith, 1999, p. 59) The fact remains that many local people felt unsure of themselves or even inferior, as they could not understand what the foreign 'experts' were saying expressed, as it seemed to them, in a strange and obscure language. But, as Lerner points out what and who constitutes the experts as experts? This is done, supposedly, by some objective entity called *Science*. The problem is that science is not the only or the best way to organize our experience according to our current needs. As Lerner concludes, in failing to understand the real limits of science as an approach to reality we tend to dis-empower ourselves (Lerner, 1986, p. 203).

Such a relationship between the Great and Little Traditions, between élite and popular culture, is found in all class-based or otherwise stratified, colonial and neo-colonial situations. As Gramsci showed, they create a hegemony of economic, political, ideological and cultural practices and systems (Gramsci, 1971, Borg et al, 2002) Although as Dascal points out, one should not regard 'western culture' as monolithic, nevertheless its 'orientations, sub-cultures and philosophical tribes display enough of a family resemblance in order to make talk of it not entirely inaccurate' (Dascal, 1991, p. 292). This self-confident and domineering 'Western science' has, historically, been globalizing in intention and in practice. According to Edward Said, the universalizing discourses of modern Europe and the United States have: '... assumed the silence, willing or unwilling of the non-European world. There is incorporation, there is inclusion; there is direct rule; there is coercion. But there is only infrequently an acknowledgement that the colonized people should be heard from, their ideas known (Said, 1993, p. 58). This is aggravated by the way in which *development* has become institutionalized and the people who work on its projects professionalised. This raises important issues: '... concerning the production and uses of knowledge, about the legitimacy or otherwise of the 'experts' who provide advice, about the level of participation of local people in projects and about the intended and unintended economic and political consequences of the whole development enterprise as it is carried out across the world' (Gardner and Lewis, 1996, p. 155). The same malaise also affects social policy provision, including education, in the developed world with the emergence of the so-called 'nanny state.'

Elements of the Little Tradition have been and still are being taken up and re-interpreted by the Great Tradition. At the same time, elements of the latter are filtered down to the former, where they are adapted according to local customs, practices and values. In recent decades, this has been shown most clearly in the systematic attempts at rural modernization and development and in rural de-population and migration to cities and other urban settlements. As Bellonelle pointed out thirty years ago: 'All our 'modern 'agronomists must be persuaded ... that they are not working a void. The men they deal with are peasants in the truest sense of the word and women who, for generations, have accumulated a capital of experience which constitutes the indispensable point of departure' (Brokensha, 1980, p. 5). The point is that indigenous or local knowledge should be complementary to modern science. This approach is still needed. Modern science has, on its own, proved unable to solve problems of rural development. This has stimulated greater recognition, among anthropologists at least, of Indigenous Knowledge Systems (IKS). These have been defined as: '... as systems of knowledge and practice, developed over generations ... these systems have mainly evolved outside or in contrast with Western-oriented, 'scientific' or 'modern' systems of knowledge and technology generated through universities, research institutes and industries. [it] ... formed the basis for local-level decision making in sectors of the society such as human and animal health, agriculture and food production, natural resources management and fisheries' (Slikkerveer, 1999, p. 513).

Contemporary Globalisation and the Need for Roots

Current theories and practice of globalisation continue to reflect this. It is defined simply by the International Monetary Fund as '... worldwide integration through trade, financial flows, technology spillovers, information networks and across cultural currents' (IMF, 2003)

It is seen also as both inevitable and desirable, politically and economically progressive, a contemporary historicism. There is now enormous economic pressure towards contemporary globalisation, that is accompanied by technological and cultural trends, international migration and 'brain-drain' and a trend towards a border-less education encouraged by the World Trade Organization and the General Agreement on Trade in Services. The GATS was adopted by the Uruguay Round and covers all internationally traded services. It is also the first multilateral agreement to provide legally enforceable rights to trade in all services including cultural ones.

While it is recognized that the inter-linked economy is not yet full formed, nevertheless the paradigm for economic behaviour is moving rapidly in the direction of what Kenichi Ohmae, has called '... the weave of economic and intellectual dependence of nations.' Ohmae, an evangelist of globalisation and former Chief Executive Officer of the international consultants McKinsey, claims that: 'Inevitably, the emergence of the inter-linked economy brings with it an erosion of national sovereignty as the power of information directly touches local communities; academic, professional and social institutions; corporations and individuals. It is this border-less world that will give participating economies the capacity for boundless prosperity (Ohmae, 1990, p. 269).

However there is a strong human need for identity and roots. Hence Simone Weil's emphasis on 'real, active and natural participation in the life of a community which preserves in living shape, creation particular treasures of the past and certain particular expectations for the future. Every human being needs to have multiple roots. It is necessary for him to draw well nigh the whole of his moral, intellectual and spiritual life by way of the environment of which he forms a natural part' (Weil, 1952, p. 41). Yet, '... if one's native land is regarded as a vital medium, there is no need for it to be protected from foreign influences. (yet exchange).... is only possible where each preserves his own genius and that is not possible without liberty' (Weil, 1952, pp. 155–156) This is a fundamental insight that needs now, more than ever to be recognized and acted upon. The experience of the indigenous peoples of the Peruvian Amazon since the 1970s may be taken as an example. The spread of formal schooling led to a loss of identity and self-esteem. At first local people believed that if they and their children learned the outsider's knowledge, they would become as prosperous. Yet they have ended up with the worst of both worlds. They were taught everything from a western world-view but actually acquired very little knowledge that would be of value to them, while their own indigenous culture was ignored, even vilified (Trapnell, 2003, p. 9). The local response was to establish in 1988 the Intercultural Bi-lingual Education Teacher Training Programme, sponsored by the Amazonian Indigenous Confederation. Its aim is to defend indigenous people's collective and individual rights and to challenge: 'a school curriculum based entirely upon the concepts of an urban colonial society' (Trapnell, 2003, p. 9). This programme has developed slowly, but steadily over the past fifteen years, but still only affects fifteen out of the forty indigenous societies in the region. The Programme does, however, recognize the importance of using the knowledge of parents: 'Many elders now work side by side with teachers in the transference of their people's knowledge. Parents who previously felt that they had nothing to teach their children, are once again taking pride in passing down traditional knowledge, while their children are learning for themselves the value of their people's traditional ways' (Trapnell, 2003, p. 11).

The parallel between bio-diversity and cultural diversity was first made by the UN/UNESCO World Commission on Culture and Development report *Our Creative Diversity*, published in 1995. This report called for concerted action to address development challenges and to sustain cultural diversity in a global world. Further discussion took place at Stockholm during the Inter-Governmental Conference on Cultural Policies for Development in 1998, with the issue being raised at successive conferences of the World Trade Organization in relation to goods and services. The argument is that: 'just as policies of bio-diversity preservation are needed to guarantee the protection of natural eco-systems and the diversity of species, only adequate cultural policies can ensure the preservation of creative diversity against the risks of a single homogenizing culture' (Cano et al, 2000, p. 39). It must be said that, while this recognition of cultural ecology is welcome, its substantive achievements are very limited. Formal recognition of cultures and their acquisition of the tourist appeal, fancy-dress of the folk museum is very far from providing the conditions in which they may thrive autonomously and authentically.

Another aspect of the tension between globalisation and local knowledge that is worth noting is in religious belief and practice. Modernization, acculturation and the now increasingly rapid process of globalisation has clearly destroyed and damaged many indigenous or belief systems in recent centuries, though it could be argued that this is simply an inevitable process of historical change. Yet the world remains culturally and religiously pluralistic and notably some Christian churches have argued the value of rooting theology in the local environment. The Conference on Theological Education in South East Asia, held in Bangkok, Thailand in 1956 argued the following: 'The teaching of theology must be relevant to the environment. It must, on the one hand, be grounded in the Bible, and on the other, related to the actual situation...The Christian faith should be presented in relation to the totality of questions raised by the local situation, and it should not be assumed that certain questions are relevant to all times and situations' (Koyama, 1983, p. 291). The culture shock comes because, as Koyama says: 'History no longer flows. It is forced. In its response indigenous theology [and local belief systems] must be able to discern the negative and positive aspects of modernization [and by implication globalisation]. It must critically suggest a possibility of human meaning...by indicating a competent understanding of this complex phenomenon ...' (Koyama, 1983, p. 294).

Globalisation and Local Knowledge: Is Compatibility Possible?

Such an effort at effective cultural ecology would also be of value if applied to highly developed Western societies; the pressures of cultural uniformity, for uniform curricula and the development of education as a formal professional process are having increasingly negative consequences. The re-discovery of family learning is one response. At a society level, a significant consequence has been that the indigenous cultural nationalities of Europe are now seeking to recover and protect their identity under the umbrella of an 'Europe of the Regions.' In this context, Morgan and Tuijnman (2000, p. 60) argue that Europe, and for that matter other regions of the globe, should not be regarded primarily as a geographical concept, covering a clearly delineated territory. Rather it is an imagined space, with a diverse, yet in certain respects common history, patterns of social, cultural and political interaction and distinctive values and national identities. The latter should be defined both in terms of nation-states and 'nations of regional communities' that are often quite local and which may transcend state borders e.g. the Basques.

Another aspect, driven by the process of globalisation, that is a major concern of public policy is that of trans-nationalism, with its related questions of identity politics, migration and human rights. In 1995, an article in *The Annual Review of Anthropology* linked this to the re-emergence of ethnicity: '...at a time when, according to modernization theory, it was to have been attenuated by robust nation-states' (Kearney, 1995, p. 559). These issues have grown in importance quite dramatically in recent years, with immigration, asylum and ethnic and inter-faith relations; central and highly sensitive issues in the European Union in particular. Morgan and Tuijnman suggest that to ensure peace, justice and prosperity in Europe over the coming decades it will be necessary to evolve an authentic civil society. This may act as a 'shock absorber' between the individual, the local community and the nation on the one hand and the state and the globalizing pressures of the international economy, information and communication technologies, and migration on the other. International developments demand that: '... the need for roots and for local belonging are balanced by the need for tolerance and accommodation, of migrants, guest workers and tourists, students and teachers, but also of science and technology, new economic activities and new attitudes, tastes and values' (Morgan and Tuijnman, 2000, p. 60). If we tip too far in either direction there is the very real danger of narrow reaction on the one hand and of alienation and disastrous loss of cultural continuity on the other. Compatibility, which means the capacity to exist together in creative harmony, is possible, but only on these terms of equality, tolerance and balance.

It will not be easy to achieve as Jacques Delors, the former President of the European Commission, has warned. He has pointed out that while culture is steadily being globalized, this has yet been achieved only partially: 'We cannot ignore the promises for globalisation nor its risks, not the least of which is the risk of forgetting the unique character of individual human beings; it is for them to choose their own future and achieve their full potential within the carefully tended wealth of their traditions and their own cultures which, unless we are careful, can be endangered by contemporary developments. People today have a dizzying feeling of being torn between a globalisation whose manifestations they can see and sometimes have to endure and their search for roots, reference points and a sense of belonging. Education has to face up to this problem now more than ever as a world society struggles painfully to be born' (Delors, 1996).

In the space of a very few decades, globalisation has reduced rapidly and increasingly the possibilities of isolation, splendid or otherwise. The school teacher and moral philosopher F. C. Happold recognized this trend almost forty years ago when he wrote: 'There is 'now only one world, of which each of us is a part; with a consequent change for good or evil in our attitudes and thought patterns' (Happold, 1966, p. 22). This change was expressed very vividly he said in Martin Skinner's satirical poem, *Letters to Malaya*, quoted by Happold and published originally by Putnam:

Gone are the days when madness was confined
By seas and hills from spreading though mankind;
When though a Nero fooled upon a string,
Wisdom still reigned unruffled in Pekin;
And God in welcome smiled from Buddha' face,
Though Calvin in Geneva preached of grace.
For now our linked-up globe has shrunk so small,
One Hitler on it means mad days for all.

References

Anderson, B. (1991), *Imagined Communities: Reflections on the Origin and Spread of Nationalism*, Verso, London.

Brokensha, D., Warren, D.M. and Werner, O. (eds) (1980), *Indigenous Knowledge Systems and Development*, University Press of America, Washington D.C.

Borg, C., Buttigieg, J. and Mayo, P. (eds) (2002), *Gramsci and Education,* Rowman and Littlefield, Lanham, Boulder, New York and London.

Cano, G.A., Gazzón, A. and Poussin, G. (eds) (2000), *Culture, Trade and Globalisation: Questions and answers,* UNESCO, Paris.

Dascal, M. (ed) (1992), *Cultural Relativism and Philosophy: North and Latin American Perspectives,* E.J. Brill, Leiden.

Delors, J. (1996), *Learning: The treasure within, UNESCO International Commission on Education for the 21st Century,* Paris.

Fei Xiao-tong (1939), *Peasant Life in China: A field study of country life in the Yangtze valley,* Kegan Paul, Trench and Truebner, London.

Fei Xiao-tong (1992), *From the Soil: The foundations of Chinese society,* University of California Press, Berkeley.

Gardner, K. and Lewis, D. (1996), *Anthropology, Development and the Post-Modern Challenge,* Pluto Press, London.

Geertz, C. (1983), *Local Knowledge: Further essays in interpretive anthropology,* Basic Books, New York.

Gramsci, A. (1971), *Selections from the Prison Notebooks,* G. Nowell Smith and Q. Hoare (eds), Lawrence and Wishart, London.

Guidance, L. and Porter, G. (eds) (2001), *Imagined States, Nationalism, Utopia and Longing in Oral Culture,* University of Utah Press, Logan.

Happold, F.C. (1966), *Religious Faith and Twentieth Century Man,* Penguin Books, Harmondsworth.

Hechter, M. (1975), *Internal Colonialism: The Celtic fringe in British national development 1536-1966,* University of California Press, Berkeley and Los Angeles.

Hudson, W.H. (1936), *A Shepherd's Life,* J.M. Dent, Everyman Library, London.

Hung, C.-T. (1993), 'Re-educating a Blind Storyteller: Han Qixiang and the Chinese Communist storytelling campaign', *Modern China,* vol. 19(4), October, pp. 395–426.

Hutchinson, J. (1987), *The Dynamics of Cultural Nationalism: The Gaelic revival and the creation of the Irish nation-state,* Allen and Unwin, London.

International Monetary Fund (2003), *World Economic Outlook,* www.imf.org.

Jones, G. and Jones, T. (1973), 'Introduction, *The Mabinogion',* J.M. Dent, Everyman Library, London, pp. ix–xxxiv.

Kearney, M. (1995), 'The Local and the Global: The anthropology of globalisation and transnationalism', *Annual Review of Anthropology,* vol. 24, pp. 547–565.

Koyama, K. (1983), 'Indigenous Theology', A. Richardson and J. Bowden (eds), *A New Dictionary of Christian Theology,* SCM Press, London.

Llewellyn, K.N. and Hoebel, E.A. (1941), *The Cheyenne Way: Conflict and case law in primitive jurisprudence,* University of Oklahoma Press, Norman, Oklahoma.

Lukács, G. (1962), *The Historical Novel,* The Merlin Press, London.

Lerner, M. (1986), *Surplus Powerlessness,* Prometheus Books, Oakland, California.

Majasan, J.A. (1969), 'Folklore as an instrument of education among the Yoruba', *Folklore,* vol. 80, Spring, pp. 41–59.

Malinowski, B. (1926), *Crime and Custom in Savage Society,* Routledge and Kegan Paul, London.

Marx, K. and Engels, F. (1967), *The Communist Manifesto,* with an Introduction and Notes by A.J.P. Taylor, Penguin Books, Harmondsworth.

Maxwell, K.B. (1983), *Bemba Myth and Ritual: The impact of literacy on an oral culture,* American University Studies, Peter Lang, New York, Frankfurt am Main, Berne.

Morgan, W.J. (2003), *Communists on Education and Culture 1848–1948*, Palgrave Macmillan, Basingstoke and New York.

Morgan, W.J. and Tuijnman, A.C. (2000), 'The challenges for adult education in Europe: De-construction and re-construction of nations and states', A. Bron and M. Schemmann (eds), *Language, Mobility, Identity: Contemporary issues for adult education in Europe*, Lit Verlag, Muenster, Hamburg, London, pp. 47–62.

Nairn, T. (1977), *The Break-up of Britain: Crisis and neo-nationalism*, New Left Books, London.

Ohmae, K. (1991), *The Border-less World: Power and strategy in the inter-linked economy*, Fontana, London.

Panniker, K.M. (1953), *Asia and Western Dominance: A survey of the Vasco da Gama epoch of Asian history*, Allen and Unwin, London.

Postiglione, G. (ed) (1999), *China's National Minority Education: Culture, schooling and development*, Falmer Press, New York and London.

Prebble, J. (1963), *The Highland Clearances*, Penguin Books, Harmondsworth.

Ranger, T. and Hobsbawm, E.J. (eds) (1983), *The Invention of Tradition*, Cambridge University Press, Cambridge.

Redfield, R. (1956), *The Little Community and Peasant Society and Culture*, Phoenix Books, The University of Chicago Press, Chicago and London.

Said, E.W. (1993), *Culture and Imperialism*, Chatto and Windus, London.

Said, E.W. (1995), *Orientalism: Western Concepts of the Orient*, Penguin Books, Harmondsworth.

Scott, W. (2000), *Ivanhoe* with an introduction and notes by David Blair, Wordsworth Classics, London.

Slikkerveer, L.J. (1999), 'INDAKS: A bibliography and database on indigenous agricultural knowledge systems and sustainable development in the tropics', D.M. Warren, L.J. Slikkerveer and D. Brokensha, *The Cultural Dimension of Development: Indigenous Knowledge Systems*, Intermediate Technology Publications, London, pp. 512–516.

Smith, T. (1999), *De-colonizing Methodologies: Research and indigenous peoples*, Zed Books, London and New York and University of Otago Press, Dunedin.

Trapnell, L. (2003), *Identity Crisis, Development*, Issue 22, Second Quarter, pp. 8–11.

Weil, S. (1952), *The Need for Roots: Prelude to a declaration of duties towards Mankind*, Routledge and Kegan Paul, London.

Williams, R. (1975), *The Country and the City*, Paladin, London.

Chapter 5

Cross-Cultural Transference in Educational Management

Marion Shaw

Introduction

The theme of this book concerns the impact of globalisation of educational praxis on culture; this chapter is concerned specifically with cross-cultural transference in educational management. It is a widely-recognised fact of global economics that the parts of the world which have enough money to indulge in research tend to exert influence on other parts of the world where such research is impossible to fund. The mechanism is straightforward: research findings are turned into journal articles, which later evolve into textbooks of educational models and theories. With globalised marketing, such books are then found on shelves around the world, and, with the hegemonic power of the printed word, and in the absence of anything more locally suitable, these can easily be seen as 'how to' texts – but the assumption that materials are equally relevant everywhere is simply not sound.

Although there is currently a greater awareness of cultural difference, and hence also of suitability, there nevertheless appear to be a number of built-in mechanisms – human, cultural and systematic – which have a tendency to neutralise culture-relevant practice. A decade of supporting educational development in a wide range of developing countries and nations in transition has furnished me with sufficient empirical evidence to believe this to be true.

This chapter first contextualises educational consultancy by briefly examining the relationship between funding agencies and the recipients of 'aid'. The rest of the chapter is then devoted to an examination of how serious misunderstandings can arise when training and consultancy do not pay sufficient attention to inherent cultural assumptions – on both sides. An analytical framework is provided by cross-cultural theory, and a well-known leadership model is deconstructed in order to demonstrate not only how culture-centric theory is but also how the cultural assumptions built into theory can misfire when recklessly introduced into another culture. Finally, a model designed to interrogate theory from a culture-neutral perspective is introduced, and then applied illustratively to a few other well-known theories.

Power Relationships in Development Aid

A great deal of evidence exists to indicate that over recent decades projects operated in the developing world by consultants from the developed world have not had outstanding success in achieving their aims (e.g. Psacharopoulos, 1989; Lockheed and Verspoor, 1991; Reilly, 1987; Leach, 1994). Indeed, in 1984 Porter was moved to note that 'the effects of the last 35 years of intense consultative and expert activity from the developed to the developing world has been only too often to give brilliant answers to the wrong questions' (1984, p. 18).

James (1999) identifies two reasons for this sort of failure: (a) because the changes introduced were not culturally embedded, and (b) because of unequal power relationships between donor and recipient. He suggests that the second argument has become more persuasive to donors than the first, and certainly there has, over the last decade since the Jomtien Agreement (1990), been a stronger – or, at least, a more overt – emphasis on empowerment. Donor aid has been channelled more into providing sector-wide support than into individual projects, and enabled by, for example, the policy of the UK's Department for International Development (DfID) to put in-country advisers in place. This has resulted in some large-scale educational programmes with multiple facets, usually with considerable effort put into counter-parting and other ways of ensuring a more equal partnership. This, on paper, is designed so that 'the Western partner acts as the expert in Western technology and the local partner as the expert in local culture, habits and feelings' (Hofstede, 1997, p. 84) – but this ideal does not always measure up to reality.

As aid agencies themselves point out (e.g. Gustafsson, 1999), for various reasons this approach has had limited success. Fox (1997) articulates a key factor for this failure: the requirements of the agencies are for the planning documents to be expressed in language, as well as linguistic patterns, which are alien to the recipient partner:

> Much of current educational development assistance continues to be planned by international and First World agencies along rational, technical lines. The metaphors of development are not based on notions of social justice, but on economic, structural images of building models, drawing analogies to the formulation of ground plans, making a blueprint for programme implementation, delivery of materials, the sending 'in' of a 'team,' the tight time line, inputs and outputs, product flow, monitoring, and so on.
>
> (Fox, 1997, p. 60)

But this type of rational social paradigm of Western planners contrasts starkly with the more interactive, subjective paradigm which 'has, at its core, the notion that individuals create the world in which they live, and that any understanding of society, its institutions and its emergent social processes, *depends on the vantage-point of the participant*' (Adams, 1991). The consequence of this is that, while consultants in the field talk about strategic planning and delivery, their counterparts in-country 'move within the more fluid and broader cultural framework of their ongoing educational context, speaking of people's lives' (Fox, 1997, p. 60).

Analysis that has been done on failed projects, then, often locates the problem, as in London's research, with 'the principles of planning and implementation that were engaged' (1993, p. 274). As any consultant who has had to configure, and evaluate, their work in a tightly-worded 'logical framework'-type format knows, the planning process takes place to a Western agenda, and the very documentation which is meant to support the project can be inaccessible to the specific group(s) most in need of understanding it. This may seriously disempower the client partner.

The rationale for this fragmentation of projects into individually-evaluated sections is ostensibly the greater accountability for public spending in the donor countries. In bidding for projects, the funding body needs to be able to account for effective and efficient use of resources, so consultants need to be given clear aims and objectives, and to be able to identify (justify?) at any given stage what they have achieved from the 'log-frame' and what they will be doing next.

But does a more covert issue of control exist as well? Governments of needy countries have learned the hard way how to leap through the hoops of aid donors, and altering policy in order to meet defined criteria is not uncommon. In order to encourage democracy, for example, Harber notes that 'international agencies increasingly attach political strings to loans and aid – no democracy, no money' (1995, p. 2). In these circumstances, a genuine dialogue cannot be said to be taking place; it is rather a 'strategic manipulation of power' (Fox, 1997, p. 48). In what might be described as a form of neo-colonial hegemony, the rich wield the power, and the poor have to conform to donor-set rules if they are to 'deserve' development funding. As I was once told in Africa, *'we will do what you* (i.e. we, as representatives of the British Council) *want: we are beggars'*.

Returning to James' reasons for the lack of success of consultancy in the developing world, one might argue that his two elements are closely inter-related, as illustrated by the following incident.

> In a revealing outburst from our Russian counterpart (the Deputy Director of Education) during a planning discussion at the start of a new project, she snapped in Russian to her (English-speaking) subordinate, *'You* deal with them. I don't understand how these English think,' (Shaw and Ormston, 2001, p. 125). On further examination, hers was a dual frustration. Firstly, she was immensely irritated at having to confine her thoughts about the complex project to the tight boxes demanded of the logical framework: it did not allow her to develop her considerable creativity in the way she felt most comfortable with, and she felt disenfranchised. Furthermore, the concepts under discussion were almost impossible to grasp in translation. The task in this case was to embed in the region 'management training by active learning techniques', but these words met a linguistic barrier in Russian, 'management' implying authoritarian administration, 'training' denoting something that subordinates have done to them (i.e. passive, one-way transfer – certainly not an appropriate thing to do to managers), and the verb 'to learn' being conveyed in Russian by the reflexive of the verb to teach, i.e. 'is-taught'. A triple conceptual mismatch existed before the project even started.

In this case, the problem happened to be with a European language, but the potential for misunderstanding across languages with quite different structures is enormous, and may compound the issue of cross-cultural transfer even further.

'The words of a language.....are the vehicles of culture transfer' (Hofstede, 1991, p. 213), and to ignore language is perhaps eventually to jeopardise the project.

Closely related to the issue of accountability is a more demanding attitude towards time. In the past, a less-frenetic and more anthropological approach to educational support overseas was possible: people could spend a reasonable amount of time living in the country and understanding how the culture worked before intervening. As Arthur and Preston found in their illuminating research for the British Council (1996), today's consultants tend to have greater pressure placed on them to achieve targets within a hugely condensed time-frame, leaving little time to get to know the local culture. Aggregated across the world, the consequence of this time pressure is an increased likelihood of the same models and theories being recycled everywhere, regardless of cultural suitability, by well-meaning – but hard-pressed – consultants who spend half their lives accumulating air-miles.

The resulting lack of cultural embeddedness plays a powerful role in the success or failure of educational consultancy; adaptability for cultural appropriateness is axiomatic.

Culture and Responsibility in Educational Consultancy

Education is a particularly sensitive area to work in, as it represents the formative stages of social development – the cradle of attitudes for the next generation. It is bad enough that many developing countries employ the use of European textbooks, models, examinations and staff, teaching to inappropriate curricula and perpetuating dependency (Watson, 1985). If, in addition, the models, techniques and materials used for the professional in-service development of the leading educationalists in the country are also not adapted to the culture, the outcome of the project is at best ineffective (Leach, 1994), and at worst dangerous (Shaw and Welton, 1996). Rodwell (1998) debates whether the best way ahead for the development of materials is via 'indigenisation' (i.e. making models and theories suitable inside the culture) or 'internationalisation' (i.e. neutralising models so that they may be used in any environment).

In effect, the latter tends to mean one-sided globalisation. Rodwell is forced to conclude that until we have enough information about *how* to indigenise effectively, it is inevitable that Western materials will fill the void – again perpetuating the inequity. However, the former is not easy either, and well-meaning attempts to indigenise recognised models have been disastrous, as this next illustration of an inappropriately-modified management training model shows.

During a management training course in sub-Saharan Africa, where one of the Ministry's main challenges was to motivate managers in the education service, help them to delegate effectively, emphasise their responsibilities and gain commitment to duty, a senior member of the Ministry produced a case study entitled 'Who makes the decisions?' that he had received on a previous management training course. It was based on Blanchard and Johnson's *The One Minute Manager* (1982), originally written to demonstrate to hyperactive American managers that they could make life easier for themselves if they used the human capital in their teams better by adopting a more 'hands-off' approach, delegating more, and employing a more participative leadership style. The authors use an idiosyncratically USA-centric and exaggerated image of a manager, who, in contrast to those managers who are over-stressed and who tend to micro-manage, is so relaxed about his job that he only appears to works for a couple of hours a week.

In order to 'indigenise' the model, the authors of this case study had re-named the people and places, carefully choosing local names from the particular region in question. They had nevertheless retained the original metaphor and exaggerated it even more, depicting the ideal manager, Amos, in these words: 'In the middle of the following week, Ndapewa popped in on Amos unannounced. [...] She found Amos lying on his sofa, half asleep. His secretary did not look very busy either. Ndapewa's arrival seemed to jar Amos awake ...'. Amos was held up as a model manager because his total weekly work commitment was apparently one two-hour meeting, as *'ever since I decided not to decide, I've got nothing to keep me busy'*. It was apparently commendable for him to spend the rest of his week flat out on his sofa, while leaving the real decision-making to everyone else.

Given the still-developing skills of public sector employees in the country where this management tool was being so inappropriately used, a manager who demonstrated such apparently laid-back and inappropriate leadership was the very last thing needed by a ministry attempting to build capacity by coaching, mentoring, enthusing and engaging.

The only positive thing that could be said about this case study was that at least someone had made an effort to change something rather than use it unadapted. Nevertheless, this is a case where a highly *injudicious* attempt to indigenise materials could only have served as a negative role model; it was probably, in fact, more dangerous than the unadulterated original would have been. By localising the names, but leaving the rest of the model intact, the content was made more accessible to the local ministry employees; it made them more inclined to follow Amos' example, but without his hinterland of knowledge, without his capacity to delegate, and certainly without his team of highly-skilled and motivated personnel to carry out the tasks autonomously. The consequence was that this well-intentioned transference was not only irresponsible but entirely counter-productive to the original intention, and it produced considerable confusion over desired leadership behaviours in the context of *that* ministry, at *that* time, and in *that* culture.

This was just one example of a model that was poorly transposed across cultures. Many others include assumptions of what is, or is not, possible in terms of behaviour among the people concerned. It is not uncommon for educational consultants to be asked to introduce into different parts of the world some of the following concepts, all examples of behaviours or policies which have been found to be either desirable or effective (or even both!) in educational systems in the developed world. But they raise – or should do – serious questions of suitability when used in different cultures, for example:

- A strong feature of many management development courses emphasises Western-style assertiveness, but is it reasonable to expect a woman in a traditional society to behave assertively to her male colleagues?
- In encouraging the development of participative styles of leadership, is it equally feasible in all societies that an employee who does not fully understand how to do the job might ask for help from their line manager?
- If the employee in (b) *did* pluck up courage to ask for help, would line managers in all societies be equally able to admit not knowing the answer to a question without losing face?
- In developing mentoring skills would it be realistic in all cultures to expect a manager to work closely with a junior colleague from a different cultural group?
- Can performance appraisal be used as a professional development tool in a national or organisational climate which is largely bureaucratic and punitive?

Clearly, there are responsibilities incumbent on the visiting educational consultant or trainer to ensure that s/he uses the models that are most suitable, and introduces them in a culture-sensitive way, and these issues are addressed on page 63. Awareness of the potential dangers in using familiar and well-documented theories and models is simply the first step: the more challenging question is how to make an informed choice of materials. If none others exist, how is it possible to interrogate these for suitability? If adaptation is needed in order to make an appropriate suitable transference, what resources do consultants have to guide them?

Reference to cross-cultural research is most helpful, and is the catalyst for effective transference of praxis from one culture into another – if sufficient care and sensitivity are applied. This body of theory explores the assumptions and communication patterns within groups of people, and can therefore throw light on the potential misunderstandings that may occur when people from different cultures communicate.

Cross-Cultural Theory

A number of research projects have sought to help people understand better what is going on between cultures. The assumption is that they should then be able to communicate more effectively, and thus eventually to improve organisational performance at all levels. There is a key difficulty in carrying out research of this nature, however: it is impossible to do a scientific piece of experimental research, as there are so many human variables. Nevertheless, between 1967 and 1973 a seminal piece of work was carried out , involving so many different cultures, and such huge numbers of people, that broad generalisations were able to be made with confidence.

Hofstede, a social psychologist, was engaged by a multinational computer firm to carry out a 'values survey' on their employees worldwide with a view to improving morale. This study was designed to find out how people preferred to work, about their relationships with colleagues, and about their expectations of, and reactions to, each other. In all, 117,000 people in 53 different countries were surveyed – a massive sample. After completing the work for his client, Hofstede realised that this huge bank of data, collected from an equivalent sample in each country, might potentially be used to analyse and interpret cultural attitudes and expectations; this work led to his international recognition for ground-breaking work on cultures and organisations, and set the scene for many further investigations.

Before going on to examine the relevance of his work, the concept of 'culture' needs clarification. Hofstede defines culture as 'the collective programming of the mind which distinguishes the members of one group or category of people from another. Culture is learned, not inherited. It derives from one's social environment, not from one's genes' (Hofstede, 1991, p. 5). Brislin, from the East-West Centre in Hawaii, echoes this:

- Culture consists of ideals, values, and assumptions about life that guide specific behaviours;
- Culture consists of those aspects of the environment that people make;
- Culture is transmitted from generation to generation, with the responsibility given to parents, teachers, religious leaders, and other respected elders in the community.

(Brislin, 1993, Ch. 1)

These definitions focus on values and assumptions as opposed to the more general use of the word which embraces the art/performance manifestations of a group of people.

Hofstede uses a graphic onion metaphor to illustrate the concept: the outer, more visible layers of the onion are represented by symbols and practices, while the concealed innermost core, once the other layers are peeled away, consists of *values*. Unlike the outer layers, which are relatively easy to observe and to understand, the core values are usually hidden; these are the assumptions inherent in the culture. They define the norms by which people of the same group live, and, because they *are* assumptions, they are not discussed. It is widely assumed that this inner core of cultural values is learned at an early stage: Hofstede suggests that 'developmental psychologists believe that by the age of 10 most children have their basic value system firmly in place, and after that age, changes are difficult to make' (1991, p. 8).

Discussing culture is fraught with difficulty: no-one is neutral – each perceiving the world from her/his own perspective, and there are many meanings – a confusion which Hofstede himself points out (1991). Values – and therefore culture – may be derived from various sources, such as national or ethnic group, generation, work organisation, gender, class and religion – and these are not necessarily all consonant with each other (Hofstede, 1991, p. 10). The researchers argue that cultural values are attached to groups of people, and that such groups are often defined by nationality. At the same time, it is recognised that nationality alone may be problematic. The nation state itself, for example, may consist of many different cultures; perhaps groups of people may have emigrated to another land through war or famine, taking their cultures with them. Whatever the cause of cultural affiliation, the researchers have sought to find a reliable way of categorising cultures into various dimensions, and nationality is one such way, so, for the purposes of this chapter, the term culture is used to mean the *values and assumptions of groups of people bound by their ethnicity.*

As a result of his research, Hofstede proposed four cultural 'dimensions', later augmented by a fifth. A dimension is 'an aspect of a culture that can be measured relative to other cultures' (Hofstede, 1991, p. 12), and his are summarised in Figure 5.1 in order to provide a vocabulary for the discussion which follows. Hofstede's numerical data for the countries on these dimensions, which are the key to the practical application of his work, are not repeated here, but can be found in his book, Cultures and Organisations (1991). Although seated in the world of corporate business, his conclusions can be applied across many aspects of work and non-work relationships, including here to education. His research has frequently been critiqued, applauded, condemned and replicated (see Søndergaard, 1994), and will not be commented on further here, except to say that his was the first substantial piece of research to allow a real cross-cultural comparison in a difficult area to assess, and that it generated much excitement.

Power distance (PD) is defined by the amount of emotional distance between employers and employees. In high power distance cultures, employees typically tend to prefer their managers to lead visibly, and paternal-autocratic leadership styles are seen as caring. In low power distance cultures, the opposite is true; employees tend to express a preference for consultative management styles.

Individualism - collectivism is defined as the degree to which people see themselves or their collective group as more important. Individualistic societies tend to emphasise the 'I' above the 'we', while collectivist societies respect the goals of their own group more than individual achievement.

Uncertainty avoidance (UA) is defined by the amount of anxiety about the future that can be tolerated. It is usually linked to the degree of freedom in the country; where control is strong and rules are plentiful, UA tends to be high, and vice versa. People from cultures with a high UA index tend to expect teachers and managers to have precise answers for everything, and to give detailed instructions for every job, while people in low UA cultures tend to feel comfortable with more ambiguity and to take unfamiliar risks.

Masculinity-femininity is concerned with the degree of achievement-orientation built into the culture, taking its name (unhelpfully, arguably) from stereotypical gender expectations. High masculinity cultures value status, challenge and achievement, while high femininity cultures value good working relationships and co-operation.

Confucian dynamism (long-term vs. short-term orientation):
This dimension emerged after the others following studies of entrepreneurial development in East Asia, which did not fit into the previous dimensions. It represents an emergence of the long-term orientation of "virtue" (persistence, thrift, ordering relationships by, and observing, status, and having a sense of commitment to others) out of the more traditional short-term orientation of "truth" (personal stability, protecting "face", respect for tradition). The interaction between the two makes up this cultural value.

Figure 5.1 Hofstede's cultural dimensions (1991)

In addition to Hofstede's dimensions, other researchers have defined ways of analysing what they have observed in cross-cultural encounters. Ross (1977) noted that, as the actions of other people tend to be judged through the value system of the perceiver, incorrect conclusions about the motive for the action are then formed. This generated the term *fundamental attribution error* – the mistake of making judgements about the characters of others without taking situational factors into account, often to the detriment of the person being judged.

Another polarity of terms, universalism vs. particularism, indicates the degree of objectivity which is the norm in a culture. In *particularist* cultures, it is not only normal, but expected by everyone, that people give preference to those closest to them (e.g. family, village, tribe). In more *universalist* cultures, this practice might be regarded as unhealthily nepotistic, because people here tend to apply the same rules to everyone equally.

Another area where cross-cultural communication can run into difficulty is about expectations. If people expect, or assume, that something will happen in a certain way, and then it does not, then any deviation from their first expectation is perceived as greater than it really is (Helson, 1964). This is very real: in Brislin's words, 'disconfirmed expectancies are certain in intercultural encounters' (1993, p. 44).

If the above makes it sound as though cross-cultural research has produced problem-solving formulae, one must remember that this area is immensely complex, and not without problems. For example, such research is largely Western-centric (Trompenaars, 1993); the research tools are not appropriate in all cultures, which means suspect validity (Riordan and Vandenburg, 1994); it is mainly industry-based, and can be easily misused when attempt at transference is made to other areas (Jameson, 1994); and it has tended to attach stereotypes to nation states (Hofstede, 1980; Trompenaars, 1993). Crossley and Vulliamy (1997) also highlight the dangers of carrying out research in developing countries, where 'cultural imperialism continues to take many forms' (p. 11).

Nevertheless, despite of the problems around their misuse, stereotypes can be useful: they help us categorise, and provide a point of reference, as 'people have so many decisions about their behaviour during a given day that they need guidance, hints, helpful rules, and so forth. Stereotypes serve this purpose.' (Brislin, 1993, p. 173). But, carried to extremes, this sentiment carries the further danger of labelling individuals – believing that everyone of a certain nationality thinks and behaves in the same way; the researchers themselves are keen to highlight this danger (Hofstede, 1991, p. 253; Brislin, 1993, p. 174). A related danger is that cultural stereotypes may sometimes be used as an excuse – a reason why something cannot happen, rather than enabling a thorough examination of the processes under the surface (Kanter and Corn, 1994; Goffee and Jones, 1995; Tayeb, 1994).

Bearing in mind these potential traps, the cross-cultural literature can nevertheless become an important tool for analysis, as the next section starts to explore.

Why Culture Matters When Using Theoretical Models: An Illustration

In order to demonstrate the importance of the origins and destinations of theories, a well-known model is examined next through the lens of a culture other than the one in which it evolved. I hope readers who are familiar with it will forgive the explanatory detail, but it is central to the argument in the chapter that the model is understood. The situational leadership model of Blanchard et al (1985) gives managers a structured approach to flexible leadership tailored to each member of their team, depending on the level of development of each individual. Its principles are summarised in Figure 5.2 for those who are not familiar with it.

Applied judiciously in training courses, this model shows how a leader can increase team members' skills developmentally by using appropriate styles of leadership sequentially:

The purpose of this model is to help team members to develop their skills by judicious application of leadership behaviours. In it, the leader is encouraged to provide:
- the right style of leadership for....
- a specific individual, for....
- his/her level of development for....
- a specific task.

Each member's "development level" is found by analysing the relative combination of commitment (knowledge and skills) and competence (confidence and motivation). The most appropriate leadership style (directing, coaching, supporting, or delegating) is then selected *for that individual for the task in question.*

If someone does not know how to do a task (i.e. their development level is low for that task) they would need a lot of directional help (**directing** style) from the leader to carry out the task successfully.

At the other end of the spectrum, if a team member is familiar with the task, skilled at performing it and motivated to do it, the leader can distance herself by fully **delegating** the task, confident in the ability of that person to complete it.

The intermediate leadership styles of **coaching** and **supporting** are useful for those team members who need closer personal attention from the leader for the specific task, giving feedback, encouragement, etc. so that they will become more skilled at the task in hand.

The model encourages a progression from directing, to coaching, to supporting and finally to delegating styles as the team member develops skill at certain tasks..

The benefits are all-round: better sharing of tasks by the leader, a greater chance of success in task completion due to stronger ownership in the team, and individual team members can also develop their professional skills in a natural and work-based environment.

Figure 5.2   Summary of situational leadership model, Blanchard et al (1985)

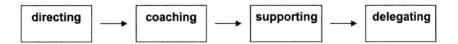

This has been found to be a flexible and successful training tool in helping educational managers to analyse their team composition and their own leadership behaviour. It supports the development of a participative management approach. However, it was 'made in the USA', a culture with a stereotypically low power distance index and a high individualism index. Consequently, the model was based on certain culture-bound implicit assumptions. For example, it might reasonably be assumed that, in the average organisation in the USA:

- close interpersonal interaction is possible between manager and each team member;
- both praise and frank feedback are acceptable in the culture;
- team members expect to be treated as individuals;
- communication is open and two-way;
- team members feel relatively at ease with team leaders (e.g. able to ask questions when an individual is uncertain).

When using this model with teams from the culture in which it evolved, a management consultant or trainer might typically work through the logic of its stages, discussing the implications of the four leadership styles, and asking members to analyse their teams, and identifying the development-level for each person for the key team tasks. The result is a revealing grid, giving team leaders insight, and helping them to select the most appropriate styles to use with different staff for the various team tasks. Although the occasional, idiosyncratic character-clash may adversely affect some of the assumptions above, in general they hold good *because they are implicitly understood*, and nothing in the model seems to counter-act anything in the culture.

The assumptions implicit in this model, however, do not pertain to all cultures, which is why caution is needed when using it elsewhere, as the following illustrates.

Where the model is used with *high power distance cultures,* status is revered highly. It is normal for team members to expect the leader to make the decisions, for the leader to tell members what to do rather than to consult them, and for team members to feel that, even if the boss *did* try to consult them, this would be a sign of weakness, not strength (Hofstede, 1991).

Under these conditions, where there tends to be a lot of emotional distance between leader and team member, interpersonal interaction across 'levels' is likely to be relatively restricted, and in such an environment it is easier for a leader to issue instructions and supervise (i.e. to direct), or to hand something over entirely (i.e. to delegate, regardless of development level), than to enter the closer relationship required for the coaching and supporting styles. Furthermore, in such a culture, individual members often find it more difficult than their counterparts in a lower power distance culture to ask for advice or help from a superior in performing a task, as to ask *appears* to be an admission of inadequacy – a prime example of fundamental attribution error. There is not only an expectation that all managerial tasks will continue to be carried out by those in managerial positions, as that is what they are paid to do, but there is also the fear of failure if they, the subordinates, get it wrong. On this basis, then, there are powerful forces subverting the model.

If the team is also composed of *collectivists*, members tend to see themselves as members of this collective rather than as individuals. They tend towards 'group-think'; the model may not feel comfortable, therefore, as it emphasises the specific skills of the individual.

In such cultures, leaders tend to use the directing and delegating styles more than the coaching and supporting styles, which involve substantial close 1:1 work. There is a quantum leap from directing to delegating, so the progress from one leadership style to the next is interrupted, and there is no smooth developmental pathway (Shaw, 2001):

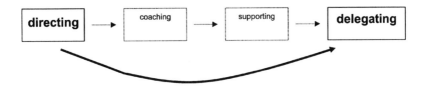

If introduced in the normal 'Western' manner into high PD collectivist cultures, therefore, this model can be largely a waste of time; people are often polite enough to accept what consultants say to their face, but the model is quietly subverted in order to suit everyone's comfort level, and eventually nothing is likely to change.

The situation is compounded if this training tool is introduced to a *mixed-culture* team of collectivists, where people are more likely to perceive greater differences between their own group and others. Telling people what to do, and 'dumping' (as opposed to effective delegating) are the styles which are easiest to adopt with an employee from a different group, as these involve most distant forms of communication. Use of coaching and supporting needs, as well as closer co-operation, empathy and understanding, more determination to help the other succeed – not very easy when working with someone who is distinctly from another group (Fadil, 1995, p. 199).

A further complication arises in *ex-colonial* countries, where a management style of 'tell and blame' has often been inherited from the civil service of the colonising power. As a result, the processes by which the countries' public services operate may be quite rigid. Such organisational climates do not lend themselves either to participative leadership styles, or to employees volunteering for new responsibilities.

Under any of the above conditions, encouraging teams working in a high power distance (PD), collectivist culture to use the original situational leadership model is not only largely unsuccessful, but, if attempted, it may be positively damaging, increasing inequalities, and potentially upsetting established relationships – as demonstrated by the case of 'Amos'.

If these are the dangers, what can be done to avoid them? This section has gone into some detail on one model in order to demonstrate the potential dangers in transferring models thoughtlessly across cultures; the next section examines how a consultant might interrogate 'received Western wisdom' so that it may be turned into something more appropriate for any given culture.

Interrogating Theories For Cultural Suitability

Rather than start from the Western-centric perspective, which many consultants do instinctively, it is helpful to view theory through different cultural lenses. A cultural relativist might, for example, adopt a progressive line of questioning, such as:

- In *which culture* did this model/theory originate?
- What are the stereotypical *characteristics* of this culture (e.g. Hofstede's analysis, 1991)?
- What are the *cultural assumptions* that the model makes (e.g. stress on the success of the individual or the group, what counts as appropriate behaviour in given circumstances, when it is OK to ask for advice from those above, tolerance of mistakes in the interests of professional development)
- *What is known* about the culture(s) where the management development is to be carried out? (e.g. Hofstede's research, 1991)
- How do the *cultural norms match or differ* from those of the model's culture? Is a wide range of cultural norms represented in the client group?
- What, then, might the *misunderstandings* (e.g. Ross' fundamental attribution error, 1977) be in using this model in a different cultural context?
- Under the circumstances, then, is the model *likely to be useful or not*?
- If useful, does it need *adapting, or presenting in a different way*? If so, how? (e.g. more emphasis on one part, omission of another part, altering part of it, etc.)

(Shaw, 2001)

Once any theory or model has been interrogated in this manner, it is possible to judge whether one can use the model, and, if so, how it might be best adapted. Returning to the example of the situational leadership model being applied in the high PD and collectivist culture, as discussed above, adaptations to turn this model into a functional management training tool might include some or all of the following:

- Discussion in more depth about what is involved in each of the four styles, opening the possibility for real choice.
- Open discussion of the suitability of each of these styles inside *this* culture, evolving into a broader discussion about barriers which might prevent these styles being used in *this* team.
- Exploration of specific behaviours that are needed for successful coaching and supporting, examining the degree to which they might be appropriate in *this* culture.
- A focus on the culturally acceptable leadership behaviours which might enable genuine upwards communication inside the team.
- Keeping open the possibility that the members of the team (or whole organisation) could exert some influence on the team climate themselves if they so wished (within the acceptable cultural framework of society).

There is a world of difference, as any trainer/consultant knows, in the manner of presentation – the nuance of assumption. Depending on the climate in the training forum, such a process as this may result in whole-team agreements about explicit 'rules of procedure' by which the team wishes to operate in future, encouraging choice of style, limiting overuse of the two extremes and contributing towards a mutually-agreed organisational culture.

Issues raised in the case above have already thrown light on some of the questions raised in Section 3, but we can now use the research drawn from generalised situations and apply it to more educational ones to analyse the other questions as well.

- *Is it reasonable to expect a woman in a traditional society to behave assertively to her male colleagues?*
  In a high power distance culture, where there are deference patterns of behaviour from subordinate to boss, it often follows also that the same patterns pertain from young to old, and from women to men, though this does depend on local tradition. In any case, while developing assertiveness skills may form a strong feature of many management courses in the West, it would be a mistake to assume the same sort of training approaches would make sense, or be appropriate in all places.
- *In encouraging the development of participative styles of leadership, is it equally feasible in all societies that an employee who does not fully understand how to do the job might ask for help from their line manager?*
  Not very feasible in high PD cultures, as discussed above: they may suspect that their boss will judge them badly if they show that they do not understand.
- *If the employee in (b) did pluck up courage to ask for help, would line managers in all societies be equally able to admit not knowing the answer to a question without losing face?*
  Not in high PD cultures, again, as already discussed in Section 5: the boss is expected to demonstrate to the subordinates in their care that they are fully knowledgeable. This may be even less likely in the Far East, where maintaining 'face' is a strong feature of society (Hofstede, 1991, p. 165).
- *In developing mentoring skills would it be realistic in all cultures to expect a manager to work closely with a junior colleague from a different cultural group?*
  As demonstrated in Section 5, mentoring and coaching involve considerable close interpersonal communication, this would be difficult in highly collectivist, mixed-culture culture teams. There is a greater psychological barrier in relating closely with 'out-group' colleagues than with those in the same group. If the team consisted of individualists as well as collectivists, the individualists may well have less difficulty in relating to the collectivists than vice versa (Hofstede, 1991).
- *Can performance appraisal be used as a professional development tool in a national or organisational climate which is largely bureaucratic and punitive?*
  There is a current emphasis on performance appraisal in the West, and so it is

not uncommon to find it being requested in other educational services as well. However, in the West this initiative evolved historically in the context of other policies, and largely within a *universalist* culture where objective evidence is used in forming a rounded view of the teacher, or ministry worker. In a climate which is punitive, performance appraisal is far more likely to be used as a weapon against employees.

If we extend this last case a little more, and attach some financial reward to the performance appraisal process, the issue is made more complex still. This requires that certain individuals above others get the rewards, so, in a *particularist* culture, the situation could become bloody; by the laws of local custom, family and tribe deserve – and get – the choice options. So, in the words of an African colleague from a particularist culture on being introduced to this policy by a senior Ministry official: 'if this becomes policy, there will be war'.

The whole concept of a performance-related pay (PRP) policy is interesting in the domain of education, in fact. It was invented originally in industry, where an individual's effort could be accurately assessed, and it is probably more feasible in those systems with *masculine* cultures, where achievement and challenge are highly rated. But in a more *feminine* culture, where collaboration is the desirable quality, such competition – for such PRP is – among one's colleagues is seen as both undesirable and counter-productive. One might argue that, the relatively high masculinity quotient that Hofstede gives Britain may well have been over-ridden in the educational service by the *organisational culture* that has developed. Schools have worked very hard to build teams, to make teaching less of an individual pursuit and more of a collaborative, sharing activity. All the training that has gone into the embedding of new initiatives over the last three decades has emphasised this, which is why, even in a relatively high masculinity national culture, PRP has appeared to counter-act all that teachers stood for.

To end this section, some commonly-used management tools are re-examined (See Figure 5 3) through a broad cultural lens, raising the sort of questions that a consultant wishing to transfer across cultures might reasonably ask.

Conclusions

This chapter has aimed to show that cross-cultural transference in educational management is both necessary and complex, that it takes research, sensitivity and emotional intelligence, but that perseverance with the research base pays dividends, and eventually develops a way of seeing things through different lenses. If a line of theory-interrogation, such as the model presented here, is followed, alternative approaches become possible.

While there is no intention to compare management consultancy with warfare(!), it was interesting to note that, during the early days of Gulf War II, when the contrasting approaches of the American and British forces to winning the 'hearts and minds' of the Iraqis were becoming daily more obvious, British military leaders were talking about the essential commodity of, in their terminology, 'situational awareness'. By this, they meant a grounded understanding of the local conditions and attitudes, not only physical, but also psychological. Without this, they said, their approach would be much more of a blunt instrument; they would be making strategic decisions based solely on a British-centric perspective of what they *expected* the 'enemy' to be doing and thinking, which would have had less success in the theatre. Nevertheless, acquiring this situational awareness is not a trivial matter.

In the words of Churchill, 'time spent on reconnaissance is seldom wasted', and the principles are the same in cross-cultural transference of educational management praxis: in the absence of the luxury of time spent in the field before engaging with consultancy work, the growing body of cross-cultural research is the

Management tools *(all evolved in relatively universalist, high individualist, low power distance and low masculinity cultures)*	Examples of questions that might be asked to inform adaptation of management tools in different cultures
Maddux's model: "groups" or "teams" Maddux's concept is that a group of people operating together in an organisation are more effective when they become more productive units: teams. He contrasts various behaviours of groups and teams, indicating the value to the organisation of the greater openness and participation of communication in the team (Maddux, 1988).	▪ Are the 'team' behaviours all compatible with mixed-culture teams? ▪ Is it realistic, for example, to expect a team led by a high power distance leader to express their disagreements publicly, or for conflict to be worked through? ▪ Do leaders have to strive harder or more consistently to make it work? ▪ Is there a sense of failure if things do not work as intended?
Stages of Team Development Tuckman attempts to characterise the various developmental stages through which a newly-formed group of people pass in order to become a well-functioning and effective team, i.e. forming, storming, norming and performing (Tuckman, 1985)	▪ In a management group containing people with different presenting cultures, what sort of understanding and effort is needed by the leader to reach and maintain the goal of the performance stage? ▪ Should the process of transition from one stage to another be examined more closely? ▪ Can we identify selective leadership behaviours that are effective in the development of teams embracing more than one culture?

Figure 5.3   Examples of the thinking needed in order to transfer theory successfully

Maslow's Hierarchy of Needs Maslow's model suggests that people's needs can be ordered in a hierarchy, each need depending on the level below being achieved first. Thus physiological needs must be met before safety, then a sense of belonging, followed by esteem, and finally self-actualisation as the most supreme motivator (Maslow, 1970).	▪ Should other needs, not recognised by Maslow at that time, be added? ▪ In a collectivist culture, is the ultimate goal of *self*-actualisation appropriate? ▪ Where is team achievement accommodated? ▪ In a low masculinity culture, would, as Hofstede (1991, p. 125) suggests, a sense of belonging be a more supreme motivator than self-esteem?
Lewin's Force Field Analysis This is the model that helps analyse the environment in which a proposed change will take place. It requires the forces working for the change and those working against it to be identified, and then, working systematically through these items, searches for ways in which the former can be strengthened while the latter are diminished. This model is ideal to help teams working with thought processes which are linear, logical and deductive (Lewin, 1951).	▪ How persuasive is this sort of model in a holistic culture? Tedla (1995) argues that it is not. ▪ Even if the model is completed to plan, how realistic - or appropriate - is it for people in a particularist culture to carry out the plan with dispassionate objectivity?
Various conflict-handling models Many of these depend on the mutual recognition and acceptance of objective criteria and logically-deduced behaviours for their success in reaching agreement (e.g. Fisher and Ury, 1981), e.g: ▪ focus on interests, not positions ▪ separate the people from the problem ▪ generate options ▪ identify how decision will be made	▪ When trust has broken down, what impact does using objective criteria in selecting appropriate responses have in a strongly collectivist society? *(When trust has broken down, it takes skill and diplomacy to establish the situation where this can happen, even when both parties come from the same cultural background. Evidence from the media indicates that when applied across cultures they are notoriously unsuccessful in creating a lasting peace.)* ▪ In a culture that affiliates strongly to the 'in-group' (particularist), what strategies are most successful in meeting the needs of *both* parties? ▪ What role does language 'context' play in negotiation (Triandis, 1994)?

Figure 5.3　Continued

consultant's reconnaissance resource. But even this would be useless if we, the consultants, were not open to different ways of working, and actually prepared to *do* things in a different manner. Elliott-Kemp sums up the sentiment of this chapter much more powerfully and succinctly than I can:

> The first task of any consultant worth his (sic) salt, then, is to break free from his initial socialization, to transcend his training. To develop and temper those qualities most valuable to the consultant it is necessary to have years of experience in which one can test knowledge to destruction, dissolve and reform conceptual categories and question assumptions and beliefs. Above all, there is the necessity to avoid that most deadly and pernicious of professional diseases – certainty. Honest doubt is a quality to be treasured, even though it may be painful to live with.
>
> (Elliott-Kemp 1988, p.192)

References

Adams, D. (1991), 'Planning Models and Paradigms', in R. Carlson and G. Awkerman (eds), *Educational Planning: concepts, strategies, practices*, Longmans, New York.

Arthur, L. and Preston, R. (1996), 'Quality in Overseas Consultancy: Understanding the Issues', British Council.

Blanchard, K. and Johnson, S. (1982), *The One Minute Manager*, Fontana/Collins, London.

Blanchard, K., Zigarmi, P. and Zigarmi, D. (1985), *Leadership and the One Minute Manager*, Fontana/Collins, London.

Brislin, R. (1993), *Understanding Culture's Influences on Behaviour*, Harcourt Brace Jovanovich College Publishers, New York.

Brislin, R., Cushner, K. Cherrie, C. and Yong, M. (1986), *Intercultural Interactions: A Practical Guide*, Sage, Newbury Park.

Cray, D. and Mallory, G. (1998), *Making Sense of Managing Culture*, International Thompson Business Press, London.

Crossley, M. and Vulliamy, G. (eds) (1997), *Qualitative Educational Research in Developing Countries*, Garland Publishing.

Elliott-Kemp, J. (1988), 'Management Consultancy in Schools', in H. Gray (ed), *The International Consultant: some principles, problems and pitfalls*, Cassell, London.

Fadil, P. (1995), 'The Effect of Cultural Stereotypes on Leader Attributions of Minority Subordinates', *Journal of Managerial Issues*, vol. 7(2), pp. 193–208.

Fisher, R. and Ury, W. (1981), *Getting to Yes*, Business Books, London.

Fox, C. (1997), 'Metaphors of Educational Development', in T. Scrace (ed), *Social Justice and Third World Education*, Garland, New York.

Goffee, R. and Jones, G. (1995), 'Developing Managers for Europe: a re-examination of cross-cultural differences', *European Management Journal*, vol. 13(3), pp. 245–250.

Gustafsson, I. (1999), 'Are Genuine Partnerships Evolving? Some reflections from an agency perspective'. Paper presented at The Oxford Conference, Oxford.

Harber, C. (1995), 'Democratic Education and the International Agenda', in C. Harber (ed), *Developing Democratic Education*, Education Now Publishing Group, Derby.

Harber, C. and Davies, L. (1997), *School Management and Effectiveness in Developing Countries: the post-bureaucratic school*, Cassell, London.

Harber, C. (1998), 'Voices for Democracy', Education Now, in association with British Council, Nottingham.

Helson, H. (1964), *Adaptation Level Theory*, Harper and Row, New York.

Hofstede, G. (1980), *Culture's Consequences*, Sage, Newbury Park.

Hofstede, G. (1991), *Cultures and Organisations*, HarperCollins, London.

James, M. (1999), 'Participation in Education and its Evaluation: some caveats about a new paradigm', Paper presented at The Oxford Conference, Oxford.

Jameson, D. (1994), 'Strategies for Overcoming Barriers Inherent in Cross-Cultural Research', in *The Bulletin for the Association for Business Communication*, vol. 57(3), pp. 39–40.

Kanter, R.M. (1983), *The Change Masters*, Unwin-Hyman Ltd, London.

Kanter, R.M. and Corn, R. (1994), 'Do Cultural Differences make a Business Difference? Contextual Factors Affecting Cross-Cultural Relationships', *Journal of Management Development*, vol. 13(2), pp. 5–23.

Kraiger, K. and Ford, J. (1985), 'A Meta-Analysis of Ratee Race Effects in Performance Ratings', *Journal of Applied Psychology*, vol. 70, pp. 56–65.

Leach, F. (1994), 'Expatriates as Agents of Cross-Cultural Transmission', *Compare*, vol. 24(3), pp. 215–231.

Lewin, K. (1951), *Field Theory in Social Science, Selected Theoretical Papers*, Harper, London.

Lockheed, M. and Verspoor, A. (1991), *Improving Primary Education in Developing Countries*, Oxford University Press, Oxford.

London, N. (1993), 'Why Education Projects in Developing Countries Fail: a case study', *International Journal of Educational Development*, vol. 13(3), pp. 265–275.

Maddux, R. (1988), *Team Building*, Kogan Page, London.

Maslow, A.H. (1943), 'A Theory of Human Motivation', *Psychological Review*, vol. 50(4), pp. 370–396.

Psacharopoulos, G. (1989), 'Why Education Reforms Fail: a comparative analysis', in *International Review of Education*, vol. 35, pp. 179–195.

Reilly, W. (1987), 'Management and Training for Development: the Hombe Thesis', *Public Administration and Development*, vol. 7, pp. 25–42.

Riordan, C. and Vandenburg, R. (1994), 'A Central Question in Cross-Cultural Research: do employees of different cultures interpret work-related measures in an equivalent manner?' in *Journal of Management*, vol. 20(3), pp. 643–671.

Rodwell, S. (1998), 'Internationalisation or Indigenisation of Educational Management Development? Some issues of cross-cultural transfer', *Comparative Education*, vol. 34(1), pp. 41–54.

Ross, l. (1977), 'The Intuitive Psychologist and his Shortcomings: distortion in the attribution process', *Advances in Experimental Social Psychology*, vol. 10, pp. 173–220.

Shaw, M. and Ormston, M. (2001), 'Values and Vodka: Cross-Cultural Anatomy of an Anglo-Russian Educational Project', *International Journal of Educational Development*, vol. 21, pp. 119–133.

Shaw, M. and Welton, J. (1996), 'The Application of Education Management Models and Theories to the Processes of Education Policy Making and Management: a case of compound cross-cultural confusion', conference paper at *Indigenous Perspectives of Education Management*, Kuala Lumpur, 19–24 Aug.

Shaw, M. (2001), 'The application of Western educational management praxis in different cultural contexts: a case study in Namibia'. Ph.D. thesis, University of Birmingham.

Smith, P. and Bond, M. (1993), *Social Psychology Across Cultures*, Harvester Wheatsheaf, Hemel Hempstead.

Søndergaard, M. (1994), 'Research Note: Hofstede's Consequences: A Study of Reviews, Citations and Replications', *Organization Studies*, vol. 15(3), pp. 447–456.

Tayeb, M. (1994), 'Organisations and National Culture: Methodology Considered', *Organisation Studies*, vol. 15(3), pp. 429–446.

Tedla, E. (1995), *Sankofa: African Thought and Education*, Lang, New York.

Triandis, H. (1994), 'Culture and Social Behaviour', in W. Lonner and R. Malpass (eds), *Psychology and Culture*, Allyn and Bacon, Boston.

Trompenaars, F. (1993), *Riding the Waves of Culture*, Nicholas Brealey, London.

Tuckman, B. (1985), 'Development Sequences in Small Groups', *Psychological Bulletin*, vol. 63, pp. 384–399.

Watson, K. (1985), 'Dependence or Independence in Education? Two cases from post-colonial south-east Asia', *International Journal of Educational Development*, vol. 5(2), pp. 83–94.

Chapter 6

Broader Horizons and Greater Confidence: UK Students' Learning from Mobility

Helen Jones

This chapter focuses on research concerning the learning from experience of British students who undertook work placements of between three and six months outside the UK. The students were all engaged in courses leading to vocational qualifications in the field of youth and community work (YCW) embedded within degrees at universities in England and Wales. The majority of students spent time in other western European countries whilst a minority went to developing countries across the Commonwealth.

The countries of Europe and the Commonwealth, to which students travelled, faced common issues or 'problems' involving young people and communities. These included crime, homelessness, prostitution, unemployment, drug abuse, HIV/AIDS and other health matters. In addition, the countries shared a tendency to problematise adolescence. Chisholm explains that young people are seen both as presenting a problem to society and as having problems themselves (1993, p. 59). Roche and Tucker note: 'young people ... are seen as either a source of trouble or in trouble' (1997, p. 1). In tandem with the perception of problems is found the assumption that interventions by appropriately trained professionals are needed to bring about future change. However, the responses to the globalised phenomena are essentially local, enshrining one of the contradictions of globalisation. The way in which the 'social professions' are constituted is subject to national variation, grounded in differences of culture, religion and of the way in which policy is designed and the shape of responses which include the authoritarian, welfarist and ostensibly empowering. The phrase 'social professions' provides a useful shorthand term for a field which includes youth and community work, social work, social pedagogy and animation but it conceals great differences. These differences include the routes leading to entrance to professional training and education and curricular design and content which are products of particular national cultures and education systems. Moreover, terms like social pedagogy themselves conceal a myriad of frameworks.

The students opted to go on placements outside the UK from a desire to explore other cultures, a liking for travel and the wish to meet a challenge. They also hoped to encounter 'new' ways of dealing with the common issues and new approaches to working with young people. They set out with varying experiences of YCW in the UK and at least one year of full-time study behind them to provide a starting point for understanding what they saw and for extending their knowledge and skills. This chapter looks at the perceptions of students and their lecturers, gathered through focussed interviews. All of the students were enthusiastic about their experiences although some knew of colleagues who were less positive but who had chosen not to be interviewed.

Entering the Social Professions

Professional work placements are included in training and education for the social professions throughout western Europe although expectations and emphases differ. Lorenz describes placements as 'far more than mere "work experience" ... [they are] a highly specialised form of "reflective practice-related studies" with a high academic content' (1998, p. 37) although he notes the 'glaring discrepancy in Europe over what constitutes a supervised placement' (ibid, p. 30). In the UK, YCW students are expected to take on the professional role in practice, albeit closely supported, and need to be provided with developmental supervision. Placements must provide more than opportunities to 'shadow' or 'observe'. The theories on which the promotion of learning are based emphasise reflection on practice and draw on the work of theorists including Kolb (1984) and Schön (1987).

Across Europe, there are differences in the backgrounds of people studying for entry to the social professions. In the UK alternative routes into many HE programmes have been created for people without formal entry qualifications, encouraging applications from 'non-traditional' students. Many YCW programmes have a 'minimum age' requirement which prevents school leavers entering. Lyons outlines the UK system for entry to the social professions and emphasises the considerable differences to other states:

> Many are selected who lack normal academic attainments required for university entrance, but whose life and work experience demonstrate their potential for professional roles ... students tend to be both older than the general student population and more representative of minority groups within the community
>
> (Lyons, 1996, p. 7).

The UK is unusual in positively encouraging non-traditional and mature students. Some European countries require practical experience in the professional field alongside academic qualifications before students start their studies, resulting in slightly older cohorts, whilst others direct school leavers onto courses with little consideration given to their personal aptitude or preference.

Learning from Mobility

The role of 'learning from experience' is key in YCW and emphasised by the importance attached to the opportunity to gain experience through the fieldwork placement. However, the precise manner in which such experience is relevant to the YCW student requires interpretation mediated by theories of learning. The design of appropriate methods of defining and assessing fieldwork has been influenced by theorists of experiential learning including Mezirow and Dreyfus and Dreyfus. Mezirow suggests ways of 'understanding the world' are learnt through socialisation in childhood: 'These culturally determined perspectives usually remain unconscious in adulthood, but they are very important in determining the way we interpret experience' (1991, p. 35). He shows the role of 'naming' reality in developing as transformative learners and identifies the significance of experience which 'strengthens our personal meaning system by refocusing or extending our expectations about how things are supposed to be' (ibid, p. 5). The impact of the 'otherness' experienced by students participating in mobility programmes forms a significant aspect of the learning as the temporary 'loss' or suspension of the 'known' and its replacement by the 'other' returns the individual to the most fundamental stage of learning. The cultural, linguistic and professional unfamiliarity provides a framework within which intensive and holistic development is achieved. Through mobility students experience the absence of things being as they are supposed to be, a consciousness of reality is fostered and an awareness is able to develop of the nature of the previously unconscious 'culturally determined perspectives'. This knowledge of one's own expectations and consequent prejudices provides a means of developing a more 'open' and accepting approach to other people and communities: the promotion of a mild cultural relativism. Goodwin's concern that a 'side effect' of mobility is 'intellectual and cultural disorientation' (1996, p. 368) does not identify a learning process where the removal of the known and its accompanying disorientation form part of a positive cycle. The positive results of disorientation are particularly significant for students who intend to join the social professions, as will be shown later in the chapter.

Theories concerning the acquisition of professional skills developed by Dreyfus and Dreyfus provide further relevant ideas. They focus on the acquisition of professional skills, examine learning and conclude there are five steps: novice, advanced beginner, competent, proficient and expert (1986, p. 21). Introducing their taxonomy, they consider 'know how', starting with the example of riding a bicycle, 'which you acquired from practice and sometimes painful experience' but for which most riders could not provide written instructions. They add:

> You know how to carry on a conversation ... appropriately in a wide variety of contexts with your family, your friends, in the office, at a party, and with a stranger. Not only do you know what sorts of things to say ... but how far to stand from your conversational partner and what tone of voice to use ... you take your know how so much for granted

that you don't appreciate the extent to which it pervades your activities except in situations in which it has deserted you (ibid, pp. 16–17).

Unlike riding a bicycle, the skills of engaging in appropriate conversation are socially, culturally and linguistically particular. The learning which takes place under conditions where the 'taken for granted' largely has been removed adds a new dimension. For many YCW students, aspects of the work are familiar in the UK and some skills have been developed to 'advanced beginner' or 'competence' level. However, the elements which combine to form the framework in which the proficient practitioner practices have been removed in the context of 'otherness' for proficiency, requires an ontological familiarity. The 'proficient performer' draws on previous experiences in the identification of patterns which inform action. Dreyfus and Dreyfus refer to this as 'intuition' or 'know how' and explain it is 'the sort of ability we all use all the time as we go about our everyday tasks' (ibid, p. 29). They add that it is an ability 'that our tradition has acknowledged only in women, usually in interpersonal situations, and has adjudged inferior to masculine rationality' (ibid). For Dreyfus and Dreyfus, it is an intrinsic part of the development of skills in practice.

Similar ideas are also considered by Mezirow. He notes the difference between 'tacit memory', which is 'memory of culturally assimilated habits of expectation that allow us to scan and censor the experience of our senses' and 'explicit memory' which is 'memory that we can produce upon demand' (1991, p. 31). The former assists in interpretation and the latter in perception. The latter leads to explanation and reflective action. 'Tacit memory' appears to correspond with intuition. On the one hand, if the experience does not 'fit' with cultural expectation the result may be a new awareness of the nature of the assimilated expectation and, in consequence, the naming of the expectation. On the other hand, an erroneous expectation may be drawn on in order to interpret and make sense of the experience. This echoes the hermeneutic circularity of explication although the role of additional experiences in extending 'habits of expectation' contribute to the potential for learning. The extension of the range of experiences within the explicit memory will be reflected in the growth in internalised, tacit memory and the scope for interpretations.

The goal of YCW fieldwork is proficiency, where students have developed a high level of meta-cognitive awareness. As with high grades, this is not a level attained by all students. The complete change of context and the encounter with otherness returns the student to the novice level of learning, where almost every element of professional know how has been removed. This offers scope to develop awareness of the skills, knowledge and values which have been taken for granted and thus has the potential to nurture understandings which contribute to skill development. For professional success in YCW, meta-cognitive awareness of 'otherness', developed on a grounding of personal experiential learning, is of significant exchange value. The student is able to return to view their own system with the knowledge gained from seeing another.

Ontological Awareness

As indicated, professional 'know how' is significant in the professional development of YCW students. One dimension is the development of awareness of difference and the encounter with / experience of being the 'other'. A further dimension is the growth of appreciation of the aspects of one's previous existence which have been assumed or taken for granted. Thompson addresses the issue of the 'taken for grantedness of everyday life'; 'the way in which members of a particular cultural group become so immersed in its patterns, assumptions and values that they do not even notice they are there' (Thompson, 1998, p. 15). This takes Dreyfus and Dreyfus's consideration of 'know how' further. Thompson explains there are both positive and negative aspects of taking things for granted. With regard to the positive dimension, 'it contributes to 'ontological security', a sense of rootedness and psychological integration – an important element of mental well-being' (ibid). Ontological security involves knowing, at instinctive level, the basic frameworks of one's societal and cultural context. However, negatively, it presents potential for ethnocentrism as it 'refers to the tendency to see the world from within the narrow confines of one culture, to project one set of norms and values on to other groups of people' (ibid, p. 16). This also results in the belief that one culture is inherently more desirable, valuable or significant than another. The projection of norms and values means using one's own frameworks which leads to errors in understanding or failure to comprehend other cultures.

In addition to ethnocentrism, ontological security, taken to its extreme, produces social and cultural myopia and generates prejudice. Thompson draws a continuum, stretching from 'excessive reliance on security, producing defensiveness and rigidity' to 'insufficient security, producing anxiety and low levels of coping skills' with a central, balanced point: 'a "healthy" balance of ontological security, neither too rigid nor too insecure' (ibid, p. 32). Giddens explains, 'Emphasising the interdependence of taken for granted routines and ontological security does not mean that a sense of 'the beneficence of things' derives from a dogged adherence to habit' (1991, p. 40). A self-restrictive quasi-ritualistic attachment to routine results in stifling: Giddens shows that ontological security does not require such an approach. Ontological insecurity, on the other hand, is characterised by chaos. Ontological security and taken for granted routines are interdependent but they are not inseparable. Overseas placements involve the separation of the ontologically secure individual from their familiar environment. This presents the scope to reflect on the previously taken for granted: the situation of YCW students who engage in international mobility schemes highlights aspects of the relationship between international mobility and ontological security. They are encouraged to explore aspects of themselves, their values, skills, knowledge, attitudes, culture and society which they had accepted unquestioningly. Investigating the relevance and effect of international mobility is highlighted when the 'taken for granted' is removed and the student is confronted by a new perspective from which they are better positioned to interrogate their own home context and are able to draw on comparative material. Students who have seized the opportunity to cross international boundaries have temporarily removed the material fabric of their ontological security whilst opening up the opportunity for the development of ontological awareness. Ontological awareness is the capacity to identify the component parts of the previously taken for granted.

To be able to identify, reflect on and 'name' the components of one's cultural security is to achieve a new degree of ontological awareness which is of key significance in the training and education of YCW practitioners. Lupton, drawing on Giddens, makes an interesting link between the individual's 'cocoon of invulnerability' which 'enables them to get on with life, to fend off their knowledge of the risks that await them at every turn' and having the confidence or trust to take risks (Lupton, 1999, p. 78). To embark on a mobility programme needs to be considered as a form of risk taking. Successful achievement of a risky activity generates confidence in the individual's ability to cope with comparable situations in the future. The nature of the risk of an overseas placement is different to that faced when engaging in forms of extreme sport or other life endangering activity but individuals have consciously taken a risk, based on their own assessment of the situation, to participate. The decision taken as the outcome of individual risk assessment is the demonstration of choice: the exercise of agency. As such, it is directly relevant to debates concerning the relationship between structure and agency. Adolescence and other periods of intensive learning in adulthood are characterised by an emphasis on agency: the individual's developing scope for choice, change and influence. Adults who become mature students characterise their earlier experiences as bounded by social divisions and expectations: by structure (see, for example, Thompson, 1989). Freire, the inspired and inspirational adult educator, identifies the 'dichotomy between human beings and the world' which is 'implicit in the banking process'. In this context, the person is 'merely *in* the world, not *with* the world or with others; the individual is a spectator not re-creator' (italics in original) (Freire, 1996, p. 56). The traveller, or tourist, may remain a spectator, a cultural voyeur waiting for the world to fill her/him with knowledge just as school teachers once did. The YCW placement, however, demands that the student remains a dynamic, active learner rather than a passive vessel: to endeavour to be 'with' or 'in' the community rather than observing.

Research Methods

The techniques used encapsulated YCW's stated underlying principles and values and brought them together with aspects of the continuum of opportunities provided by practitioners from 'planned' to 'spontaneous' (NYA, 1997, p. 6). The collection and generation of data had three phases: an initial survey across all universities offering YCW courses endorsed by England's National Youth Agency, pilot interviews with lecturers and students at two universities and actual interviews with lecturers and students at ten universities across northern and central England and Wales. The initial survey was structured with brief questions designed to elicit quantitative and other factual data in written form. The importance of interpersonal interaction, central to YCW, was enshrined in the subsequent interviews. Interviews were piloted then honed, following analysis, reflection and modification. The hierarchical focusing technique employed for the final implementation of interviews was derived from Tomlinson's model (1989) which provides a means of ensuring material is gathered on all the topics where data are sought whilst leaving interviewees the maximum scope for spontaneity. Tomlinson explains that the interviewer:

> Starts from the more general end of the agenda hierarchy and elicits the elaboration of interviewee accounts. Insofar as this fails to produce coverage of the research agenda, the interviewer checks on the interviewee's exhaustiveness of coverage under any given heading and, if necessary, then raises the next most specific sub-topic her/himself (1989, p. 165).

Hierarchically focused interviews provide sufficient flexibility for respondents to explore aspects they themselves deem to be of importance. Although Robson notes the 'considerable experience and skill on the part of the interviewer and great flexibility' (1993, p. 241) demanded by less formally structured forms of interview, these skills are those associated with YCW. Thus the practical experience and the understanding of the skills, particularly groupwork, required by university staff engaged in the delivery of YCW courses provide a strong foundation for the use of the technique and, indeed for its understanding by interviewees.

In the research phase, twelve individual interviews were completed with lecturers at ten universities. Fifteen students were interviewed, either in groups or individually. The group interviews in particular generated spontaneous debates which included valuable data but it was not always possible to meet with more than one student. All interviews were taped and transcribed with interviewees' agreement. Participants were assured of anonymity but not confidentiality due to the intended use of the material.

Learning from the Experience

In considering the outcomes for students, lecturers identified aspects of personal development as the most significant outcome for students: learning was not situated primarily in the professional practice engaged in during placements. Echoing the findings of Teichler and Maiworm (1997), such aspects were key, with language outcomes and knowledge of the destination secondary and professional or academic knowledge last in importance. In addition to the growth in confidence, both lecturers and students used phrases relating to the 'broadening' of 'horizons'. The extension of both experience and vision presents an important learning tool for the student, adding to the range of life experiences. A lecturer spoke of 'breaking with insularity' and explored literal and metaphorical interpretations of the phrase. In literal terms, the limited extent of students' previous experience was mentioned and examples were given, whilst in metaphorical terms 'insularity' implied inward-looking. The concept of ontological security offers a means of understanding both the positive dimension of a 'sense of rootedness' and negative aspects such as ethnocentrism (Thompson, 1998, p. 15).

Whilst lecturers spoke of generalised personal outcomes for students, the students themselves focused on specifics. They mentioned a range of aspects which had been highlighted because they had previously taken them for granted, from the ability to read posters and leaflets to find out what was going on to knowing about money and grocery shopping. The experience of encountering difficulties in basic tasks generated reflection on the wide range of aspects of life which they had done previously without thinking or had taken for granted. The challenges presented were recounted with amusement (one student spoke of 'playing detectives' and another of a daily 'fact-finding mission') but the learning was significant. The learning from meeting the challenges and from encountering the frustrations of day-to-day life was focused on to a far greater extent than the learning from professional contexts. It appeared that the experience of buying the preferred type of milk and using laundrettes and public transport had had more impact than being on placement alongside social professionals. The extent of the 'know how' inherent in daily life is highlighted by its removal. Reconstructing the foundations of knowledge required for living, building a basic ontological security, outweighed the development of professional skills. The benefit of hindsight may, in the longer term, modify the students' accounts: several lecturers, whose motivation for involvement hinged on their own participation as students, located their development at a profound level. None of them spoke of the skills they had encountered but rather of the impact on their personal development. For them, the passage of time had diminished the impact of the satisfaction felt by recently returned students who had negotiated the challenges of coping in an unfamiliar society.

The key outcome for the students who participated, as perceived by both lecturers and students, was the growth in self confidence. This emerged from the successful engagement with risk generated by the 'removal of ... normal support networks'. The 'disorientation' identified by Goodwin (1996, p. 368) is certainly a positive rather than negative feature. Future challenges could be weighed against the experience of coping successfully in a different country. As Goodwin notes (1996, p. 368), the difficulty of measuring 'some of the less tangible consequences of academic mobility like personal transformation' may lead to its being overlooked. However, using techniques of reflection-in-action and drawing on work concerning the acquisition of professional skills may provide scope for measuring such development.

Supervision and Assessment

The issue of developmental supervision was identified by some lecturers and all students who had undertaken work placements in other countries as presenting an area of weakness. The opportunity to engage in reflection, guided by a skilled and experienced practitioner or fieldwork supervisor, is seen as providing the supportive means to explore learning. In the UK, the placement exposes the student to the opportunity to rehearse their use of practical skills in the YCW context; to build links between their college-based learning of theory and the practice encountered. There is considerable emphasis on the role of the fieldwork supervisor. This was generally agreed to be absent in international placements although the use of alternative systems and models was seen by some lecturers as providing a transferable approach ensuring parity. YCW's emphasis on high quality developmental supervision as an aspect of the training and education of future practitioners is identifiable as part of the professional ideology.

One lecturer, believing that professionals from different social professions in other countries did not understand what was required and that 'some practice is not as rigorous as ours', described attempting to inculcate the YCW approach through brief trainings so that they would provide this model of supervision. Not only had the professional terminology of the university's documentation been a source of difficulty but also the different approaches typical of different professions had contributed further. The lack of shared approaches to supervision was identified as a weakness although the interpretation of the validity of the alternatives varied. Lecturers tended to generalise from single examples and to extrapolate national professional models from their own students' accounts and from their own meetings with staff. There was belief that 'the issues of supervision' were not understood. The extent to which alternative approaches to supervision have the potential to offer equally meaningful opportunities for development was not raised; lecturers dismissed alternative approaches to supervision. The validity of this could be questioned: staff seemed to assume a single valid approach whilst emphasising, in a different context, that the value of international work is providing the opportunity 'to see that there's more than one way of doing things'.

Understanding Paradigms

None of the students or lecturers encountered youth work practice which they believed to be situated within entirely unfamiliar methodological paradigms. With the exception of accounts of projects working with street children in developing countries, none of the interviewees encountered unfamiliar intractable problems or contexts. Projects focused on young people, drug users, homeless people, health education, refugees and other examples with direct parallels in the UK. The unfamiliar was limited to operational and physical arrangements, for example, a large-scale circus project and a dinosaur-shaped building. Staff and students encountered work with young people and communities which was essentially familiar, yet they remained convinced that an elusive and profound difference existed. This certainty was based on intuited impressions rather than on evidence from practitioners or users of services, or written material. The approach to the work was 'similar' but a lecturer added that it was complicated by 'different cultures', 'different languages' and 'different histories'. The lack of 'YCW as we know it' was widely acknowledged. Another individual was, 'Constantly having to explain what we mean to European colleagues because they only know about social pedagogy'. Understanding social pedagogy posed a particular challenge for the lecturers and students who visited countries where it forms one of the panoply of social professions. It was generally identified as a composite of familiar professions; of youth worker, community worker, teacher and counsellor. Although one lecturer believed that social pedagogy lacked the 'transformative social change aspects of radical community', the value base remained unclear to other interviewees. Explanations could only be given in terms which were linguistically accessible to translation but they required understanding of the framework requiring comprehension. The interpretation of words incorporated in explanations could only be undertaken within the familiar, arguably resulting in flawed understandings as engagement with different and unfamiliar discourses was framed within the UK's YCW framework or 'tradition'. The outcome tended to be tentative and the interviewees believed that they were not able to put what they had sensed into words. For several interviewees, social pedagogy turned out to be a frustratingly elusive entity, not quite corresponding with any known form, and intuited rather than consciously learned. Writers too have lamented the inadequacy of materials available to them to facilitate comprehension of unfamiliar approaches. There is a common assumption that an ontological and epistemological Rosetta Stone for the social professions would not only be a feasible creation but would also succeed in achieving understanding. Information concerning different approaches was difficult to acquire and indicated the significance of national systems of compulsory education in the design of HEI programmes for the education and training of social professionals. However, the extent to which written expressions would provide the actual information sought is not certain: interviewees tended to 'feel' that there was a difference and the extent to which this was located in the national and cultural as opposed to the primarily abstract or academic was unclear. In addition, there appeared to be a generally held assumption that social pedagogy was a single entity. The precise form varies from country to country.[1]

Lecturers and students alike voiced frustration at being unable to comprehend fully the theory behind the approaches they saw and designed their own explanations, sometimes generalising from single examples. They perceived that interpreting and understanding what they saw in its entirety depended on their interpretation of aspects and vice versa: the potential 'Catch 22' of the 'hermeneutic circle': they dealt with the task of understanding the work they encountered by employing familiar interpretive frameworks. Inevitably, when raising the issue with practitioners in other countries, their questions were framed within interpretive frameworks with which they were familiar. Such questions were not necessarily comprehended on epistemological, semantic and linguistic grounds and they did not gain answers in the terms anticipated. This approach corresponds precisely with Usher's explanation of the role of existing knowledge in understanding (Usher, Bryant and Johnson, 1997, p. 182) and highlights the dangers inherent in using the known to explain the unfamiliar. Two examples offer illustrations. First, a lecturer recounted asking about the nature and scope of work in a particular community centre, presuming the reply would be framed within a Freirean discourse of 'transformative change'. However, the answer was that people who were unemployed were targeted with the aim of training them for employment. Drawing on the British radical community development approach based around 'countering injustice and inequality', the interviewee's assumption had been that the worker would be involved in 'questioning the reason for them being unemployed'. However, whilst a developed 'awareness of social issues' was apparent, as far as the interviewee was concerned, this did not appear to be grounded in structural analysis. Further examples were given by the same interviewee, whose expectation that the rationale for the work would be framed in familiar terms was not met. Secondly, a student asked the manager of the youth club at which they were on placement about the aims of the work with young people. The student had expected a reply framed in the rhetoric of personal and social education. The manager explained that the aim was 'to keep them off the street and out of trouble'. The student perceived that they had presupposed a shared understanding grounded in YCW. A weakness in seeking to explain the unfamiliar in terms of the familiar appears to be the use of known 'good practice' as the starting point. The two interviewees who had been seeking refined, conceptually sophisticated explanations of the aims of the work they had seen were both taken aback to receive answers which they considered suggested superficial thinking. Both had used what they considered to be 'good practice' to frame their expectations but encountered responses which were not theoretically grounded. There are several potential explanations. First, they could have been using inappropriate forms of existing knowledge as the starting point: structural analysis was not involved but an alternative theoretical framework was being employed. This possibility highlights the flaw inherent in the hermeneutic circle. Secondly, linguistic difficulties could have prevented the people they were asking from responding in English using the terms anticipated. Thirdly, the thinking behind the work could not be expressed in English which the interviewees could interpret. Fourthly, the work indeed was situated at a superficial level and not grounded in structural analysis. The lecturer believed that this could be the explanation but the student concluded that the thinking behind the work was present but not necessarily operationalised. The use of single examples as the starting point for generalisations is notable. In the UK, examples of good and poor practice would be anticipated but, when dealing with practice in other European countries, the expectation seemed to be that a single example characterised the work.

Sharing Epistemologies

Placements provide the opportunity for students to develop subjective strategies for knowing. The privileging of ostensibly objective knowledge located in publications and expressed by 'experts' over the subjective and felt has been identified as gendered by authors including Belenky, Clinchy et al (1986) and Dreyfus and Dreyfus (1986). Students are studying in contexts where there exists a clearly implicit hierarchy which places abstract conceptualisation beyond subjective knowledge. Although interviewees potentially had the skills to analyse what they saw, heard and experienced, their academic grounding impelled them to seek the information expressed in terms of values, aims and objectives. This could have been seen as seeking validation of their perceptions or as lacking confidence in their own interpretive abilities. Difficulties encountered around communication resulted in limited potential to use professional language or 'jargon' to explain the work and expectations, either with regard to placements or the professional field. In particular, staff and students identified difficulties concerning the terminology included in their institutions' documentation concerning fieldwork placements. Nonetheless they had persevered and continued to use the same material for both UK and overseas. No interviewees mentioned any methods to enhance understanding: all had focused on verbal and written forms of communication of value bases, aims and objectives and on watching and interpreting the face-to-face work. There appeared to be an artificial limitation of approaches to understanding which did not make use of the full range of options used in YCW educational and training contexts. Upon reflection, one which provides potential scope for exploration is the emphasis on the influence of the work of Freire on the field. Across Europe, practitioners cite his work as inspirational and there is arguably scope for using it as a conceptual touchstone.

The interviewees who had sought to develop a deeper understanding of the theories on which practice was constructed and the aims of the work had expressed themselves in abstract terms. They anticipated similarly abstract answers. A lecturer noted that this required sophisticated multilingual skills in their respondents and also highlighted their own presuppositions. A second opportunity to develop a greater degree of understanding could be through describing professional ethical dilemmas affecting different countries and cultures. Interviewees identified familiar contexts: work with youth club members, with drug users, with avowed racists and described the work going on. This presents a better potential starting point for understanding value bases than asking about value bases per se. Focusing on discussion of 'typical' dilemmas could provide a route towards understanding the different professional bases through the use of linguistically less sophisticated material. Discussion of values arguably privileges the abstract and theoretical. It incorporates potential linguistic difficulties in requiring the translation of codified knowledge whilst focusing on ways of dealing with ethical dilemmas in a contextualised form could offer scope for the use of less sophisticated language and provide the opportunity to ascertain whether comparable tasks are undertaken but expressed in different rhetoric and to identify whether the difficulties are linguistic, semantic or conceptual.

Know-How and Knowledge

All interviewees had to rely on others' linguistic skills to discuss the practice and to relate the practice to theory. In terms of language acquisition, being able to discuss theoretical concepts in abstract terms would appear to be at a more sophisticated level than being able to engage in fluent debate concerning concrete examples of work. Eraut identifies a difference between 'technical knowledge' and 'practical knowledge'. Whilst it is possible to express the first verbally, given access to the vocabulary, the second includes aspects which lay beyond the scope of language to encapsulate. Eraut says, 'some kinds of practical knowledge are uncodifiable in principle. For example, knowledge which is essentially non-verbal [such as] the expression on a face' (Eraut, 1994, p. 42). Although he explains that 'to recognise that uncodifiable practical knowledge exists need not imply that stored written knowledge is irrelevant to such situations', he adds 'the unscripted and intuitive nature of much verbal action makes attempts to describe or criticise it equally difficult' (ibid). The development of professional intuition is the ultimate goal of the YCW student. The difficulty of expressing the instinctive is enshrined in its nature.

The acquisition of professional skills, values and knowledge and the challenge of developing intuitive expertise form the basis of the work of theorists of situated and contextualised knowledge development. The nature of the relationship between the codified technical knowledge and practical knowledge results in what Eraut terms the 'problem' which arises from the significance of professionals' instinctive use of 'experience-derived know-how' (Eraut, 1994, p. 42). The 'problem' lies in the fact what the know-how is implicit rather than explicit. The extent to which it may be explained verbally is limited. On placement it is intended that YCW students are able to see examples of good YCW practice in operation, from which they may learn consciously through developmental supervision and structured forms of reflective journal or recordings but on whom they are also able to model themselves at an instinctive level.

This point is relevant where students are not placed within a YCW setting and have to make sophisticated links between their day-to-day experience and a different professional paradigm: international placements highlight the issue of the relevance of the practice to the YCW student's learning. The model of practice is constructed on a different professional basis, the direct relevance of which is an area for debate but which is clearly not framed within the principles and values identified by England's National Youth Agency. Furthermore, the 'codified technical knowledge' which informs the professional's practice is that of the particular, and different, profession. The extent to which such knowledge is based on ideas and approaches derived from the same theorists provides scope for future research. As noted above, the absence of effective developmental supervision removes the scope for discussion and understanding of the unfamiliar.

The 'experience-derived know-how' or 'uncodified practical knowledge' from which professionals derive their ability to act and react instinctively is framed within a series of contexts. First, it exists within the professional framework and context. The response to a specific situation is not common to different professions. For example, the intuitive responses of a YCW practitioner and a midwife to a pregnant teenager are framed by professional responsibilities and expectations. The nature of the relationship between the professional and the young woman are professionally situated and the differing professional cultures inform the interpretation of the situation. Secondly, professionals' instinctive responses are situated within their own national or local cultures and subcultures. Whilst the existence of social professions is arguably an identifiable aspect of European culture, the different manifestations are products of localities. Practitioners in different countries have their own instinctive knowledge which informs and affects their actions in practice. Eraut notes the assumption that technical knowledge, 'is used systematically and explicitly while practical knowledge is used idiosyncratically and implicitly' (Eraut, 1994, p. 47). The difficulties inherent in articulating such knowledge in one's own language to somebody sharing the same codified knowledge and access to the same cultural understanding have been identified. Where these may not be presumed, further profound barriers exist.

The impact of engagement with practice conducted in different cultural contexts and possibly using different languages on the acquisition of professional expertise provides the additional element existent in international placements. The problem of accessing the codified aspects underpinning the practice presented students with an acknowledged area of difficulty whilst they used their own burgeoning professional understanding as the means of comprehending the practice. The role of culture in the construction of the context within which the 'experience-derived know-how' has developed adds a further level of complexity to the task of comprehension. For although some human expressions of fundamental emotion are a global form of non-verbal communication, much non-verbal communication is culturally constructed and influenced. The experienced worker, for example, notices and identifies the implications of the choice of a particular item of clothing or insignia in terms of current youth culture and local subgroups. In verbal terms, the use of specific modes of speech provides further communication of the cultural groups to which people belong or with which they identify. Although the Eurocentric nature of culture has been identified , the national and local have a major impact on aspects of the subcultures which have especial significance during adolescence.

The taken for granted also includes aspects of communication. Deprived of the scope to be understood in spoken English, students had to develop alternatives and became much more aware of what they had assumed hitherto. A student who spent a placement in a country where she was unable to understand the language thought that being unable to understand what was being said was 'really good', explaining the value of 'being put in a position where I couldn't make any judgements about what people are like because of the way they spoke ... that I would naturally do without thinking about it'. This enhanced her understanding of oppressive behaviour and how it is possible to stereotype people based on their speech. Other students explored alternatives to speech, drawing on aspects of non-verbal communication with apparent success. One talked about using alternatives to verbal communication: 'I don't speak [the language] but my facial expressions and body language – I had to take it to the maximum to get them to understand'. A lecturer identified the same situation: 'How do you overcome barriers of communication? ... They have to look at ways to work their way through that'. No interviewee identified any instances where there had been significant misunderstandings by any people involved in exchanges although Usher notes how 'an apparently simple [physical] action ... is immersed and inseparable from a network of culturally conditioned beliefs and practices, assumptions and presuppositions' (Usher, Bryant and Johnson, 1997, p. 183). This could be seen as a warning: confidence that non-verbal communication has been interpreted accurately could be misplaced: Jaques explores the potential for distortion in verbal communication (1991, pp. 51–54); a potential likely to be present in alternative forms of communication and Nelson-Jones identifies cultural and national differences in aspects of body language including eye-contact and gesture (Nelson-Jones, 1990, pp. 56 ff). Indeed, certain misinterpretations of gesture could have unfortunate consequences. Nonetheless, students became more sensitive to issues of communication; an aspect of learning likely to be of relevance to their future practice as difficulty in understanding the content of verbal messages led to students relying on their reading of other forms of communication.

Transferability

An assumption which this research confounded was that there would be key ideas and methods from other countries which had impressed interviewees and which had been 'borrowed' or subsumed into their own range of skills and knowledge. The interview format provided interviewees with the opportunity to mention aspects they considered significant. Prompts around transferability and learning did not elicit any such responses. Nobody recounted seeing professional methods which they intended to import and employ. Only one lecturer cited the potential of intercultural pedagogy as an alternative to anti-racist work. The learning had been of a different nature. For students, the consciousness of the contexts in which they operate is heightened by their awareness of their own situations. The 'ontological awareness' shown to be a necessary facet of comprehending and countering oppression includes an awareness of the elements comprising the cultural and societal. The ability to 'name' the elements is important in fostering change, a point reminiscent of Freire's suggestion that transforming education presents people with the opportunity to 'perceive critically the way they exist in the world'

(Freire, 1996, p. 64). This is the vision which a lecturer felt was missing in the examples of work encountered in other countries but which may be developed by students through the international experience.

The necessity for the development of YCW skills in bringing about changes at individual level requires an understanding of the elements which constitute the ontological level: the taken for granted. The students interviewed did not explore extensively their experiences at this level of depth. Some lecturers suggested that time needed to elapse before the impact was felt. An alternative interpretation might be located in the nature of the learning resulting from the experience and the need for reflection to transform this knowledge into something which may be expressed. The lack of the anticipated model of developmental supervision and lack of clearly designed processes to assist students in making sense of the experience may also present explanations.

Students undertaking international placements do not have the opportunity to encounter YCW but they are sometimes in a position to demonstrate their own practice. The practical display of informal education techniques, accompanied by the necessity to explain the rationale, provides a useful opportunity to articulate the skills, knowledge and values and to answer direct questions. The modelling and explanation of good practice can provide a useful further opportunity to explore the taken for granted. Examples were cited, from joining street children on the floor rather than sitting on chairs to engaging in informal groupwork. However, without the presence of competent YCW practitioners, poor practices could go unquestioned and become more deeply entrenched.

Conclusion

Interviewees returned with a more developed understanding of YCW despite the fact that they had not been exposed to it. Exposure to examples of what YCW is *not* resulted in a clearer appreciation of the key elements of what it *is* and what practitioners are aiming to achieve. Furthermore, the growth in understanding of alternatives, of appreciating that there were different ways to 'see' different frames of reference and truths, was mirrored by enhanced certainty in the validity of YCW's particular approach. The group interviews generated thoughtful questions between participants which enhanced the reflection undertaken and which served to indicate the potential of supervision. A contradiction may be identified in the way in which developing acceptance of ways of perceiving situations also fostered greater confidence and determination to engage in YCW. Significantly, no interviewee's experiences resulted in the decision to move out of their chosen profession. YCW was no longer presumed to be appropriate but had been selected having been weighed up against alternatives, resulting in certainty. Aspects which were highlighted were YCW's emphasis on the voluntary nature of young people's engagement, the issue of social control in working with young people and the role of structural analysis in addressing oppression. These were identified as distinctive features of YCW since they were not evident to outside observers in other countries' professional paradigms.

It was shown that students, who had worked with projects which focused on 'familiar' intractable issues such as unemployment and drug abuse, did not identify any 'unfamiliar' approaches to practical work. The shared identification of common issues or 'problems' involving young people and communities was reflected in shared responses although the frameworks, within which professions are positioned, differ. It would be tempting to extrapolate the global situation from these findings, given the range of countries in which experiences have been gained. However, the countries of the European Union and Commonwealth share the Indo-European linguistic heritage / influence and the epistemological framework created by the monotheistic religions. Whilst students recognised what they had taken for granted in their own context when they experienced the unfamiliar, it could be suggested that UK students draw upon a shared heritage which predates the current rapid form of globalisation. The impact of living and working in countries with less commonality would form an interesting adjunct to this particular research.

Note

1 A comprehensive overview of European countries' social professions may be found in W. Lorenz and W.F. Seibel (eds) (1998), *Erasmus Evaluation Conference – Social Professions for a Social Europe*, Koblenz: European Centre Community Education.

References

Belenky, M.F., Clinchy, B.M., Goldberger, N.R. and Tarule, J.M. (1986), *Women's Ways of Knowing*, Tenth Anniversary Edition, Basic Books, New York.

Chisholm, L. (1993), 'Young People in the European Community', *Youth and Policy*, vol. 40, pp. 49–61.

Dreyfus, H.L. and Dreyfus, S.E. (1986), *Mind over Machine*, The Free Press, New York.

Eraut, M. (1994), *Developing Professional Knowledge and Competence*, The Falmer Press, London.

Freire, P. (1996), *Pedagogy of the Oppressed*, (1996) Edition, Harmondsworth: Penguin.

Giddens, A. (1991), *Modernity and Self-Identity*, Polity Press, Cambridge.

Goodwin, C.D. (1996), 'Academic Mobility in a Changing World' in Blumenthal et al (eds), *Academic Mobility in a Changing World*, Jessica Kingsley Publishers, London.

Jaques, D. (1991), *Learning in Groups*, Kogan Page, London

Kolb, D.A. (1984), *Experiential Learning*, Prentice Hall, New Jersey.

Lorenz, W. (1998), 'Erasmus Evaluation – The Experience of the Social Professions', in W. Lorenz and F.W. Seibel (eds), *Erasmus Evaluation Conference – Social Professions for a Social Europe*, European Centre Community Education, Koblenz.

Lupton, D. (1999), *Risk*, Routledge, London.

Lyons, K. (1996), 'National Report: UK', in W. Lorenz and F.W. Seibel (eds), *Erasmus Evaluation Conference – Social Professions for a Social Europe*, European Centre Community Education, Koblenz.

Mezirow, J. (1991), *The Transformative Dimensions of Adult Learning*, Jossey-Bass Publishers, San Francisco.

Nelson-Jones, R. (1990), *Human Relationship Skills*, Cassell, London.

NYA (1997), *Professional Endorsement Of Qualifying Training In Youth And Community Work*, National Youth Agency, Leicester.

Robson, C. (1993), *Real Word Research*, Blackwell, Oxford.

Roche, J. and Tucker, S. (1997), 'Youth in Society: Contemporary Theory, Policy and Practice', in Roche J. and Tucker, S. (eds), *Youth in Society*, Sage / Open University Press, London.

Schön, D.A. (1987), *Educating the Reflective Practitioner*, Jossey-Bass, San Francisco.

Teichler, U. and Maiworm, F. (1997), *The ERASMUS Experience: Major findings of the ERASMUS evaluation research project*, Office for Official Publications of the European Communities, Luxembourg.

Thompson, N. (1998), *Promoting Equality*, Macmillan, Basingstoke.

Tomlinson, P. (1989), 'Having it Both Ways: hierarchical focusing as research interview method', *British Educational Research Journal*, vol. 15(2), pp. 155–76.

Usher, R., Bryant, I. and Johnson, R. (1997), *Adult Education and the Postmodern Challenge*, Routledge, London.

Chapter 7

Overseas Students in Higher Education

Christine Twigg

Introduction

Higher education institutions continue to undergo fundamental change because of the influence of globalisation. Brown and Scase (1994) stated that universities will be called upon to educate a new generation of internationally competitive overseas students, to create a climate in which innovation and change can take place, to create links between global and local areas and to integrate economic policies with social and cultural initiatives.

Saha (1996) considers the extent to which universities are related to the social and cultural development of a society, and thus to national development and nation building as follows:

> One of the best documented research findings is that, compared with those with no higher education, persons who have attended some form of higher education tend to be less traditional, less family-oriented, more secular and more change-oriented in attitudes, value and behaviour. Although it is debated whether or not attendance in universities 'causes' these modernising effects, or whether a self-selection is the cause, the association is nevertheless clear.
>
> Saha (1996) p. 84.

Saha explains that the modernising impact of universities on students may be nothing more than an extension of general education. However, the impact on the individual's values, attitudes and lifestyle will ultimately have an affect on society.

Humfrey (1999) describes some of the advantages of international education as follows:

> At its highest level, the benefits of such education could be global understanding and harmony – more realistically, they should at least include the facilitation of friendships across international boundaries, more effective development of the global knowledge base and more interesting programmes for students at every level.
>
> Humfrey (1999) Preface.

Humfrey (1999) explains how further education provides an opportunity for home and overseas students to work together in academic programmes and that international education belongs to those who leave their countries to obtain it and expand their intellectual horizons in doing so.

This chapter is based on a study of students within the Department of Computation, UMIST, England. The students were studying on MSc, MPhil and PhD programmes and were at various stages of their study. The sample consisted of 42 students from 24 different countries, which was representative of approximately a third of the postgraduate overseas students in the department at that time. The countries were segmented into five areas of the world ranging from America through to the Far East of Asia.

The author discusses the issues which may have an impact on overseas students due to the change in culture and their surroundings which will vary depending on such factors as their initial expectations, their country of origin and previous knowledge and experience. The author attempts to explore the concepts which may be related to the behaviour of students when interacting with their new environment.

Culture

Ronald Barnett (1990) addresses the inner culture of higher education which works on two distinct levels and is an essential ingredient in the development of the system. The first is in relation to the academic community. He asks:

> What if anything, is characteristic about the culture of academics? Is there one, in fact, or are there now only the multitude of disciplinary sub-cultures? Can we, at a deeper level perhaps, identify elements of a form of life, with its own values, which is distinctive of the academic community in general?
>
> Barnett (1990) p. 96.

However, he states that those questions are separate to those that can be posed on the second level of culture. This is the level of the process of higher education itself which comes close to that of the student experience. The questions to be asked at this analytical level are:

> What kind of cultural enlargement, if any, can higher education hope to offer the individual student? Is it a matter of exposing students to some kind of culturally rich material or is it more a matter of a particular educational experience? In other words, is it a matter of content or process?
>
> Barnett (1990) p. 96.

He queries that if it is a matter of process, then what are the limitations on the process of learning considered as human transaction, if the sought-for cultural enlargement is to take place? On the other hand, he states that culture as content seems to point to different answers for different kinds of educational programme. Whilst he distinguishes between the culture of the academic community and the cultural dimension in the student's educational experience, he believes that there has to be a strong connection between the two. Logically, the character of the life of the academic community affects the quality of the student's experience.

Barnett (1990) describes the culture as:

A shared set of meanings, beliefs, understandings and ideas, in short, a taken-for-granted way of life, in which there is a reasonably clear difference between those on the inside and those on the outside of the community. Part of the sharing, and sense of community, resides in the taken-for-granted aspects of the culture. The unquestioned stock (of dominant ideas, concepts, theories, research practices) bestows personal identity and sustains the community as a community. The recognition takes several forms, including modes of communication. All these features of a culture are apparent in the academic community.

Barnett (1990) p. 97.

Barnett then goes on to discuss the other dimension of culture within higher education, namely higher education as a cultural experience for students. He refers back to the 19th century where education evolved through its tutorial system, an educational process in which the student's character was developed and the face-to-face interaction between the student and tutor was crucial. Higher education stood for an overriding and widening development of the mind. Therefore, he claims that higher education was a cultural experience in several senses.

An explanation of the generality of culture is given as follows:

Having a sense of culture and its related skills are unique human attributes. Culture is fundamentally a group-solving tool for daily coping in a particular environment. It enbles people to create a distinctive world around themselves to control their own desinies, and to grow in self-actualisation. Sharing the legacy of diverse cultures advances our social, economic, technological and human development on this planet. Culture can be analysed in a macrocontext, such as in terms of national groups, or in a microsense, such as within a system or organisation.

Harris and Moran (1993) p. 23.

When a student first arrives, the change in culture may be quite overwhelming. The student will have gone from a familiar environment into one that is unfamiliar and unknown. In addition to this, they not only have to familiarise themselves with the national culture of the country but also the sub-cultures which may exist within the town, university, department, accommodation etc. A couple of students described the initial apprehension they felt shortly after arriving at the airport as follows:

When I arrived at the airport it was raining and of course people were speaking in English. I was very worried about the foreign life and looked around me and found the 'Arrivals' and 'Departures' signs. I wanted to go directly to the Departures!

PhD 3rd Year student, South Korea

It was my first time in England and I was on my own. It was very scary the first day. When I arrived on the first day, I thought 'can I go back now please?' I felt a bit lonely and wondered what I was going to experience in the next year.

PhD 3rd Year student, Thailand

A student may be worried as their distinctive world has disappeared and they no longer feel in control of their own destiny. The skills used to cope daily in the culture which they have come from may be useless or irrelevant in the new culture.

However, the extent to which one has prepared themselves may help the student to develop the new skills and knowledge needed to understand and adapt to their new environment.

Wierzbicka (1991) explains how humans are inevitably guided by certain principles and certain ideals which are not necessarily shared by the entire human race. However, it is important to determine the specific features of the culture to which one happens to belong, and what can be, with some justification, regarded as simply human. Wierzbicka suggests that to achieve an understanding one must learn to separate within a culture its distinctive aspects from its universal aspects and that human nature must be found within every particular culture. This is necessary not only for the purpose of studying 'human nature' but also for the purpose of studying the particular aspects of any culture that one may be interested in. To study different cultures in their culture-specific features we need a universal perspective and a culture independent analytical framework.

Nevertheless, a student may experience a situation that they are not prepared for as it may not exist *at all* in their own culture, therefore they have no basis for reference. Until they come to Britain, they may not have been aware of the phenomena and may simply not know how to deal with it because they cannot comprehend it in any way. Some student reactions to such situations are as follows:

It was my first time in Manchester. The gay festival was on and it was very strange for me. You had a festival and a village. I was living close by so I decided that for 2-3 days I wouldn't go out. I wanted to avoid the whole thing as I just couldn't understand it but afterwards I got used to it. In my country they don't have it. I was also surprised that they have a gay group in the university.

PhD 2nd Year student, Sudan

I think alcohol is part of the British culture. I don't like it. I don't know why. We are not allowed to drink so it seems completely different to me.

MSc student, Indonesia

Therefore, it could be said that the aspects of human nature required to gain insight into a different culture are human understanding and empathy. Although some students did not understand the British culture they attempted to either understand it or accept the differences as part of their new way of life as follows:

When I see a new environment and I see new ideas, I compare it with my ideas. I question what is the reason for accepting a new belief. I give myself the opportunity to think about new things, if it has a good reasoning then I accept the idea.

MSc student, Iran

I am here alone. I didn't find it difficult to adapt. I just came here and enjoyed it. I understand culture and I didn't think it was good or bad – it is just a different culture. Because I am living in this country I just accept it. If I am having a bad time other people will not change their culture for me. I must change my culture for others because I live in this country.

MSc student, China

> I came here on my own but now have a British girlfriend. It wasn't that difficult to adapt. The most important thing when learning a new culture is what you shouldn't do first. You have to observe and see what happens. People here expect you to be polite, so when in the UK you have to do what the Romans do!
>
> PhD 3rd Year student, Malaysia

> My country is Islamic and there are a lot of different things. The style of dress is different and the relationship between the family is different. The men and women are separated. I just accept that British culture is different. If I don't, I might as well stay at home!
>
> MSc student, Libya

Hofstede et al. (2002) believe that people from different countries are more different from one another than people from the same country. 'National culture' is the term they give to distinguish people from different countries which they describe as follows:

> National culture runs deep. It is taught to children from the day they are born. Does it matter whether a child is female or male? What about social class? Do children accompany their mother's all day? Does the family sleep in one room or even in one bed? Do grown-ups teach their children to use different behaviour toward the elderly, the young, men, women? To stand up and fight or to sit down and talk? To speak their mind or to save others' face? To wear skirts, shorts, veils, caps? Are all these things theirs to decide, and if so, from what age?
>
> Hofstede et al. (2002) xviii.

They also stress that although much of what happens among people from different countries depends on culture, not everything does as every human is unique to some extent and no two people will act exactly the same due to differences in their personal experience and personality. In addition, people are social beings and behaviour is learned through the groups they associate with.

It is self evident that the overseas student population consists of people of different experiences and personalities which will affect their perception of, and adaptation to, English culture. However, a number of the students felt a sense of familiarity, not only with those from the same country, but also with those from the same part of the world as they may share similar experiences, values or cultural background. This connection could refer to the national culture as described by Hofstede et al. (2002). Furthermore, some students believed it was impolite not to acknowledge the presence of another co-sojourner even if they didn't like them. Some examples of this association are as follows:

> I normally have friends from Asia like Japan, Malaysia, Indonesia and Taiwan. I find it easier to talk to people from China, maybe we are from a similar culture and from somewhere far away. I feel they are not that different from my country. It is not that difficult to make friends with them.
>
> PhD 3rd Year student, Thailand

It is easier to make friends with people from Asian countries as the background and culture is similar – it is not just the language. In China people come from a different history, cultural background and legal system but for Western countries they are totally different. My friends from Europe are not very close.

MSc student, China

Personally I talk to everyone from everywhere because I try to get to know the culture from each country. But as time goes on you find it is easier to go for someone who has quite a similar culture to your own country because the Europeans and Asians are totally different in some aspects.

PhD 3rd Year student, Thailand

When I didn't drink the English people really respected that. They were proud of me and said it was very good. Sometimes they even admitted they were drunkards! But after about a year I started drinking with my Sri Lankan friends. The English people were more accepting but with the Sri Lankans I had to drink to be part of the group.

MSc student, Sri Lanka

A lot of people from my country, I don't like them, even the ones in Manchester. Interactions also depend on experience not just culture. It depends on how you are raised and how to interact.

PhD 2nd Year student, Mauritius

I have friends from all over the world. I find it easier to make friends with Africans because I am African. Although sometimes we have different cultures it is easier because we have this familiar feeling that we are away from Africa and we are interested in why the other is here.

PhD 3rd Year student, Botswana

Social Behaviour

In an attempt to understand the complex meaning of culture, it may be helpful to firstly understand the basics of human behaviour. Roth (1990) explains that from babyhood, all humans are both social and individual beings. However, to become integrated into the social world and differentiated from it are complementary processes, and the growing child develops sociability and individuality at the same time.

The first of the two complementary processes of social development is socialisation, which includes all the influences that make us accepted members of society and help us to establish and maintain relationships with others. As such, socialisation is the integrating process which allows the child to become a full member of society. There are many ways in which the growing child is given incentives to conform, from the direct instructions of parents to the more subtle influences of images in the media.

The second process of social development is the development of the individual's personal identity, or self. Children need to develop a sense of their own personal characteristics, abilities and attitudes and, at the same time, they need to reconcile their individuality with the many requirements of the social world, such as those of status, gender and occupation. This process is the differentiating role of social development, whereby individuals distinguish themselves from others and find a personal position within the social network. Both the integrating and differentiating processes in social development are equally essential to an individual's ability to operate successfully in the world, and they are deeply interconnected (Roth, 1990).

However, these processes can become confused when a student enters a new setting as their social skills and roles may need to change. For example, some students come from civilisations where the need to conform is necessary to keep the society functioning in a certain way. In some countries the community structure can be a great support to those who would find it difficult to live or otherwise survive alone. Everyone has a role to play and people's expected behaviour is controlled by the group. However, there are also disadvantages where non-conformity can lead to ostracisation or stigmatisation by the community members or society itself. Some of the students commented on the dynamics of such societies and how they may differ from British life, as follows:

> A community is like helping each other. You can actually rely on people. The country people live together in big families but in the towns it is like the Western culture, people move out. In villages they live in huge compounds where everyone is related and it has a name. The people are poorer and stick to their traditions more.
>
> English people are allowed to express themselves. People are not shocked by someone trying to be an individual. In my culture, Jesus Christ!, there are rules and regulations and if I wanted to express myself I would be limited by the people. That is what I admire about this society – people are allowed to be individuals and do whatever they want without anyone thinking it's not right.
>
> Here you can have debates and you still have as many people supporting you as not supporting you but back home they decide, in advance, that something is not right. By the time you do it you know it's not right or they have set their mind on that. It is a unified response and can come from anybody.
>
> PhD 3rd Year student, Botswana

> You try to struggle and stay afloat – it is an everyday struggle. But here, if you are healthy and working, 'afloat' is to lead a normal life. At home, just to keep food in the fridge for the next day you have to think really hard and sometimes you have to create 'magic'. It's impossible. The employment rate is quite high and the salary is very low but the food was imported so was expensive. Just because of friends and relatives, we somehow got along.
>
> MPhil student, Mongolia

> There is a lot of freedom here. For example, the press can say what they want – too much really. In general people do tend to be able to express opinions. In our country some people would be put in jail but you obviously get people who abuse the system here. But the fact that you do have it is something to be cherished. At home, and a lot of places I know, you don't have to say anything particularly 'bad' just a criticism of anything and you would probably find yourself in the bad books. When I was very small one guy was criticising some papers and he lost his job afterwards.
>
> PhD 2nd Year student, Mauritius

At home what another person does is other people's concern. People are afraid about what other people say. I am a bit quiet there because I don't go out that much. I mainly go out at night to do things, as I have to hide away from people.

Information flows so fast. It restricts you in so many ways. For some families it has really ruined their lives because they listen to other people and it has put their children in trouble. Even if someone wants to get married that can be broken.

MSc student, Sri Lanka

According to Roth (1990) the child gradually becomes an accepted member of a society when they understand and use the rules and roles of that society which are passed on to the child through interaction with experienced members of society.

It could be said that the overseas student could be compared to a growing child who is subjected to the processes of social development. However, unlike the child, the overseas student has to re-evaluate their integration and differentiation processes in order to assimilate their new domain. As a result, the student may experience difficulty and stress in the transition of roles and status which may have a detrimental affect on their behaviour, health and academic achievement.

Motivation

One particular social motive is the need for affiliation, or interaction with friends or acquaintances. Most people need to be with and communicate with other people. Social relationships, particularly with people in whom one can confide, are important for both physical and mental well being. Humans are creatures of both biology and culture and belonging to communities channels their innate motivational tendencies so that their expressed motives fit local social and economic conditions. Social roles represent a major part of the individual's self image and this becomes more apparent with age. One reason why it is so important to conform to these expectations is that most social roles are interdependent – they do not exist in isolation but constitute social systems. If society is to function properly each member of the role set must be able to rely on all the others behaving in an appropriate way. This interdependence is particularly striking in the case of complementary roles e.g. teacher-student where one role cannot really exist in the absence of the other. However, when role expectations are not sufficiently clear to guide the occupant's behaviour and interactions with others a person may not know how they are expected to act (Westen, 1999).

According to White (1959) the 'master reinforcer' which keeps most of us motivated over long periods of time is the need to confirm our sense of personal competence which is defined as our capacity to deal effectively with the environment. It is intrinsically rewarding and satisfying to feel that we are capable human beings, to be able to understand, predict and control our world. Unlike hunger which comes and goes, competence seems to be a continuous, on-going, motive. Competence motives often involve the search for stimulation which can be sought through curiosity and exploration. Therefore, it could be said that the 'competence' motive is an important factor in a student as they are normally stimulated by the curiosity and exploration of seeking new knowledge.

However, the extent to which the competence drive is active in a student may also reflect their ability to understand and adapt to their new environment. For example, students who are from traditional cultures may be excited by their new lifestyle and may change their behaviour, opinions and even their identity. Nevertheless, although it may be desirable here, it may be of concern to the student when they return to their own society. Some examples are as follows:

> I enjoy life here. I sometimes like the individual life. If you live on your own you will be more mature. I feel more independent which is quite a problem when I go back. I used to do things straight away but now I don't and my parents get annoyed. Most people have a problem with living when they go back.
>
> PhD 3rd Year student, Thailand

> When I go home I have to adjust immediately and think 'there are limits here'. If you don't get along they will do something about it and being ostracised by society is not a good thing. But that is how it is in a community. You lose more by not going along.
>
> PhD 3rd Year student, Botswana

> In this country I have to express my own ideas, which motivates me more. I don't have to agree with my supervisor. In research it is inevitable to have some argumentative situation if you have good ideas. In my country I have to follow my supervisor's suggestions but here you can negotiate with each other. I think one of the good things about the Western system is that they can distinguish between the formal and the informal, but in my country it's a bit ambiguous and may become aggressive. Korea has a very strict hierarchical system. We are always worried about what happens if you express your ideas but in Western systems they separate the work and the personality.
>
> PhD 3rd Year student, South Korea

> It is also the freedom, the bravery to come up with your own ideas and talk about them. A friend in Indonesia doing research just followed her supervisor. Since our childhood we were always told to stay quiet, listen to the teacher and if we didn't we would be punished in some way. I expect this to be a problem when I go back. When I speak to people and do things I will have to use a different approach. I still know a lot about my people, about their habits and my habits so I will try and do it in a psychological way.
>
> PhD 2nd Year student, Indonesia

> Normally we eat spaghetti and English food. We only eat Chinese food when we cook together. Actually, we like Western food more – especially steak. We also like mushrooms and pasta which are expensive in Malaysia. We will eat them more when we go back. We can't get Malay food so our diet has changed a lot. We are willing to try new food and went through a stage of trying out new restaurants. We even went for a British meal on our first wedding anniversary!
>
> MSc student, Malaysia

> At first people must have thought I was quite boring. The other Chinese thought I was from Hong Kong or Singapore because I was talking English all the time. At this moment I am more English and have also changed my hairstyle. In China I had long hair but short hair is easier to deal with and feels quite free.
>
> MSc student, China

It was not difficult to adapt. Maybe I am strange! I wanted to know more about differences. Why and how? Maybe others may take months to adapt if they stay with their own people but to me I like being alone. Everything is exciting! I felt as though I was out of the cage, out of the room – if you open a window you get fresh air. But everything has its price. You have to do many more things but you begin to understand more about life. I have become more mature here.

MSc student, China

Being abroad is a course in itself, a degree in itself. I have learnt many things – some good, some bad. In my country I never had to protect my car so when I go back there my behaviour has changed. I have to think about things that I never thought about. My attitude has changed. When you are inside the circle you don't see the circle but when you go abroad you can see it very well. I have seen some advantages and disadvantages about my own country. I have a wider perspective and feel that my personality has changed by living abroad.

PhD 2nd Year student, Saudi Arabia

It took me about 3 months to feel comfortable. It takes time to learn about things like bus systems, shopping and where to go for things. I think I became more used to learning new things. It gave me more courage and made me more adventurous as I didn't worry about making mistakes.

MPhil student, Taiwan

According to Berlyne (1960) exploring the unfamiliar increases arousal. However, if the unfamiliar is too different from what we are used to, arousal will be too high and we may feel anxious and tense. Alternatively, if it is not different enough, arousal is too low and we soon become bored. Our optimum level of arousal is partly determined by how relaxed we are feeling initially. When we are relaxed we are more likely to welcome novel and challenging experiences whereas when we are already tense, we prefer to deal with what is already familiar and relatively undemanding.

This explanation could be associated to 'culture shock' as a student may feel ill at ease in a new environment because, initially, everything is too different. One of the students gave a realistic portrayal of homesickness as follows:

I did know the feeling of homesickness. It wasn't physical; it was like emotional emptiness in a way. You wanted to say something or share something but it was as if part of your life was taken away. I couldn't say what it was, it wasn't tangible, but some part was missing and you couldn't fill it with anything either. Probably it was the way of life and day to day routine which was totally changed here. It was like that for about a year. I couldn't go with my problems to anybody. You had to make friends but even friends would go away, like students, and there wouldn't be enough time to make good friends.

MPhil student, Mongolia

Mental Programming

In an attempt to understand social behaviour it is important to grasp the basics of human thinking which affect all human beings of all cultures. Hofstede (1984) argues that people carry 'mental programs' which are developed in early childhood and reinforced through educational establishments. These mental programmes contain a component of national culture and are normally expressed through different values. He states that the mental programmes can be found at the universal, the collective, and the individual level and that social systems can only exist because human behaviour is not random, but can be predicted to some extent. He attempts to explain this as follows:

> I predict that Mrs X will be in the office at 8.25 a.m. tomorrow; that the taxi driver will take me to the station and not somewhere else if I ask him; that all members of the family will come if I ring the dinner bell. We make such predictions continuously, and the vast majority of them are so banal that they pass completely unnoticed. But for each prediction of behaviour, we try to take both the person and the situation into account. We assume that each person carries a certain amount of mental programming which is stable over time and leads to the same person showing more or less the same behaviour in similar situations. Our prediction may not prove true but the more accurately we know a person's mental programming and the situation, the more sure our prediction will be.
>
> Hofstede (1984) p. 14.

Hofstede then comments further on the issue of mental programmes and that every person's mental programming is partly unique and partly shared with others. He illustrates the three levels of uniqueness as given in Figure 7.1.

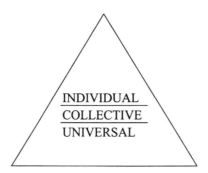

Figure 7.1　Three levels of uniqueness in human mental programming

The most basic is the universal level which is shared by almost all mankind. He refers to it as the 'biological operating system' which includes a range of expressive behaviours such as laughing and weeping and associative and aggressive behaviour which are found in higher animals. This may also be associated with the belief that all human beings are innately the same and are subject to human nature. The second level is the collective level which is shared with some but not with all other people. He states that it is common to people belonging to a certain group or category, but different among people belonging to other groups or categories. This level includes the language in which we express ourselves, the respect we show to others, the physical distance we maintain from others in order to feel comfortable and the way we perceive general human activities. In overseas students, this level could be associated with the national culture. The process of socialisation and the extent to which they are governed by the rules and roles of society will affect how they familiarise themselves with certain groups or categories.

However, Hofstede explains how the individual level is the truly unique part as no two people are programmed exactly the same even if they are twins who have been raised together. It is the level of individual personality, and it provides for a wide range of alternative behaviours within the same collective culture. He reveals that the borderlines are a matter of debate among anthropologists as it is difficult to draw sharp dividing lines between individual personality and collective culture or to distinguish exceptional individuals from their cultural systems. In overseas students this level defines the difference in experience, knowledge and behaviour between students from the same country. Despite similar backgrounds, these factors distinguish the individuals from their cultural heritage. One student aptly explained the dilemma which may exist at this level as follows:

> I think people change sometimes but you don't know if it's the culture or your personality changing. Your behaviour may change but it may be because you are learning, getting more knowledge and experience.
>
> MPhil student, Malaysia

Hofstede believes that mental programmes can be inherited or learned after birth and that the universal level is most likely to be entirely inherited as it is that part of our genetic information which is common to the entire human species. But it is at the collective level that most of our mental programming is learned, which can be shown by the fact that we share it with people who went through the same learning process but who do not have the same genes. This may also explain that although the overseas students who come here have individual experiences, they may still feel the need to acknowledge others who share their national culture. It may not just be because they are going through a similar experience but because they actually feel a sense of familiarity as they are intrinsically connected.

Social Interaction

During their academic study an overseas student will most likely interact with people from diverse cultures for numerous purposes.

> People affiliate, or seek out and spend time with others, for many reasons. Sometimes they interact to accomplish instrumental goals, such as raising money for charity or meeting over dinner to discuss a business deal. Other interactions can reflect family ties, shared interests, desires for companionship, or sexual interest.
>
> Westen (1999) p. 821.

One factor that influences attraction is similarity. People tend to choose casual acquaintances, as well as friends, on the basis of shared attitudes, values, and interests. Surrounding one self with likeminded others seems to be rewarding (Westen, 1999). Although all students will interact to obtain their main goal, the overseas students will most likely make friends with those that share the same attitudes, values and interests as themselves. However, it is apparent in the study that those who do not have many English friends do not adapt as well. Although some were aware of this they still found it difficult to make friends with English people which they explained as follows:

> Initially, coming across natives was quite difficult. People are not very open here but once you get familiar with the system you become part of it. There is not much warmth towards the foreigners from the natives. I have been lucky enough that everything has been fine with me but on the whole when you interact with people they are not very receiving of foreigners. I think it is something to do with the culture and people value their own independence too much.
>
> MSc student, India

> I don't know much about the British because I only know a few British people. One of my British flatmates was very nice and friendly but that was all. I think English people are friendly but it is very difficult to make friends as they don't tell you about their personal life even though you may know them a long time. I think they are very similar to the Japanese who are very polite and kind but do not open their mind to you.
>
> PhD 3rd Year student, South Korea

> It creates a problem for me discussing the lectures with my Arabic friends and I regret not speaking to native speakers. My friends were very helpful and I spent a nice time with them but I spent my time working and studying with them. But it would have been better if I would have an English student as a friend.
>
> MSc student, Syria

Bochner et al. (1977) provided a functional model for the development of overseas students' friendship patterns as follows:

- **PRIMARY, MONOCULTURAL NETWORK.** Consists of close friendships with other sojourner compatriots.
- **SECONDARY, BICULTURAL NETWORK.** Consists of bonds between sojourners and significant host national such as academics, advisors and officials.
- **THIRD, MULTICULTURAL NETWORK.** Consists of friends and acquaintances from mixed cultures.

With regard to the framework, Furnham explains:

> Although Bochner did not interpret his findings within a social network framework, others have found that the degree of social interaction between the host national and the sojourner is related to the latter's adjustment.
>
> Furnham (1997) p. 19.

From the study, it is evident that the majority of overseas students remain in the bicultural network most of the time. However, those that successfully functioned within the third, multicultural network seem to adjust better to their new environment. This scenario was also compounded by Furnham and Alibhai (1985) who replicated and extended Bochner's work and found that foreign students still showed a stronger preference for co-nationals rather than host nationals or any other nationals. This had occurred despite the fact that Sellitz and Cook (1962) found that sojourners who had at least one close host national friend experienced fewer problems than those with no close host national friends. In the study, those who had English friends appreciated the effort it took but commented on how rewarding the experience could be as follows:

The English are friendly but their approach is different to that in Sri Lanka. I don't think many international students move around with English people but they should because they come to this country and they won't gain anything out of it. I have a lot of English friends and they are very patient people.

MSc student, Sri Lanka

I think the English people are friendly and I don't believe those who say that the English are 'cold'. I have some English friends from the course, from demonstrating and from a part time job and some off the internet by 'chatting'.

MSc student, Pakistan

You don't know what to expect and what people do in this society. I was lucky to have an English housemate who helped me. I think if you have a lot of English friends you can learn a lot in a group. I think it is difficult to break into a group at the beginning but if you go out with a group of English people it is better.

MPhil student, Taiwan

My best friend is British so I think compared with other people I am quite lucky. I met them in my MSc course. It is great to get to know the British culture through my British friend as I spend Christmas and New Year at her house. My friends from Taiwan don't have any contact with the locals and they stay in a group so when they go back they don't know about the different culture, different thinking and way of living.

MPhil student, Taiwan

My first friends were my landlord and his family. I go to see them every few months with my girlfriend. They always looked after you when you have problems. I only lived with them for 2 weeks but in that time they offered a lot of help. We do Chinese meals for them and they are very good friends.

MSc student, China

Furnham (1997) explains that one of the most popular explanations for the different reactions by migrants to a new environment is the neo-Darwinian idea of selective migration. It is an extension of the principle of natural selection, which states that all living organisms that cope best with the demands of the new environment will prevail. This theory is emphasised by Humfrey (1999) who explains that secure and happy students are more likely to be academically successful and have good memories of their time overseas. She explains that if they are satisfied with their stay they will recommend the institution to their families, friends and sponsors and that students who integrate well create fewer problems for themselves and the host community.

Communication

In order to interact with others it is necessary for overseas students to communicate with other people. Harris and Moran (1993) stress that communication is at the heart of all organisational and international relations and that it is the most important tool for getting things done. They describe communication as a process of circular interaction which involves a sender, receiver and a message. The process is described as follows:

> Both sender and receiver occupy a unique field of experience, different for each and every person. Essentially, it is a private world of perception through which all experience is filtered, organised and translated; it is what psychologists call the individual's life space. This consists of the person's psychological environment as it exists for him. Each and every person experiences life in a unique way and psychologically structures his own distinctive perceptual field. Among the factors that comprise one's field of experience are one's family, educational, cultural, religious, and social background. The individual's perceptual field affects the way he receives and dispenses all new information.
>
> Harris and Moran (1993) p. 31.

They explain how an individuals self image, needs, values, goals, standards, expectations, cultural norms and perception have an effect on the way input is received and interpreted, in relation to their own perceptual needs. Therefore, two people can derive entirely different meanings from the same message which highlights that communication is a complex process. When the sender is from one cultural group and the receiver is from another, the human interaction is referred to as inter-cultural communication. Harris and Moran also explain that a person transmits many kinds of unintended or subconscious behaviour besides verbal and non verbal which includes such aspects as tone of voice, gestures and facial expressions. Therefore, communication at any level can be complex and the way in which we communicate can be strongly influenced by our cultural conditioning.

Harris and Moran (1993) continue to say that every person is a versatile communicator and that language distinguishes us from other creatures. The human communication skills are diverse and include words, gestures, signs, shapes, colours, sounds, smells etc. Every individual communicates a unique perspective of the world and reality and every culture reflects that group of people's view of the world.

When overseas students first arrive in England they may have a confusing time as their psychological environment is based on their own distinctive perceptual field which is derived from experience, knowledge and social background. Initially, although they are able to speak to another human being the meaning derived from both the verbal and non-verbal interaction may be distorted. Their perception of the physical environment may also be different between students based upon how much it varies from what they are used to and the accuracy of their expectations. The landscape and people may also be perceived in different ways as follows:

It is more old in London but Manchester is more industrial in style. The buildings are quite nice but they seem squashed. In Trinidad there is more room. There is not much colour here. Not much variety. The buildings are red but there are no flowers.

MSc student, Trinidad and Tobago

When I came to London I asked my husband where the high buildings were. I was thinking that every English man and woman has blue eyes and blonde hair.

PhD 1st Year student, Syria

The buildings are very old and I like them. I expected the modern buildings like in the movies but I did not find any high ones, only 3-4 storeys. I was surprised at the traditional buildings as it was not like LA or New York.

MSc student, Libya

I was thinking 'First World, Fast World' but when I got here I was surprised to see it was the same pace as us. To be honest, I think I was exposed more to American TV and I was expecting America - that kind of life. I thought it would look like America but then I saw these normal buildings, even older buildings than where I come from. You like your history and you keep it but I wasn't expecting it. My perception of the 'First World, Fast World' were the little things you see in the media.

PhD 3rd Year student, Botswana

In China I have watched most of the films from America but New York is not Manchester and does not have high buildings, skyscrapers. In China we thought England would be the same but knew England has got more traditions than America, but I didn't think the people liked the past.

MSc student, China

The buildings and the streets gave me a shock because I thought England was a developed country and the buildings should be higher, beautiful and colourful. At first I had the impression that England was quite boring, red buildings, and nothing had changed for 100 years. But on the contrary it is really good. You are living in a cultural life and not just a stone forest.

MSc student, China

I like the old buildings as to me the modern building is like a match box. Western buildings and architecture is horizontal – they do not build very high. Shanghai does not have many spaces so it is vertical. I like the churches here very much. I like the style and it gives me a feeling of 'dungeons and dragons' which is familiar to the games I play!

MSc student, China

I expected to see high, tall buildings but what I saw were red brick houses which are different to me. In Taiwan we paint over the bricks so to see the bare bricks was interesting in a way. I was told by my housemate that it was traditional. I expected to see the tall buildings like in London or America.

MPhil student, Taiwan

London is the same as I expected as I thought it should be quite old and the architecture should be like the pictures in the travel books and TV programmes of Tower Bridge. I thought 'Yes, this is London'. Manchester was different as I thought the buildings are quite new and modern in architecture compared to London. There are not as many old buildings as London. It looked like modern stuff but in an old colour – dark and grey.

PhD 3rd Year student, Thailand

The first thing that I noticed is that the people are very colourful because in my country we almost have the same appearance i.e. black hair and same eyes. The British style of architecture is quite different because most architecture in Korea is made of wood. I expected it to be more modern but was fascinated by the old fashioned buildings.

PhD 3rd Year, South Korea

I was quite shocked at the buildings in Manchester but now I am getting quite used to red brick buildings. The buildings are old and some used to be factories. Whenever I see red brick buildings in Manchester I think of a Pink Floyd album in which they argue about how the industrial revolution affected the people. I didn't expect it to be modern but it is still different than the Far East.

MSc student, South Korea

I didn't expect it to be that gloomy. I expected to see tall and bigger buildings because England is one of the G7 countries but then I guess it is more European. The roads were OK but I thought they would be wider but then again most people's perception of England is London.

PhD 2nd Year student, Mauritius

When I arrived, it somehow was bizarre. I read a book in Russian called 'The House of Uncle Tom'. It was set in 18th century England. I was walking along the street in London and could see all these 'smiley' people, really like 'kind' looking, black or white. I thought 'Yeah! This is just like in the book'. There was a 'kind' feeling inside. There were old people walking who looked kind and happy looking and didn't care too much about their clothes – really relaxed. They say Mongolians are happy people but it was like a totally different kind of happiness – more relaxed.

Manchester was different than London. It was quite red. It's still red – all bricks. In London they are white, grey – quite mixed. Even the old buildings in the city centre are red.

MPhil student, Mongolia

In the study, it was apparent that, as noted by Harris and Moran, the overseas students received non-verbal messages about their new environment and society through shapes, colours, sounds and gestures. However, from this form of communication they were also able to derive some meaning e.g. old buildings may mean that we value our own history, very green trees may signify that it rains a lot and people queuing at a bus stop may indicate that we are a patient people. Many of the students described Manchester as 'red' due to the red brickwork or 'horizontal' due to the low height of the buildings. It was also interesting to discover that many of the overseas students expected England to be very similar to America but not Europe. This association may be due to the distorted messages that are projected by our own media to overseas countries. Furthermore, a number of students who had visited London expressed that London alone fulfilled their expectations of how they imagined England to be.

Language

The most common method of communication and interaction between students and their host environment will be through the medium of language.

> Language is a tool for communication but crucially it is also a tool of human interaction. By means of language, we express our personality, our thoughts, intentions, desires and feelings; and by means of language we relate to other people.
>
> Wierzbicka (1991) p. 453.

Wierzbicka (1991) explains that there are many different modes of interaction between people and that they depend partly upon what one feels and wants at any particular time. However, they also depend upon who the people are – both as individuals and as members of particular social, cultural and ethnic groups. She gives the following example:

> If you and I are Japanese our interaction will be different than it would be if we were both Americans or Russians. And if we were both Americans, the prevailing modes of our interaction would probably depend on whether we were white or black, Jewish or non-Jewish and so on.
>
> Wierzbicka (1991) p. 2.

She argues that all meanings involve interaction between the speaker and hearer regardless of the subject matter, and that we use language as a tool of social interaction.

Baldwin et al. (1999) state that as all human societies have language it is difficult to imagine how a society might exist without it. They say that the minimum condition for human society is ordered and regular relationships between individuals, the recognition of shared meaning and the ability to transmit knowledge and information to each other and that the use of language is usually the most efficient and effective way of doing so.

This explains how a student with language difficulties can be affected if the meaning is distorted, as they will not be able to transmit knowledge and information to English people and vice versa. Many of the overseas students commented on the difficulty of interacting with others as follows:

> I found my listening difficult at first, especially with pronunciation, as I am used to American English. It is especially difficult in Northern England. I thought I knew enough English to live and study here but the first days I couldn't understand anyone and I thought 'what am I doing here?' I thought about going back to Mexico, as I was frustrated.
>
> PhD 2nd Year student, Mexico

> My first problem was the language so I tried to speak more at my hall. I just thought 'I

have to speak English'. I tried to be present in the common room every night and spoke to everyone there! It really helped. I went out with a mixed group of people from the course to learn more about the UK, about Manchester and the culture of the people here. I thought I could only survive that way.

PhD 2nd Year student, Indonesia

When I initially arrived I couldn't understand a word of what they were saying but you have to adapt and learn how to listen. It took a few months to get used to the Manchester accent.

PhD 3rd Year student, Malaysia

I speak to everyone but it is more convenient to make friends with oriental people. English people do not like people who speak slowly. Sometimes you can't think about the right words at the time you want to say it and they have to wait for you to recall the words you want which can be a problem.

PhD 3rd Year student, Thailand

At first I found it hard to speak up because of my language and culture. Although I had studied for 10 years it is totally different when you first arrive because we are used to listening up to 3 hours a week with a Thai teacher, from a book. But when you come it changes and it is difficult as you have to listen all the time. The first couple of months was a horrible life.

PhD 3rd Year student, Thailand

English does affect my relationships, as I don't always know how to say what I want. It is easier to speak English to a Chinese person because they also make mistakes.

MSc student, Indonesia

The first problem in human relationships is attraction. The second is language. The other problem is patience. Some foreign people say that they don't understand my English and don't want to listen to me which is stressful but English people are patient. In our country we think about other people's feelings whereas Western students are individuals.

PhD 3rd Year student, South Korea

If you don't understand you can ask again but it depends on confidence. When I first started meeting people and sat in a group I didn't understand jokes or slang words which aren't used in Pakistan, but you learn over time. It is all in the process of learning.

MSc student, Pakistan

Fortunately, there are also some positive aspects of having difficulty with the English language which may be life changing! One student explained:

I used to bother about my English a lot. The main reason I first went out with my husband was to improve my English. I told him that it was a good opportunity to practice my English and he was really helpful. But the more we got to talk we started to like each other. He got quite serious after a few months but I told him I just wanted to improve my English. Now that we are married he still mocks me and says that my English is still not good enough so I will have to stick around for at least another 3 years!

MPhil student, Mongolia

Student Experiences

Hoffa (2002) aptly summarises the problems and reasons why a student living abroad may encounter difficulties with their new environment, as follows:

> It is very hard to know what life is really like in a country or region whose culture one has never experienced directly. But it is very easy to have the illusion of knowing what it will be like – from images furnished by popular communications media, from reading, or perhaps having met a few people from 'there', here on home ground. Simply 'knowing about' another culture, however is not the same thing as knowing what it will feel like to be learning and living there, on its terms. Every culture has distinct characteristics that make it different from every other culture. Some differences are quite evident, even to the unsophisticated (e.g. language, religion, political organisation, etc). Others can be so subtle that while foreign visitors may be vaguely aware of them, making adjustments is a complex process and one may remain uncomfortable and off balance for quite some time.
>
> Hoffa (2002) p. 1.

Hoffa explains how after the initial period of excitement wears off, they gradually become aware that their old habits and routine will no longer suffice. He attempts to reassure students that these feelings are a kind of 'psychological disorientation' and that it is part of the necessary discomfort needed for psychological adjustment to a different environment. Hoffa refers to this situation as an 'occupational hazard through which one has to be willing to go through and learn from in order to enjoy the pleasures and experiences of other countries and cultures in depth' (Hoffa, p. 2). However, the extent to which a student can psychologically and physically adjust to their new environment is dependent on many issues, some of which have been highlighted in this chapter.

References

Baldwin, E., Longhurst, B., McCracken, S., Ogborn, M. and Smith, G. (1999), *Introducing Cultural Studies*, Prentice Hall, Europe.

Barnett, R. (1990), *The Idea of Higher Education*, Buckingham, The Society for Research into Higher Education & Open University Press.

Berlyne, D.E. (1960), 'Conflict, Arousal and Curiosity', New York, McGraw-Hill.

Bochner, S., McLeod, B. and Lin, A. (1977), 'Friendship Patterns of Overseas Students: A Functional Model', *International Journal of Psychology*, vol. 12, pp. 277–99.

Brown, P. and Scase, R. (1994), *The Consequences of Modernity*, Cambridge, Polity.

Furnham, A. (1997), 'The experience of being an overseas student', in D. McNamara and R. Harris, *Overseas Students in Higher Education*, Routledge, London & New York, pp. 13–29.

Furnham, A. and Alibhai, N. (1985), 'The Friendship Network of Foreign Students', *International Journal of Psychology*, vol. 20, pp. 709–22.

Harris, P.R., and Moran, R.T. (1993), *Managing Cultural Differences*. 3rd (ed.), Gulf Publishing Co, USA.

Hoffa, B. (2002), *Exploring Cultural Differences*. Available at: http://www.studyabroad.com/handbook/cultdiff.htm. Accessed 22 October 2002.

Hofstede, G. (1984), *Culture's Consequences*, Sage Publications, Newbury Park, London, New Delhi.

Hofstede, G.J., Pedersen P.B. and Hofstede, G. (2002), *Exploring Culture*, Intercultural Press, USA.

Humfrey, C. (1999), *Managing International Students, Recruitment to Graduation*, Open University Press, Buckingham, Philadelphia.

Roth, I. (1990), *Introduction to Psychology*, Open University, Milton Keynes.

Saha, L.J. (1996), 'Universities and National Development Issues and Problems in Developing Countries', in Z. Morsy and P.G. Altbach, *Higher Education in an International Perspective*, Garland Publishing Inc., New York & London, UNESCO International Bureau of Education, pp. 84–86.

Sellitz, C and Cook, S. (1962), 'Factors Influencing Attitudes of Foreign Students towards the Host Country', *Journal of Social Issues*, vol. 18, pp. 7–23.

Westen, D. (1999), *Psychology. Mind, Brain & Culture*, 2nd (ed.), John Wiley and Sons, USA.

White, R.W. (1959), 'Motivation reconsidered: The Concept of Competence', *Psychological Review*, vol. 66, pp. 297–333.

Wierzbicka, A. (1991), *Cross-Cultural Pragmatics, The Semantics of Human Interaction*, Mouton de Gruyter, New York.

Chapter 8

Cultural Shock or Cultural Acquisition? The Experiences of Overseas Students

Dale O'Neill and Cedric Cullingford

Introduction

The literature on the experiences of overseas students has remained remarkably consistent in its content, conclusions and recommendations. It is also consistent in its negative tone. Studies from Sen (1970) to Burns (1994) and Osler (1998) record the difficulties and concerns of overseas students relating to practical matters such as housing and finance and to the more complex challenges of adapting to local communities and to unfamiliar approaches to education. One of the main conclusions drawn from these studies relates to the extent to which bodies of overseas students, however different in age or in background, tend to stick to each other, in a type of cultural ghetto. This socialising with fellow nationals has negative effects on their intellectual as well as linguistic progress (Geohagen, 1983). It raises two kinds of questions. One is to do with the negative impacts of the host community (Bochner, 1980). The other is to do with the way in which people adapt to new circumstances which force them either to challenge some of their own assumptions or make them mentally retreat into the familiar. It is this choice, this cultural complexity, that deserves further exploration.

It is difficult to find a survey of overseas students which does not contain a litany of accounts of negative experiences. It is unreasonable to assume that there are no positive aspects to the time spent studying abroad but these are rarely given much airing. One reason is the fact that relating difficulties is far easier than recalling the more subtle pleasures of the everyday. News, as in the public media, tends to be bad.

Another reason is the fact that it is far easier to describe cultural differences, in terms of symbols like food and dress, than it is to uncover cultural similarities or distinctions in terms of ideas or assumptions. The whole notion of 'culture shock' pre-supposes that there are almost insuperable barriers to mutual understanding whether problems are to do with the communal and superficial communication associated with transport, or shopping, or the more complex transactions demanded by friendship or intellectual challenges (Furnham and Bochner, 1982). The very fact that the ability to communicate with people 'in another foreign culture can be regarded as a social skill' (Furnham, 1993, p. 106) suggests that cultural demarcation lines are clear and strong.

'Culture shock' is a condition, or a theoretical base, that pervades the literature, the notion that it is an emotional reaction to the 'perceptual reinforcement from ones own culture' (Adler, 1975, p. 13). On the face of it, there is plenty of evidence for the difficulties and the challenges of confronting other people of different outlook and alternative habits. On the one hand, we have the loss of the familiar. On the other hand, we witness the effects of the gaze on others who seem to be doing inexplicable things for their own highly rational motives. Seeing the world divided into tribes and nations, into regions and languages, is seen to be at least a starting point in understanding the existence of other kinds of thinking rather than one's own. The notion of cultural disparity should be celebrated. It is interesting. It demonstrates the breaking down of parochialism. But it is so often presented, despite this, as a series of negative or unfortunate incidents.

Travelling to a different country and living there, rather than being a tourist, does pose obvious difficulties and we should be aware of the practical problems, like simply finding out how to travel to a particular destination. Travelling also poses other obvious difficulties, which are both practical and more culturally complex. Language is an obvious example. The same distinction which applies to tourists or more permanent settlers is appropriate here. The language which is perfectly serviceable in a restaurant is not necessarily adequate for the nuances of meaning and understanding expected in more extended or probing dialogues. One genuine surprise for visitors is the difference between the English used in the home country and taught as a foreign language and the demands made by native speakers. This is not a deliberate suspicion by native speakers of those who speak the language with 'foreign' accents (Loveday, 1986). It is a fact of socio-linguistic difference which permeates all kinds of communication, including the difficulties in understanding between two native speakers of English who come from, say, Newcastle and Liverpool.

Phonological differences, whilst they can be irritating, are comparatively superficial. It is the understanding of what is meant and implicit that causes difficulties. The problem is that when confronted by an unfamiliar challenge, like academic English purveyed with all the cultural assumptions of an academic lecturer, the difficulties will appear not only the more acute but be simplified.

Just as the notion of culture shock brings out the differences and even simplifies them, so a sense of linguistic alienation will assume that there are clear barriers to understanding. Students travelling abroad feel their differences to the extent that they forget all the variations of their own multiple, adaptive, multi-cultural backgrounds (Osler, 1998). Being abroad heightens a sense of otherness and also a sense of self-identity.

Students choose to study abroad. Indeed, many feel privileged to do so. One might expect them, therefore, to be adaptable for the sake of academic progress. The irony is that it is with the various aspects of studying itself that the students find most difficulty. They worry about the attitudes of their tutors (Geohagen, 1983). They are concerned with the lecturers' apparent lack of support by encouraging them to learn by themselves, autonomously, rather than being told explicitly what to do (Eyre, 1992). Students worry that lecturers do not always understand that what the students are supposed to learn is geared towards their ultimate goal, a qualification (Brew, 1980). The very instrumentalism of their own approach to studying causes difficulties. It brings out the sense of cultural alienation the more strongly, in the very place they least expect it. It also causes the same students to look differently at all the other experiences they have had. It certainly pervades surveys of their attitudes. The negative impression of much of the research could be that students naturally look for reasons outside themselves for any hint of inadequacy or discomfort.

Students working overseas experience two influences. One is the realisation of differences both obvious and subtle. The other is the sense of loss of the familiar, both at a level of the pragmatic, like family and friends, and at more complex levels. If much has been made of cultural 'shocks', it is because they are both easier to describe and more collective. That yearning for what is familiar defines far more personally and deeply what a culture means. It is the mixture of the two which is worth exploring further. That there are cross-cultural misunderstandings is clear, with confused expectations of what is appropriate to say in certain circumstances (Geohagen, 1983). These should not simply be attributed to xenophobia. All kinds of differences can be overcome in the creation of friendships (Bochner and Orr, 1979), whilst it is easier to be close and feel warmly towards those who are most familiar including the same sex. This does not mean there should be automatic suspicions of anyone who is different.

In a time when there is so much more global communication and so much more physical as well as mental travelling, the more simplistic notions of distinctions need to be questioned and challenged. It is easy to relate the difficulties or the negative experiences but this does not necessarily explain either how people develop their own cultural identity or how they so often adapt to quite different circumstances without losing their own essential sense of self. There are some people who will only be able to develop a sense of individuality by creating an alien picture of others. Their very insecurity will bring out their prejudice (Cullingford, 2000).

There are many more who find it easy to adapt and to understand. Some overseas students survive much better than others but the question is why?

Not all experiences of travel are negative, although this is sometimes the impression given in the research. There are, therefore, questions to be asked about the outcome of these highly prized awards for students to study abroad. What are the factors which are positive as well as negative? What impact has travel on the individual and his or her own sense of self? How do groups, large and small, identify and present themselves effectively to others? These questions, from the motivation to travel, through the practical difficulties, to the experience of being 'other' need constant addressing. There are differences between expectations and reality and between the obvious and the subtle. There are also differences between the given mythologies and the newly created ones. Students abroad make very interesting if unwitting witnesses.

The Research

Questions about cultural inheritance, invoking discrimination and prejudice, self-awareness and responses to others, are very complex and the methodologies used to explore them need to be sophisticated. Going to live in another country does not lead simply to a list of impressions or stereotypes or fixed reactions to natives. All attitudes are formed by previous expectations and cultural habits and distinctions both left behind and brought along. Responses to new circumstances will be as much influenced by others, by fellow travellers and native language speakers, as well as the new relationships, both ephemeral and long-term, formal and personal. Travelling abroad is not just a matter of gaining insight into others but an opportunity or a necessity for greater self-awareness. Those who have lived in another country than their original one become the more acutely aware of their own cultural inheritance as well as the peculiar attractions of the new. Real understanding of the effects of travel abroad needs to take account of the cultural influences that are brought and not only those that are met.

Culture 'shock' implies a confrontation of obvious differences. Of course, those who are concerned with the notion of different habitats realise that what is inherited is as significant as what is newly met (Bourdieu, 1986). Reading the literature of people's experience of travelling, however, especially the many studies of students (a captive audience), would lead one to believe that the entry into another culture is automatically defined as alienating, as leading to a sense of discomfort and separateness.

We have already noted the negative tone of much of the research. This is partly because it is easier to define differences. It is also because much of the research is based on attitudinal surveys which in many cases fail to detail, in any substantial way, the experiences, which give rise to them. This research attempts to contextualise feelings and ideas in the light of the students' individual personalities as well as attitudes. Questionnaires were eschewed as inappropriate.

The focus of this research is a cohort of fifteen mature people who have travelled to the United Kingdom for a year in order to upgrade their professional qualifications in ways which were impossible in their own countries. This was what is called an 'international' cohort, typically not including either Europeans or native English speakers. A significant number left behind close relations as well as relatives. They were aware of what they were coming for and for how long they were coming. Their goal throughout their stay was to return. They therefore looked at the country they were in with a particular scrutiny, quick to sense any antipathy or discomfort and looking steadily for the easiest, the smoothest passage. Given this kind of gaze, it would be easy to extract lists of stereotypes.

Dialogues were held with the cohort of students throughout their stay. It was important for them to have confidence in the researcher, who was not associated in any way in the teaching on administration of the course, although the subjects would have liked to have used her as if she were a representative of it.

Gaining their trust was important so that each student could talk freely and openly about their experiences. The quotations that are used to illustrate and illuminate the findings come from the recorded and transcribed interviews that punctuated the longitudinal and continuous observation. Many of the insights derive from this peer observation, objective, careful and unhurried, but it was also useful to allow the subjects to articulate more formally their views and experiences.

'Formality' in the interviews does not here mean that sense of seeking out of what is right to say in the light of the interview questions. On the contrary, the diurnal sharing of ideas and opinions gave an authenticity and clarity to the ways in which the students were thinking. They were easy with inadvertent comments and insights. They were not cajoled into being polite. The interviews, when they took place, were confidential and anonymous.

One of the essential insights that was afforded by such continuous and close personal contact was the way in which the students would influence each other. Whilst a participant in a formal interview for a job or a place on a course will be most conscious of what the interviewer would like to hear, the mind set of the subjects here was more tuned to each other than the participant observer. One should not underestimate the strong influence of other people in a cohort, the tendency to dominate and then shape opinions in others. Some of the research on the subject is contaminated by not being aware of this fact.

Even in an anonymous interview there can be a tendency to repeat those collective attitudes that have been generated by the group rather than those more carefully considered and idiosyncratic conclusions developed by the individual. The close co-operation with the group made this clear and added depth to the interviews. Students were not just encouraged, or prevailed upon, to speak openly with confidence but clearly to reveal the distinctions between the half-held beliefs that derived from the group and those valid insights that they would present consistently and repeatedly.

The quotations from the transcripts represent the consistent findings, the shared impressions and the insights achieved through the experience, which included a degree of self-knowledge. Each person remained a unique personality but their culture and their concerns were common to all of them. The themes are summarised here. There are some who travel as if cocooned in their own cultural identity and have no insight either into themselves or others as a result of the experience. There are others who are personally changed, not by adapting to a different culture but by greater self-awareness. It is these who offer the most interesting insights into the experience of entering a different culture. Gender and age differences are not significant so that the examples remain anonymous and representative.

Findings

Whilst previous research has quite easily drawn out lists of practical difficulties and the subsequent sense of distance from an estranging culture, it is clear from this more extended exploration of student ideas over time that there is no automatic or insuperable problem associated with the welcome or the lack of friendliness of the locals. Whatever the myths about the cold and distant English and whatever incipient fears there might be because of race or language, these visitors found no difficulties in interacting with those they met, in all kinds of circumstances.

> I think people here are very good ... I got no problem with, er ... personal relationship. In
> fact, I was treated as a family.
> I don't really know much about the country, but when I come here, the people are very
> kind to me. I been lost around and I ask people and I found they react, that is the first
> thing. Second thing, when I first come I don't know how to make use of the Pound. You
> see, I was confused with all my money so I was afraid of being cheated but the people
> are very friendly.

The interpretation of culture 'shock' as if there were some kind of confrontation
with people utterly different or indifferent can be dismissed. The difficulties in
coming to terms with understanding new challenges are not based on any obvious
estrangement. Sometimes to their surprise, the social interactions that they have
had have been friendly and supportive.

Students have found themselves being treated with that respect that they would
not just expect back home but which they recognise as the courtesy that goes with
the sense of someone else's dignity. The normality of the interactions is at a variety
of levels, from the willingness to do what is necessary and polite, to the sensitivity
to do more when there is a need but without being intrusive. The first and everyday
level is politeness, being 'friendly' without cheating.

> They are the most polite people I've ever come across for one thing. Compared to places
> we have been ... they have been very helpful here. If you stop anybody, they will tell
> you exactly ... people here actually help you.

One level is the willingness to carry out an everyday transaction without rudeness
or a sense of intrusion. The second is the slightly larger human curiosity that
allows the help to go a bit further. In comparing one country with another, this
person points out that there is something more important than meeting a basic
requirement. She finds that her sense of worth is maintained because the dialogue
is directed towards her individual needs.

> People have definitely been very responsive in the sense of whenever I asked them
> something, there have always been people who wanted to help or say something on what
> I've said so it's not like they've said I've got no time for you and rushing you know. So
> I've gained a lot from them.

The ability to contrast one environment with another demonstrates cultural
awareness. More pertinent is that distinction between instrumental transactions,
however friendly, and the feeling of mutual learning, which is real understanding.
'I've gained a lot from them as well' shows the complete lack of cultural alienation
at the level of separateness. One of the assumptions in the literature is that people
will be treated differently, without respect, or even discriminated against because
of their differences, whether of colour, clothes, language or habit. This is not borne
out. Given the multicultural nature of most societies, there are constant demands on
adaptability and a need to recognise and accept superficial differences. Even if

these students face difficulties, it is not attributable simply to a lack of communication because of cultural barriers.

That there are problems associated with spending time abroad is clear, but most of these are practical and a question of universal loneliness and missing people as well as those habits taken for granted. It is the absence of the familiar that is remarked upon. The family is missed, naturally enough, but also simple things like food.

> We are cooking the food we cook at home, to except the certain foods, certain ingredients that we cannot have but we just say, you know, because for us it's only a few months and when we reach home, we can pick those foods we really like, but for the daily living, I mean we have rice every day so it doesn't matter to me.

We see here two themes; the sense of self- enclosure that means even in such a small or practical way, rethinking the usual domestic habits and also the feeling that this is an interim experience, which needs to be put up with. This and the very longing to be able to grasp the opportunity to travel – through scholarships hard fought for – should mean that the scrutiny of the alien experience should be the more sharp. The possibilities of stress are there but the students know that this is far more self-created, however good the reasons, than thrust upon them. The problem with that sense of just temporarily having to go through this particular rite of passage is that the individual might remain cocooned in a particular and unexpanded way of life. This choice, however, is not forced upon them but self-generated. They might not like English food but most adapt or submit or even grow to appreciate it, however grudgingly. The point that is being made, however, is the longing for the availability of what is familiar. Food becomes symbolic in this respect. The yearning for the homeland is often expressed in nostalgia for teacakes or Vegemite.

The sense of being in an alien, unfriendly land is not nearly as powerful as the missing of particular cultural familiarities. Of course the two phenomena belong together but they are not the same thing. It is possible to be in circumstances which are culturally comfortable and yet yearn with a powerful nostalgia for those habits of thought and mind which are perceived not as being better but as being simply more familiar. The very immersion in a more challenging environment can lead to distraction from missing home. What emerges from the research, however, is the powerful nature of accepting the fact of ones own cultural inheritance. It might not be rated that highly but it is valued as being a part of the self. Young children express the fact that they are born and brought up where they are with objective centrality (Cullingford, 1999). They know it is a matter of chance. This does not prevent the fact that it is the most significant influence in self-definition. Going to another country reminds the individual of the power of the social self, the very domesticity of the home environment and what familiarity means.

Being treated 'different' is a reminder of what has been left behind. This reminder can be inflicted as crudely as the approach of immigration officers.

> They see from our luggage that we are foreigners and that we're not white. I think that they should ... I mean in my country, I don't think this thing exists ... it might exist but very small percentage I think.

Even here, there is a realisation that the 'friendliness' perceived in one's own official is a kind of familiarity, recognition of the distinction between the role and the person. Even the expected distinctions of behaviour based on 'race' are soon perceived to be missing.

> And we were very pleased now. It was the first time I had seen an English man carry the bag of a person who is not white. I was surprised and yet, nice people. Back home you call them 'Sir' but now the 'Sirs' carry your bag. I didn't ask to carry the bags ... first impression is a nice picture.

However strong the pleasant surprise, it is still tinged with the loss of the familiar habits at home. The unobjective comparison, not between standards of living and behaviour but between what is deeply habitual and what is subtly different, remains powerful. The new country is looked at through what is personally missed:

> That's the only thing that keeps bugging us at night, when I think of home. It's homesick ... not for the sake of the country ... but the family.

Missing friends and family is natural but it is sometimes interpreted as a criticism of the country in which the people find themselves. All kinds of circumstances can be challenging but they are easier to cope with when the shared mutual understandings are implied.

> More of an adjustment to the environment, to the people and all that. I still had the worry about ... I don't understand at what level I'm going into. What role do I play there? ... because being different from back home. I feel I still want some support, still have to lean on the people you know ...

Even when the approaches to professional matters reveal inadequacies in the common practices back in the home country, the familiar routines will prevail. Many of the students are critical of the lack of new initiatives in their own professions. They have witnessed and tried out a number of new styles. Yet they realise that when they return they will also revert to what they were doing previously. All environments are adjusted to – one's own environment the most easily.

Missing the familiar, therefore, is not a matter of a critical judgement that concludes that ones own cultural habits are best. On the contrary, the problem is that this enclosure in the familiar goes so deep that it is difficult to shed and at some levels impossible. The sense of loneliness at the first entrance into foreign territory is universal. It pervades the subsequent adaptation to new circumstances.

> A bit distressed thinking of the family behind ... our own people are very friendly to us. I think it was a bit drizzling and it makes my heart turn, go right to the bottom.

That sense of which is missed remains a strand in the perception of all the experiences they will be going through. This is not chauvinism nor is it confined to the domestic. It is not only relations that are missed but the ordinary routines.

> What sort of civilisation do I come from ... probably from a very uncivilised and certainly appearing in a ... They're taught we must be very barbaric people. But they didn't know we have our own kind of civilisation.

'Our own kind' is the personal and the familiar that all people need to define as part of their personal identity.

Many of the concerns that are expressed by overseas students are practical. Missing family is practical. So is the need for instructions in essentials, simply in how to cope in particular places. This stresses the need for practical advice and shows how relatively unimportant are the cultural distinctions. In fact the students all say that the advice they would have most appreciated before coming to the country was to do with practical issues, like clothing and transport rather than culture. They did not want careful briefing on the ways in which the natives were supposed to behave. They did not want subtle exegesis on styles of proxemics or tokens of ethnographical habit. They were far too deeply caught up in their own. Before mutual understanding they first wanted to learn how to cope.

> About the climate, what I should expect, what shoes I should wear, what clothings I should bring and what food I should expect and all that. Some of it was not accurate. They know most of information are very encouraging but then when it really comes to your own situation, it's not true ...
>
> I get used to the weather, get used to the new customs and environment, than to go about looking for a home to rent ...

There are different levels of challenges, from food to relationships, but the crucial issues that involved prospective travellers, however inaccurate they turn out to be, are the most practical ones: 'how to' do certain things rather than the expectations of behaviour. Subtleties of cultural differences only matter when there is enough confidence in coping with the everyday.

> Got all the information. Where to catch a bus, all the areas which is good and which is not so good when you're renting a house, what to be aware of when you rent a house and all this kind of information.
>
> I think I would give them [the next cohort] a thorough briefing on what to expect. In the sense of the difficulties in moving around, getting to know people, renting a house, thinking of the things we have experienced ...

'Briefing on what to expect' could include all manner of things, from the level of tourist brochure to the historical and cultural nuances of the place. Nothing could be more complex than trying to convey the mental habits of nations and regions, that broad cultural briefing which is difficult to translate into other circumstances. Certain symbolic archetypes can be transmitted, like representation of the Arts, but the subtleties of folklore or domesticities are more difficult. Overseas students also feel they are not required. Provided the people are friendly and helpful (they are) then all that is required at first is solid advice. When they think back on what they were told, they make a distinction between many of the generalised statements they found unhelpful, even if accurate (like about the weather) and those matters they could have found useful.

> The time the bus comes to that station ... I still can't comprehend that timetable ... Another thing – they've got to talk about is clothing. You've really got to show the students this is the second-hand shop, right, this is the expensive shop. Or this is the Oxfam, they can start to realise where, because when we come here like us we spent a lot of money back home buying a lot of clothes.

The practical details that are required are domestic and parochial. They consist of useful tips, like bringing one sweater (for Heathrow) and buying clothes from second-hand shops, as well as the mysteries of transport. This suggests something about the lack of cultural 'shock' because of the hegemony of practical concern. Surviving and coping in the best way is not just considered an essential first step but remains as the core of the experience. It implies there are few difficulties with dealing with the people. All that matters is knowing what to do. Beyond that, cultural insight is not so necessary or so challenging.

That overseas students do have difficulties is understood but the nature of the impediments to their well being are both pragmatic and academic. Entering into any new course is difficult, however sophisticated the student (Salzberger, Wittenberg et al, 1983). All in-service courses seem to have the effect of reducing those who take part in them to that level of shyness and uncertainty that they recall from their undergraduate days. It is, therefore, a mistake to suppose that the difficulties that overseas students experience are all to do with their foreignness to the demands placed upon them. They might find the assumptions made about their intellectual autonomy are demanding. They might feel themselves to be suddenly exposed to uncertainty. All students who are confronted with open rather than closed questions, however, feel this uncertainty.

When we explore the feelings of discomfort, frustration or uncertainty, we need to bear in mind the themes of the loss of the familiar, the concern with practical realities and solutions and the nature of academic life, which affects all. Cultural distinctions then become far less of an issue. When a student talks of uncertainty it could be due to a number of factors:

> I'm still probing into the dark and don't know what is happening.

> Yes the feeling was terrible because we did not know what they expected of us.

It turns out that the major concern and anxiety is what is expected of them academically; what group they might be in and what the learning conditions might be. When they talk of being 'lost', it is invariably because instead of the familiarity of being with their 'own' group with people from their own country and background, they are 'mixed' with others. They are concerned not with the fact of cultural difference but the deeper level of demand that comes with it. Suddenly the level of dialogue and expectation becomes different. The 'loneliness' they talk of is the academic exposure to new demands.

> We never expect the loneliness we were experiencing when we were on our teaching practice placement ... but people here are friendly to us. They make us feel welcome, then I see it as a challenge ...

This makes clear the distinction between the demands of a new challenge, the exposure to unfamiliar surroundings and the warmth and support of people. Any student finds a new placement difficult. Nor should we underrate that strong sense of loss of the familiar.

> Although the people here are very friendly, but as we said, we are still finding that it's just a superficial conversation. We can't really talk to them about our problems and what our feelings are like.

Loss, not confrontation, is the problem. The familiarity with a cultural or domestic milieu leads to an openness and informality of conversation that both overcomes practical difficulties and alleviates the tensions of academic demands. Again, the same witness emphasises the significance of the preliminary briefing, which took place before arrival.

> Before we came, people who ... er ... people kept saying the people from – they don't know anything, they didn't learn this, they didn't learn that so we also had that in mind when we came here ... Everybody kept saying – oh, those people from – they don't know anything so when we came here, we see the value and the reasons for the way this comes.

The prejudices were set up and nurtured. Antipathy to new approaches or being 'mixed' with new challenges had been almost wilfully nourished. This overlaps with the expectation that people would generally be unfriendly and unhelpful. In the event:–

> We were taken aback how people kept saying 'hello, how are you?' and saying 'don't worry, don't worry.' It was always ringing in my ears you see ...

One of the most serious causes of discomfort is the difference between expectation and reality but this is not because of the commonly assumed reasons. Students receive a series of general myths, mostly negative in their effects, before encountering a new culture and it is these received attitudes like layers of self-doubt that undermine many experiences. Small difficulties then become exaggerated and of greater significance than they need be. That there are language problems, for example, is to be expected. The Diaspora of the English language has had the same effect as the tower of Babel in being used and reformed in so many ways, especially dialect.

> The problem is that the students cannot sometimes understand my accent, my pronunciation so that's a cause of a bit, I mean, having a barrier in terms of language.

> So somehow, when you find that your English that you were taught at school, people
> don't understand you, somehow you feel your English is no longer good.

The nuances of meaning in language, the short cuts of imprecision and the
elaborated expectations of academic complexities all make demands and cause
barriers.

This is again true of all students but more obviously so for those who have
acquired a different vernacular. The crucial familiarity of understanding, of the
sense of the small community of a linguistic domain deepens the sense of a
particular cultural hegemony. Language makes use of a series of conventions, of
particular uses of words or phrases and, like jargon, can create barriers as well as
understanding. This is a subtle matter, more complex than impenetrable accents or
dialects but equally not deliberate. Sometimes the different conventions can be as
simple as the way in which people are addressed.

> In our culture you should not call somebody by his or her [first] name if she or he is
> older than you. If there is ten years difference ... so the relationship is different here and
> using tutor's names is difficult.

There are the kinds of cultural convention that can easily be adapted to and yet
there can still be an unwillingness to do so, an atavistic longing for what one is
used to.

Having language conventions in common is one facet of the pull of the
familiar. The desire to be close to the everyday is a stronger feeling that the fear of
the new. This in itself leads to difficulties. Whilst it is not difficult to adapt to new
conventions, provided there is genuine contact with others and the friendliness is
perceived clearly, there is always a tendency to be closest to those with whom they
already have much in common.

Fear of the 'mixed' group can lead to a tendency to fall into a self-inflicted
ghetto. We know that some of the most significant friendships made abroad are a
matter of the first chance meeting; that person who is the only person one talked to
on the first day. This first meeting is often with someone from a similar
background, a fellow international student. This means that the cultural interchange
with the host country, however friendly, can remain limited.

> Probably I don't mix around with other races, I mean 'mix around' with other
> international students.

Sometimes such narrowness can be for defensive reasons.

> My husband has advised me that if you're in somebody's country, you have to be like do
> not get involved with some, like people who are not ... how shall I say it? ... socially
> involved with people, I mean men I think.

Whatever the dangers of rumour, what is clearly of most significance is the
continuing thought of reputations at home. Missing the larger family can mean
clinging to the available familiarity, being shy of any personal involvement outside

the socially complete attributes of the home country. It is far easier to be relaxed enough to be sociable with those who share exactly the same conventions. This is also true of the academic demands.

Being in a 'mixed' group means being forced to talk, to engage with others who do not automatically share the same prejudices. The students are very equivocal about the people with whom they spend time. On the one hand, they emulate the conventional attitudes of academics, a mixture of the supercilious and the self-conscious. On the other hand, they are more conscious of the attractions of retreat, of withdrawal into the familiar and the avoidance of what they also know to be both challenging and good for them.

The temptation is to stay with those who are least demanding and most familiar. To some extent this is a reflection of what it is like in their individual countries but abroad it becomes the more pointed.

> At home, I'm more independent. I don't go around in groups, I mix with everybody. I don't have any particular set of friends that I keep in touch with. Whilst here, we are staying together because that time is suited for us to study together. Sometimes we are finding that if I don't have anything to do, I go back on my own. It's just that the time is suited to us and it's more fun together – we are laughing most of the time.

> We are just staying in the same house, sharing the same interests.

> I don't think I could stay alone, when there's someone around and there is someone to discuss, to share with your interests and your problems, your happiness – everything together.

The variety of friendships is replaced by the routines of intense acquaintance and the closeness of the group. This is a common experience for those abroad, the chance creation of a new group that becomes an almost exclusive and potentially self-enclosed set. Such reliance on the easy conversations, the hiding in the undemanding, is understandable if not inevitable.

One reason for the significance of what is familiar is that a period of time in another country is a personal challenge. The student is forced to think about him or herself. Far from directing all the attention outwards in an objective analysis of what is strange or different, the rite of passage of the overseas course is one in which a personal reappraisal becomes central. Personal stress can lead to positive outcomes like greater self-knowledge, or new confidence, or can be a reiteration of all those habits that they most like. Homesickness is a very significant matter and encapsulates the depth of the hold of cultural convention. Any difficulty that is faced is exaggerated by the questioning of the extent to which it is the student's own fault. All sense of conventional objectivity is lost, whether towards the circumstances or the context.

> The both of us got the shock of our life. We are asking ourselves, 'where have we gone wrong?' 'Did we upset her or anything?' The whole day is spoilt, we do not know the reason ...

Doubt and anxiety can afflict anyone but such incidents are exaggerated by the sense that they need to be dealt with without all the friendly paraphernalia of a familiar alternative or conversation. The individuals are far more exposed and know this.

> As for me, I have come to realise what are my weakness points. I mean, when you're on your own you realise what the things are. You're not good at this, not good at that, so ... Maybe we put our own high expectations on ourselves but we feel the more tension, the stress is there, criticising our selves.

The pressure that the students feel is not from outside unless the very fact of being in an unfamiliar country is itself a pressure. It is because they are 'on their own' that they put 'high expectations' on themselves. The experience of being abroad is not just an opportunity to learn new things but crucially an opportunity to learn about themselves. All the attention is upon themselves and upon their own cultural inheritance.

Many people resist the challenge of self-awareness and will turn the demands of the experience away from self-knowledge into rejection of the circumstances that are too challenging for them. Many of the students reflect on the real opportunity that they have been through.

> I have a broader sense of seeing things, instead of being in my small world and feeling just the views which I think people see in that small world. Now it has broadened up into thinking that it is I not that narrow, it's a broader sense of it ... so I see this as personal development, not just professionally even my own self.

There are many conventional wisdoms made about 'broadening horizons' but to achieve greater self-awareness is a complex and demanding process. It does not come about simply by being in a strange place. It all depends on what is made of the opportunity. At the heart of the experience of going abroad is the very personal sense of greater self-awareness and greater insight into one's own cultural inheritance. It is not a matter of being confronted or shocked by what is alien and different but rather as a matter of missing what is most valuable and most conventional. The important lessons which are learned are those that are most personal. The 'sickness' of missing home is a realisation of all that is looked at the more fondly and forgivingly for being exposed to the scrutiny of distance. Being alone in a foreign land defines home. The mythologies surrounding both might remain but the values that are deep-seated are confirmed in all their power. They are approved of as a result of their defining control over the personality, language and the styles of thought.

Conclusion

Any exploration of individual experience over time is bound to be complex and sometimes unexpected but there are some clear patterns which emerge which lead us to question some of the shared assumptions that seem to have been made about students studying overseas. In this longitudinal research, the aim was to explore both the natural occurrences of travel and living and studying in a new environment but also some of the cultural implications. This concern is at the levels of nationalism, racism, prejudice and stereotyping but also with inter-ethnic and multi-cultural contacts and conflicts. Some of the themes that emerged at both levels make one doubt whether the conclusions of some previous research really reflect the experience of students abroad. The almost universal negativity that was supposed to be detected in students was not borne out here. The difficulties which they encountered were to be expected and were practical rather than owing to the unfriendliness or unhelpfulness of other people. Far from being wholly confronted by a sense of alien cultures and habits, students found that they missed the comfortable wadding of their own familiar styles of living, not because they were deemed superior or inferior but because that was what they had become most accustomed to. The challenge was not of the new but of a repositioning against the old. Those who wanted to gain from the experience could do so; those who were inclined to the sense of personal insecurity could maintain their narrow sense of identity in antipathy to the alternative culture.

In the days of global mass media and global economies cultural interchange abounds but so does provincialism and narrowness of vision. The opportunity to learn about other countries and the availability of information has not led to any great improvement in mutual understanding or international co-operation. Within a community like Europe, there is a strong belief that visiting other countries will provide enough knowledge to dismantle antipathies. One may gain knowledge of other places but these could merely support an established prejudice. It is possible to enter a separate domain, say as a football supporter, and be quite determined to succour one's own nationalist identity in the face of another culture and to retain all one's own familiar habits. In such cases, the previously established stereotype remains. Indeed this is intensified by the experience.

The difficulty in understanding the experience of travelling overseas to live, rather than acting as a tourist, is that there are two almost completely different levels of reality to deal with. One world is that of the images, the stereotypes, the visual symbols and the simplified facts. This is one kind of truth. There are castles and cathedrals, old towns and pageantries, abundant outdoor sports and terrible weather. The other world is that of everyday transactions, of negotiations with neighbours or checkout attendants, with the knowledge that eases coping strategies. It is the latter that is a real world and an important one that singles out the crucial definitions of personal experience.

This implies that there are all kinds of levels of cultural sovereignty. Each might be a collective identity but each one overlaps (Zetterholm, 1994). We see from these witnesses how one cultural insight into another person's way of thinking leads to a realisation of other alternatives. Awareness of other people's styles of thought depends upon the consciousness of one's own. Those who are certain of their own values cope more easily with problems they meet (Moyende, 1997). The irony is that it is those people who are most aware of their own cultural values who are also most conscious of the kaleidoscopic nature of cultures. They know that they could just as easily have been born into a different place with a different language. This does not lead them to suppose that theirs is the greatest of all possible states in any sense of the word (Cullingford, 1999). Culture, like taste, is after all, on artificial matter of upbringing and education (Bourdieu, 1984). Some of the nuances of cultural thought are so self-perpetuating that they cannot be separated from the sense of self.

The tensions of cultural experience lie between specific instances and general patterns of interpretation and involve both different kinds of ideas of what is 'individual' rather than collective (Liberman, 1989) and stresses between accepting and avoiding uncertainty (Hofstede, 1980). To understand the individual's sense of self, it is important to unpack the cultural awareness. This is why people studying overseas can give such an important insight into personal (and not just generalised) experience. For the individual, it is always difficult to unleash the 'pattern variables' that surround what can be interpreted as universal or particular (Parson and Shils, 1951).

Looking at the subjects of this study we see the difference between those who have been able to seize the opportunity to understand themselves better and those who have retreated. It should be noted that it is difficult to divide a cohort into two, since all experience degrees of self-knowledge and moments of denial. One of the results of the year abroad was clearly a distinct difference in the degree of personal (as opposed to professional) knowledge.

> Let's say your friends of another culture, the part may be different, of solving problems and if you were to talk to them you may find that you can weigh and compare the way they approach they use and the way you would have used ...

Cultural enrichment does not consist of adding or embellishing the existing norms with extraneous material. It is a matter to re-appraising ways 'you would have used'. Personal involvement with trying to see another point of view makes it possible to reassess those habits of thought long taken for granted.

> I have made the effort to overcome the problems by looking at the people here from their point of view and my point of view and putting myself in their place and looking at them from their culture and not thinking of my culture and expecting them to follow.

This is not a retreat from the 'shock' of what is different but a re-appraisal of the existing state of cultural mind.

These students appear to be subconsciously and unintentionally endorsing the point that personhood is eventually a cultural phenomenon (Harré, 1998). In all the different concepts of self, there is an awareness of the tensions between the truly individual and the collective, those obvious social characteristics that enforce an environment, like language. Even 'genetic emotions' like fear, grief or compassion have varying manifestations upon cultures (Nucci et al, 2000). The students in the study reveal in their unselfconscious and perceptive comments how an awareness of cultural hegemony (one's own) can strengthen understanding of other people. The crucial experience of being overseas is not cultural accretion but cultural self-knowledge.

References

Adler, P. (1975), 'The Transitional Experience: An Alternative View of Culture Shock', *Journal of Humanistic Psychology*, vol. 15, pp. 13–23.

Bochner, S. (1982), *Cultures in Contact*, Pergamon, New York.

Bochner, S. and Orr, F. (1979), 'Race and Academic Status as Determinants of Friendship. Formation: A field study', *International Journal of Psychology*, vol. 14.

Bourdieu, P. (1984), *Distinction: A Social Critique of the Judgement of Taste*, London, Routledge and Kegan Paul.

Brew, A. (1980), *Response of Overseas Students to Differing Learning Styles*, ELT Documents 109, British Council.

Burns, R. (1994), 'The Psycho-Social Adjustment of Overseas First Year Students at an Australian University', *Journal of International Education*, vol. 5(2), pp. 9–39.

Cullingford, C. (1999), *The Human Experience: The Early Years*, Aldershot, Ashgate.

Cullingford, C. (2000), *Prejudice: From Individual Identity to Nationalism in Young People*, Kogan Page, London.

Cullingford, C. and Husemann, H. (1995), 'Anglo-German Attitudes', Aldershot, Avebury.

Eyre, A. (1992), 'The split-degree experience: Malaysian Students in Britain', *Journal of International Education*, vol. 3, pp. 35–44.

Furnham, A. (1993), 'Communicating in Foreign Lands: The Course, Consequences and Cures of Culture Shock', *Language, Culture and Curriculum*, vol. 6, pp. 91–108.

Furnham, A. and Bochner, S. (1986), *Culture Shock: Psychological Reactions to Unfamiliar Environments*, Methuen, London.

Geohagen, G. (1983), *Non-Native Speakers of English at Cambridge University*, Bell Educational Trust and Wolfson College, Cambridge.

Harré, R. (1998), *The Singular Self: An Introduction to the Psychology of Personhood*, Sage, London.

Hofstede, G. (1991), *Cultures and Organisations: Software of the Mind*, McGraw–Hill, New York.

Liberman, R. (1989), 'Decentring the Self: Two perspectives from Philosophical Anthropology', in A. Dallery and C. Scott (eds), *The Question of the Other*–Albany SUNY Press.

Loveday, A. (1986), *The Socio-Linguistics of Learning and Using a Non-native language*, Pergamon, Oxford.

Moyende, A. (1997), *Black Families Talking: Family Survival Strategies*, Exploring Parenthood, London.

Nucci, A. (2000), I Saxe G. and Turiel E. (ed), *Culture, Thought and Development*, Lawrence Erlbaum, New Jersey.

Osler, A. (1998), 'European Citizenship and Study Abroad: Student Teacher's experiences and identities', *Cambridge Journal of Education*, vol. 28(1), pp. 77–96.

Parsons, T. and Shils, E. (1951), *Towards a general theory of Action*, Harvard U.P., Cambridge, Massachusetts.

Piaget, J. (1929), *The Child's Conception of the World*, Routledge and Kegan Paul, London.

Salzberger–Wittenberg, I., Gianna, H. and Osborne, E. (1983), *The Emotional Experience of Learning and Teaching*, Routledge and Kegan Paul, London.

Sen, A. (1970), *Problems of Overseas Students and Nurses*, Slough, ENFER.

Zetterholm, S. (1994), 'Why is Cultural Diversity a Political Problem? A discussion of Cultural Barriers to Political Integration', in S. Zetterholm, *National Cultures and European Integration: Exploratory Essays of Cultural Diversity and Common Policies*, Berg, pp. 65–82, Oxford.

Chapter 9

Students' Perceptions of Lifestyle Changes in a Remote Community Following the Availability of New Technologies

Tony Charlton and Charlie Panting

Introduction

We have only a meagre knowledge of humans' early social interactions with others. Likewise, we know little about how these dealings increasingly began to impact upon others, as the years passed by. Yet, what is irrefutable is that this impact has burgeoned with the passage of time. In far off times, for instance, an individual's or a group's influence was usually restricted to the immediate neighbourhood. More recently, this influence has acquired a global capability, of a kind that Giddens (1990) writes about as:

> the intensification of world wide social relations which link distant localities in such a way
> that local happenings are shaped by events occurring many miles away and vice versa (p. 64).

Much of this capability, or intensification, is inextricably linked to remarkable advances in transportation, and communication technologies. Even so, the effect of these advances upon individuals and cultures is not easy to assess: in recent times there have been few opportunities to observe people before, and then after, exposure to them. Thus, it is understandable that social scientists are lured to an isolated community once it gets immersed in communication and information technologies (e.g. television, the Internet, the E-mail) for the first time. Where an opportunity of this kind presents itself, an important line of inquiry would be to consider whether exposure to the 'outside world' alters the community's lifestyle, and changes its perceptions of the world outside.

From the Parochial to the Global

Ever since the genesis of humankind, individuals and groups have possessed the ability to exercise sway over others, in one way or another. In earliest times, this influence would involve only small numbers of people (e.g. another individual, a small group or community) and – for practical reasons such as transport constraints and a limited knowledge of distant places – would be confined to the immediate or not too distant locality. Over the years, the nature and extent of this influence has flourished. Most recently, it has impacted in unprecedented ways upon communities, cultures and societies, as well as continents. Hence, in the 21st century few people (even the information-poor and geographically isolated) remain unaffected by the effects of globalisation, for the scope to exercise worldwide authority and other influences has flourished. We can witness this influence most vividly in organisations such as the United Nations, multinational commercial conglomerates, in supermarkets stocking merchandise from around the world, and in the way that information can be broadcast to countries worldwide, without delay. Some refer to operations and influence of this kind as part and parcel of the globalisation process.

Globalisation at Work

Globalisation, thus far, has effected remarkable changes upon the world; most markedly by shrinking distances and by overlooking time. To illustrate, Cairncross (1998) talks about 'The Death of Distance' brought about by communication technologies which allow information to flow more rapidly and to reach further; information which (almost instantly) traverses oceans, mountains and rivers, whilst remaining oblivious to countries' borders, to climatic variations, war theatres, devastations and famines. So, countries become interconnected through myriad threads of information, which can be accessed almost anywhere, and at any time. Thus, information flows of this kind have helped engender, and subsequently sustain, globalisation trends.

In contrast to the usefulness of this information speedflow, some have cautioned that the nation-state risks being supplanted – often covertly – by a global society. Supportive of this thinking, Smith (2001) argues that states are becoming 'decision-takers' rather than 'decision-makers', and:

> As nation states of necessity, open themselves up to the global economy, they suffer a loss of political and economic authority. 'Diminished', 'narrowed', 'hollowed out' are some of adjectives used to describe the state's reduced capacity and scope of policy action (p. 117).

In a similar vein, Golding (2000) forewarns that the 'push-button democracy or electronic forum is but a few cables away' (p. 175). There is an obvious ring of truth about these words given that such practices are already customary within supranational and transnational institutions, organisations and programmes including, by way of illustration, the International Monetary Fund, World Bank, General Agreement on Tariffs and Trade, and European Union. In all likelihood, the future will see practices of this kind becoming increasingly commonplace and influential especially where nations elect to, or are obliged to, amalgamate for reasons to do with commerce, economics or defence. Thus, Fulcher (2000) is of the conviction that the nation is 'a relic of the past' (p. 524), and in like manner Van den Bulck (2001) cautions that 'national identity' is under threat, being exchanged in the fullness of time by a world where life styles, core values as well as family customs, dress, lifestyles and routines for example, become indistinguishable across countries. Hence, 'tradition' has become one of the 21st century's early addenda to the endangered 'species' list with the risk that 'Youth lose their rich cultural heritage and the systems of meanings, support and social control that were part of their traditional society ...' (Larson, 2002, p. 13). Similarly, Carlsson (2002) writes of an homogenising effect with the consequences that totally foreign cultures 'may soon be a thing of the past' (p. 7/8). An associated worry is that much of this conformity is linked to America's influence upon a global society. This concern arises, in part, because much of the world trade in informational goods (software, information services, technical services and financial services, for example) flows from the USA to the rest of the world. Likewise, others talk, somewhat disparagingly, of the worldwide diffusion of dominant cultures 'through the global market place ... reading "globalisation" as another case of hegemony, cultural imperialism, or Americanisation' (Irvine, 1999, p. 1).

Further disquiet has to do with disparities in the new technologies' availability; disparities with the potential to generate inequalities between the information-rich and the information-poor. Hence, the power and wealth of the information-rich can be used to sharpen, even more, the rich/ poor divide. However, Negroponte (1996) argues that the real divide is a generational one where the young tend to grow up alongside, and with a concomitant understanding of, the technologies whilst adults are at risk of estrangement from them.

On the other hand, as mentioned earlier, benefits are claimed for globalisation. It can encourage the reappearance, or assist with the preservation of local nationalisms (Giddins, 1999). It can herald a new era of wealth, freedom, and democracy (see Larson, 2002, for example). Moreover, organisations such as Greenpeace and Amnesty International are able to attract increasing global support (Pettigrew, 2000).

Thus, the two sides of the coin suggest that the subject of globalisation benefits remains the subject of debate, along with the usual claims and counterclaims. Yet, what is beyond dispute is that globalisation does impact upon our lives, personal and otherwise. It intrudes into our neighbourhoods, workplaces and more personal space using, for instance, new technologies such as the E-mail, television and the Internet. Consequently, it can alter the ways in which we think both of ourselves and others, as well as our culture. Additionally, it can change how we view the 'world outside'.

Globalisation and St Helena

Of particular interest to social scientists is what happens to an isolated community once it becomes immersed in recently introduced communication technologies (e.g. television, the Internet, the E-mail). Immersions of this kind are likely to incorporate novel experiences which introduce community members to new interactive communication modes, as well as exposing them to (and in some instances encouraging them to adopt) different life styles, unfamiliar core values as well as unusual family customs and daily routines, for example.

This chapter makes a cursory attempt to respond to the above question. In doing so, it reports on one from a number of research studies undertaken recently with adults and youngsters from the island of St Helena. Located in the South Atlantic Ocean, St Helena is one of the world's most isolated communities. Commercial transport to and from the island is restricted to the RMS. St Helena which visits the island every three or four weeks or so, whilst steaming on its voyage between the UK and South Africa. Broadcast television arrived in 1995 with the availability of CNN on a single channel. More recently, the service has expanded to incorporate three channels (Channel 1 – BBC World Service and Discovery; Channel 2 – MNET; and Channel 3 – Supersport). Television was then followed by the introduction of the Internet and E-mail. An earlier phase of the research provided scope to undertake a rare pre/ post-television investigation that monitored young children's social behaviour for two years before, and then for six years after television's arrival (see Charlton, Gunter and Hannan, 2002).

The following pages report on a research study undertaken recently with students from St Helena on UK higher and further education training courses. Undertaken nearly eight years after the availability of broadcast television, the interviews draw upon students' accounts of ways in which the availability of television as well as the Internet and E-mail seem to have effected wide-ranging alterations to island-life including changes in family life-styles, shopping habits, educational performance, social and recreational activities, satisfaction levels with changing life-styles and altered perceptions of the outside world.

Method

The data analysed and discussed in this chapter were taken from a larger project exploring St Helenian older pupils' students' and adults' changing views of both the outside world and the island's culture following the introduction of new technologies. Individual telephone interviews were undertaken with five St Helenian students (3 males; 2 females) undertaking higher education courses in UK universities or colleges. Students were aged between 18- to 20-years-old, and had been residing in the UK for at least 7 months on the interview occasion. Semi-structured interviews focused upon 9 questions exploring students' perceptions of changes that had taken place upon St Helena following the availability of the new technologies. Each interview lasted for approximately forty minutes and was undertaken between locations at the University of Gloucestershire (i.e. the research base) and each student's university or college residence. Interviews were audiotaped, transcribed and analysed using NVivo.

Discussion

The E-mail

Whilst some students referred to the value of using E-mail for business, more generally the new technologies were regarded as being useful for wider social purposes although some islanders (adults in particular) had little or no access to the E-mail. Even so, all of the students interviewed acknowledged 'enhanced communication' as being a fundamental benefit of the E-mail's introduction to St Helena. It improved communications with the outside world through bypassing the 'time and distance barriers, or obstacles' which, hitherto, had hindered speedy communications between the island and the rest of the world. Indeed, one student remarked how the improved facilities were becoming both more convenient and popular and were increasingly replacing long-standing modes of communication (e.g. facsimile, letter post, telephone). Others expressed similar thoughts.

> Especially with E-mail, you can communicate with people anywhere ... I would say the boundaries have fallen quite a bit now. (Student 4)

> The postal service back home is so rubbish anyway that E-mail is definitely, if not already, gonna take over. (Student 1)

> You might find people actually use telephones less because they can get so much more down on E-mail now ... especially for international stuff ... (Student 1)

Not only had the E-mail (and the Internet) refined the communication process in terms of speed, efficiency and reliability, it had also added to the number of people (on- as well as off-island) with whom islanders could 'chat'. For example, many of the islanders had now:

> got other ways of talking to people. Just having a friendly chat to someone *[at a distance]*, to a complete stranger, is a totally different concept for St Helenians. (Student 3)

The Internet

All students acknowledged the benefits of the Internet. It provided an excellent information-gathering resource; one which not only allowed many islanders to access material with a speed and convenience hitherto unknown on St Helena, but one which also supplied the means which could assist with the modernisation of the island. Additionally, the Internet supplied islanders with their first visual opportunity to access British news 'around the clock'.

> It gives, uum, the island a quicker connection with the outside world, because sometimes, although we have television it's *[mainly]* South African *[and American]*. So like, uum, sometimes the English or British news don't get there very quickly, yeah. So I think, well the Internet is quite fast. (Student 2)

Students recognized, too, that the Internet on St. Helena provided an effective educational support for assisting with school topics, assignments and examinations, as well as for preparing for higher and further education. By way of illustration, one student knew someone on the island who was undertaking a course in journalism via the Internet. Another had found the Internet to be an invaluable data-searching source whilst studying for his A Levels, especially so given that one of his teachers had resigned halfway through the school year. Other uses included obtaining up-dates on current affairs, as well as improving general knowledge.

Television

All in all, students were aware of the benefits of television. By way of illustration, one student admitted that television provided up-to-date information on global affairs (albeit, with a inclination towards North American affairs in the early days of television when only CNN was available).

> You know before the days of television ... we would probably get magazines, or whatever, which were a few months or at least a few weeks out of date and we were kinda behind the times. But now it's like an up-to-the-minute thing. (Student 4)

> TV proved more interesting than relying on the radio. You were more likely to watch TV than, hmm, listen to the World Service on radio. (Student 2)

Benefits of the New Technologies

It was unsurprising that students were agreed that the new technologies had recency, were informative and, with a modicum of training, were easy to use. When asked to contrast the printed word (e.g. books, magazines) with the new technologies, students remarked as follows.

> Well, I'd say the Internet then, because there's so much more to choose from. (Student 5)

> The Internet, because you get actual, visual images whereas you know with radio and books you read about it, you hear about it but it don't hit you as hard as when you see *[visual]* images. (Student 2)

One other student pointed out how an awareness of – and an elementary familiarity with – the new technologies was an education in its own right. It also provided an acquaintance with 'the communication mode of the future'. Nonetheless, the printed word was not dismissed out of hand, particularly in the school context. The book, for instance, still retained some uses.

> Well, in the educational sense you are more likely to concentrate on the subject in the book. (Student 5)

Even so, the consensus was that the new technologies had uses that surpassed those associated with the printed word.

What it *[the Internet]* has probably done is give youngsters a better idea as to what they can do with their education after. They can just see the opportunities there. For just generally being able to see and appreciate the outside world, which is an education in itself, then yeah, it has done a lot. (Student 1)

Accessing the New Technologies

Many islanders (although, possibly, less than a majority of the adult population) were now able to utilise both the Internet and E-mail. However, access for some was limited, for financial reasons as well as 'access' hindrances. Costs presented a problem for some St Helenians (young and old alike) as their only internet/ E-mail access was routed through the telephone dial-up connection. One student recollected that the domestic Internet cost on the island was 5 pence per minute (10 pence at peak rate). Therefore, lengthy on-line conversations and extensive Internet searches could be costly (even so, the situation appears to be improving as originally the cost was £1.50 per minute). Likewise, the initial cost of the computer could not be disregarded.

I don't think every person could buy a computer. It is more than most people can afford. Although people who get a higher wage ... *[they]* have an Internet and computers. (Student 4)

The significance of these set-up costs and running charges needed to be considered in the context of the average weekly wage of islanders of just over £60 per week; with some receiving far less.

For those who did not own a computer, limited public facilities were available on the island although students were not always mindful of either what facilities were accessible, or where they were sited.

The hotels ... I don't know if they provide network facilities for their customers. I really can't say. (Student 1)

There isn't an Internet café as such, but people tend to use the Cable and Wireless *[office]*. They go through them. But there's not really an Internet café. (Student 3)

No, they *[the islanders]* don't have an Internet café but I do believe that there is a computer available at the public library that has the Internet. Perhaps Cable and Wireless. But, no, there isn't *[an Internet café]*. There have been talks of an Internet café but as of yet; no. (Student 4)

The island's primary schools supplied limited opportunities for Internet access, but these were used principally by teachers for lesson preparation, and for computer lessons with the pupils. The one secondary school (Prince Andrew School) boasted more access, albeit this was still limited.

Yep, we've got two computer labs plus one or two areas dotted around the school (*Prince Andrew School*) that have Internet access, semi-restricted, to make sure the system isn't abused. (Student 1)

E-mail, I think, is restricted but you still tend to get people *(i.e. pupils)* who don't have a computer [*at home*] using their hotmail addresses there [*i.e. at school*] ... but Internet is definitely available to ... students. (Student 4)

New Technologies and Lifestyle Changes on the Island

Although students did not regard the E-mail and Internet to be fully integrated into islanders' lifestyles, they were in no doubt that television had become 'part and parcel' of everyday life for the majority of St Helenians. It was seen to take up more of individuals' time than either the E-mail or Internet. For most, and adults in particular (see Charlton and O'Bey, 1998), television had increasingly assumed an accepted, integral yet time-costly role in their culture. For instance, one student admitted that television had begun to rigidly regulate some of the islanders' daily routine.

You knew that people were going home to watch 'Egoli' [*a South African soap featured daily, on MNET*] at 5 o'clock, before they did anything else. (Student 1)

Television channels on the island showed predominantly South African (i.e. MNET) and North American programmes. Interestingly, some students highlighted the differential production quality between MNET and UK programmes. Thus, one student commented on differences he noted between the South African television programmes he had been watching on St Helena and the UK soap operas he has watched since moving to the UK

I knew it [*South African television*] was bad. But I didn't realise how bad it was until I saw the English soaps over here. They [*the UK programmes*] were that bit better. They weren't as far fetched. They didn't have as many murders and hijackings and stuff every five seconds in the British ones, so I just found Egoli a bit over the top ... Mind you, that's probably more to do with the South African culture ... South African culture as you know is far more violent than British culture. (Student 1)

When the students were asked whether (in their opinion) the St Helenian culture was changing given the popularity of the new technologies, there were mixed – and at times contradictory – responses. One student was confident that St Helena's culture would never change. He felt that even though the islanders' culture was being exposed to, and challenged by, so many new experiences, the islanders (with their traditions and close nuclear and extended family ties) were sufficiently strong to resist significant changes. On the other hand, another student thought change was inevitable, and necessary if the island was to survive economically in the future. In a similar vein, another thought St Helenians were becoming more liberal in terms of their lifestyles and aspirations as a consequence of their exposure to the new technologies. Thus the global society was gradually affecting (but not, yet, totally) the intimate lifestyle that had been an island characteristic for so long.

Well, no, there's no virtual community in the island cause everybody sees everybody, they communicate face-to-face rather than E-mail and so, ... you can't avoid people, they are always there. (Student 5)

There is still a distinct St. Helenian culture. It's probably less distinct than it was years and years ago. It was always gonna change anyway and it was changing before technology came. My personal view is that St. Helena has to change anyway, it has to modernise ... (Student 1)

I would say, well it's become; people's views are becoming more Americanised if you see what I mean. They, I dunno; they are becoming more open minded, as well. (Student 3)

Computer games and television games and such stuff *[like]* play stations, you find more people have those now. You might find the young kids will be swaying more towards that than doing whatever activities they would have done a few years ago. I think society in general is changing, to do with technology. People's expectations change and develop. (Student 1)

Fashion was one area that evoked especially interesting comments. The television, and later the Internet, had provided opportunities for people to gain visual updates on what others were wearing in the USA and UK, for instance. Thus, many St Helenians had become more fashion conscious, and now were able to copy current fashion trends overseas, without too much delay.

They *[the islanders]* know exactly what is in fashion at that time. You know young teenage girls, and even some boys, are gonna follow the trends, or whatever. You know before the days of television and stuff we would probably get magazines, or whatever, which were a few months old or at least weeks out of date and we were kinda behind *[fashion]*. But now it's like *[we're]* up to the minute ... (Student 4)

[Once] it took quite a while for fashion to reach the island ... now it's much quicker. Youngsters are much more aware of what's going on ... they try to follow along ... rather than catching on a few months later kind of thing. (Student 2)

So, they remarked on changes of this kind and attributed them to the new technologies that could provide islanders with instant updates on fashion trends, particularly in the western world.

I mean St. Helena is just catching up faster and faster and the rate of change on the island is increasing uum, it would be about 30 years ago that St. Helena was well behind, now its pretty much right up there except for um mobile phones (*which cannot operate on the island, as yet*), every technology that you have over here (*in the UK*), you got access to back home even though it does cost more uum, generally fashion and trends have caught up faster and faster. (Student 1)

The immediacy of this information availability was clearly affecting some of the lives of people on the island.

However, this technological facility to make off-island 'visits' to observe trends and be informed of changes was not restricted to clothes' fashions. Unsurprisingly, given the volume of advertising on television, different foods and other commodities were often sought by some St Helenians. Regrettably, although the new technologies continued to up-date the island on popular food and other commodity trends overseas, it remained difficult to access quickly the merchandise associated with them. Commercial transport, to and from the island, had not kept pace with advances in technology. In a similar vein, although grocery shopping on the island had recently improved with the opening of two further supermarkets there were often lengthy delays in importing customers' orders because of the infrequent visits by the RMS. St Helena. Paradoxically, one student told how one of the grocery stores on the island has a web site whereby the neighbouring island, Ascension Island (one of St Helena's two dependencies: the other being Tristan da Cunha) can order groceries from St Helena. Thus, the goods are shipped from South Africa to St Helena and then put back on the RMS. St Helena as cargo for Ascension on the ship's journey north. Nonetheless, trade with St Helena remains difficult due mainly to poor transport links (especially given the lack of an airport) with the outside world. Moreover, the cost of importing cargo by ship and the prolonged period of time that could pass before the RMS. St Helena visits the island combined to generate import (and export) barriers with the rest of the world.

> But uh, it's the barrier of transporting it as well. That's like the big barrier because I mean its so expensive to freight stuff from home so the price is gonna be extremely high. (Student 2)

However, the students were in agreement that the Internet had helped to place St Helena 'on the map'. One mentioned how he knew of more than a few people on St Helena who had created their own web site although these initiatives were mainly intended to promote the island, as opposed to promoting their personal business enterprises. Moreover, at least some of the websites had undertaken a useful 'business' role in terms of 'educating' browsers and, more importantly, attracting tourists to the island

> They've got these little message boards – or whatever you call 'em – and they *[the overseas browsers]* tell me *[through leaving a message on the web page]* that they would never have known about the island if it hadn't been for the web sites. (Student 4)

> I think it *[the Internet]* probably has *[encouraged visitors]* because St Helena has got its own web site and I think probably people do become aware of St Helena through their web site more. We have a few web sites with like scenes of the island and stuff and I think that probably encouraged people to come. (Student 2)

Thus, whilst the island's isolation, remoteness and poor transport created difficulties for the island in their attempts to attract tourists, the new technologies had generated some success in publicising the island to the rest of the world.

> The *[outside]* world has become more accessible so ... if you look at it that way then it *[the distance between us and other countries]* has shrunk ... it *[the outside world]* is closer to us now. Well, it's closer to us in a virtual sense but as our access still so bad *[i.e. transport connections to and from St Helena]* it's still – when you think about it in real terms – it's still just as far away as ever. You can see *[other countries on the screen]* but you still can't get to them. (Student 1)

However, the island's publicity does not succeed in reaching everyone. One student admitted how the island remained unheard of among his peers at university.

Exposure? My class mates don't even know where it [*St Helena*] is. (Student 5)

Increased Awareness of the Outside World

One of the notable virtues that students ascribed to the new communication technologies was that it had brought about a heightened awareness of, and knowledge of, the outside world to St Helena. 'Tuning in' to fashion, wars, famines, riots, earthquakes, politics, pop festivals, to mention but a few examples, more often than not became more stimulating – and was usually more informative – when accessed on a screen as opposed to listening to the local radio, BBC World Service (radio), or viewing outdated magazines or newspapers.

> At first we just had the CNN news channel and that was great. You could soon be up-to-date with current affairs all the time, and then you realise there really is a world out there. (Student 1)

> You're not quite as naïve as you were before we had television ... . You're not so sheltered really. (Student 4)

> You just got a better understanding, a better picture of what the world was like outside of St. Helena. (Student 1)

> Yeah, I would say, like uum, you just realise like how big the world actually is outside the island; you know. It's like being in the same place all your life and you get used to your thoughts and ... your train of thought is like small and narrow. (Student 5)

Another important way in which television had helped the islanders was by showing them how events can impact upon, or otherwise affect, other countries and, on occasions, the world in general.

> ... and it's stuff like, I remember seeing things like watching a space shuttle, and a space shuttle news station and watching it live on television and being amazed by all this technology 'cause you can watch something not even happening on earth, live. The Mars' landings and stuff like that sort of hits you and makes you realise how advanced the [*outside*] world actually is. (Student 1)

> You know, like the September 11th. Just <u>hearing</u> about it, wouldn't have had the same impact as <u>seeing</u> it on television. You know, it really brings home to a lot of people how important it [*the September 11th incident*] was. (Student 4)

Yet, whilst the new technologies had helped islanders to become more focused upon the outside world, the students – who had been in the UK for less than a year at the time of interview – thought that the immediacy of viewing UK lifestyles on the Internet or television on St Helena, for example, was still inferior to the real experience (i.e. residing in the UK)

> I think that even with television you still have to get away from St Helena to get a better appreciation of the world ... . You know like with the news and stuff, you don't see the full

picture. You either perceive it as a 'land of milk and honey' or as a horrible place sometimes seen on television, it's like normally one or the other. You don't get to see the full picture either way. You have to weigh it up [*experience it*] for yourself. (Student 1)

Everything is much, like, on a much larger scale compared to over here (*on St Helena*) so like, you know it's gonna be bigger but you just don't know how much bigger and how different. (Student 2)

Thus, for islanders fortunate to have regular access to the new technologies, elements of the 'barrier' shielding St Helena from the rest of the world had been removed. However, the actual physical obstacles (i.e. distance and transport constraint) were impracticable to eliminate. When asked if these 'obstacles' had been usefully overcome by the technologies, Student 1 commented:

Reduced but not removed yet, uum, I think St Helena will only become globalised when we can improve our actual physical access as opposed to virtual access. Uum, until then we will still be shut off although we can see things, and people can see us, we will still be shut off until you know you can actually physically get there. At the moment, if you're looking at the island on the web then it is for the most part just virtual, you wouldn't be able to just dash off there for a week and then come back again.

Conclusion

In 1995, the arrival of the television enabled St Helenians to receive instant visual images from abroad, for the first time. Thus, current affairs from across the globe (albeit predominantly from a North American perspective in the early viewing days) could be viewed at the same time as overseas' viewers. Since then, the Internet has augmented the island's choice in accessing worldwide news. So, islanders became able to bring themselves up to date on global affairs including fashion, political affairs, celebrity gossip and sport. Moreover, the Internet allowed individuals to undertake searches for more personal information needs. So, many – if not the majority – of the islanders could focus their attention upon distant horizons. By way of illustration, they could watch world affairs on television, they could utilise the E-mail to interact with individuals, groups and organisations anywhere in the world, and they could 'talk' in Internet chat rooms. Equally important, St Helenians could communicate with an unaccustomed anonymity (on- and off-island), away from the watchful eyes within their island community.

The students interviewed, acknowledged that St Helena's physical isolation and relative inaccessibility had not improved with the new technologies' availability. Even so, they accepted that television, E-mail and the Internet had gone some way in circumventing the physical and other barriers isolating the islanders from the world outside. As a result, (although in a 'virtual' sense) the new technologies enabled many islanders to observe and talk with the outside world, expeditiously and comparatively inexpensively. They could also surf for global information with the same convenience as their overseas' counterparts. A further benefit of these improved communications was that the island had placed at least a foot in the global marketplace enabling St Helena to promote, or advertise, itself to potential tourists.

However, some St Helenians had elected not to engage with the new technologies (although few islanders rejected the television). For other St Helenians the cost of a computer and Internet set-up was beyond their means. Thus, the 'economically poor' were placed at risk of becoming the 'information poor'.

The facilities and opportunities offered by the new technologies had produced other changes upon islanders' lifestyles. For many, the technologies had gone some way in lessening feelings of isolation, as well as improving the facility for personal and commercial interchanges, worldwide. Yet, there is a – more intrinsic – dimension unexplored in the study, one concerned with psychological functioning and associated behaviour. After centuries of colonial rule, an engagement with the new technologies suggests the potential to enhance islanders' self-worth, and heighten their feelings of personal control in particular. It will be of interest to note how changes of this kind – should they take place – impact upon matters to do with the island's governance.

Another unattended area concerns displacement. Clearly, some changes in the islanders' lifestyle have taken place (and these changes are likely to spawn others). For most islanders, a significant proportion of their leisure-time is being dedicated to viewing television, and for less than the majority, perhaps, some of this leisure-time is preoccupied with the Internet and E-mail. What was unaccounted for in this chapter was exactly where the time dedicated to the new technologies was being displaced from. Interestingly, Hannan (2002) undertook an inquiry to determine where young pupils' television viewing time was displaced from. In summary, he found that after initial preoccupations with the recently available television, many youngsters returned much of their TV-viewing time to those activities that were popular during pre-television days. However, Hannan's inquiry did not study television displacement effects in the adult population. In any case, displacement effects are likely to be more manifest where islanders experience the three new technologies, as opposed to only television. A few years ago an omnipresent characteristic of island life was the contact time that islanders tend to share with each other. For example, gossip constitutes an integral part of island life (including, for example, shopping excursions in both streets and shops) of a kind seldom experienced in the UK. There is evidence that social intercourse of this kind underpins community spirit and makes important contributions to a community's social capital (Laub and Lauritson, 1998). It could be a matter for regret if the new technologies were displacing time away from such 'community building' practices.

To conclude, the students' interviews provided more than a cursory indication that local happenings on St Helena such as the introduction of new communication modes, unprecedented access to latest clothes' fashions, new foods, novel educational support resources and burgeoning advertising efforts to promote the island, were being shaped by events which had occurred, or were occurring, thousands of miles away. These changes may work to the advantage, and for the convenience, of the islanders and the island. Such outcomes may be especially important to a microstate of a type that Rogers (1996, p. 8) refers to as 'ecologically fragile and vulnerable'. Nevertheless, a potential cause for disquiet has to do with where time is taken from to give to viewing, surfing and E-mailing. Hopefully, the sources of these displacements will be of neither a kind, nor a magnitude, which leads to untoward consequences for St Helena, and the islanders.

References

Cairncross, F. (1998), *The Death of Distance. How the Communications Revolution will Change our Lives*, Orion, London.

Carlsson, U. (2002), 'Foreword', in C. von Feilitzen and U. Carlson (eds.), *Children, Young People and Globalisation*, Goteborg, The UNESCO International Clearinghouse on Children, Youth and Media, at Nordicom.

Charlton, T., Gunter, B. and Hannan, A. (2002), *TV effects in a remote community*, Lawrence Erlbaum Associates, Hillsdale, New Jersey.

Charlton, T. and O'Bey, S. (1997), 'Links between Television and Behaviour: Students' Perceptions of TV's Impact in St Helena, South Atlantic', *British Journal of Learning Support*, vol. 12, pp. 130–134.

Fulcher, J. (2000), 'Globalisation: the nation-state and global society', *The Sociological Review*, pp. 522–543.

Giddens, A. (1990), *The consequences of modernity*, Stanford University Press, Stanford, California.

Giddens, A. (1999), *Runaway World: How globalisation is shaping our lives*, Profile Books Ltd, London.

Golding, P. (2000), 'Forthcoming Features: Information and Communications Technologies and the Sociology of the Future', *Sociology*, vol. 34(1), pp. 165–184.

Hannan, A. (2002), 'The impact of television on children's leisure', in T. Charlton, B. Gunter and A. Hannan (eds.), *TV effects in a remote community*, Lawrence Erlbaum Associates, Hillsdale, New Jersey.

Harris, J. (2001), 'Information technology and the global ruling class', *Race & Class*, vol. 429(4), pp. 35–56.

Irvine, M. (1998), 'Global Cyberculture Reconsidered: Cyberspace, Identity, and the Global InformationalCity',http://www.georgetown.edu/faculty/irvinem/articles/globalculture.html.

Larson, R.W. (2002), 'Globalisation, Societal Change and New technologies', *Journal of Research in Adolescence*, vol. 12(1), 1–30.

Laub, J.H. and Lauritson, J.L. (1998), 'The interdependence of school violence with neighbourhood and family conditions', in D.S. Eliott, B. Hamburg and K.R. Williams (eds.), *Violence in American Schools: A New Perspective*, Cambridge University Press, Cambridge, England.

Negroponte, N. (1996), *Being Digital*, Coronet, London.

Hon. Pierre S. Pettigrew, Minister of Trade, 'On Seattle: A Collision Between Two Worlds'. Speech to the Global Forum 2000, Washington, DC., 15 May 2000, <www.dfait.maeci.gc.ca>.

Rogers, A. (1966), 'Adult continuing education in small states and islands: Concept Paper', *Convergence*, vol. XXIX(2), pp. 8–20.

Smith. P.J. (2001), 'The impact of Globalisation on Citizenship: Decline or Renaisance?' *Journal of Canadian Studies*, vol. 36(1), pp. 116–140.

Van den Bulck, H. (2001), 'Public service television and national identity as a project of modernity: the example of Flemish television', *Media, Culture & Society*, vol. 23, pp. 53–69.

Chapter 10

Globalisation, Cultural Diversity and Teacher Education

Elwyn Thomas

Introduction

As we enter the 21st century most people in the world will be affected by the impact of globalisation on their lives. The nature of the impact will be different for each of us, and while the context and nature of globalisation will also vary, there are a number common consequences that will be felt by all. A key concern harboured by many people is the nature and extent to which global influences will affect positively and negatively our daily lives, and particularly the cultural values we hold. Transitional societies with their emerging economies, are in the main, highly traditional and conservative in outlook. In such societies, the consequences of globalisation are often seen as a threat to the cultural and religious values which these societies hold dear. Even in the richer and better off countries of the world, the increasing pace of globalisation is a cause of serious concern to many citizens, as globalisation is perceived to be coupled with excessive reliance on market forces and the dominance of corporate culture, resulting in often intense anti-globalisation movements. At the base of these concerns, is the extent to which individuals and the group cultures to which they belong, may become marginalised and even subordinated to the greater 'globalisation' culture.

The present chapter aims to relate three key elements which are pivotal in understanding the impact of globalisation on education with particular reference to socio-cultural values held by groups large and small. The three key elements are globalisation itself, cultural diversity and teacher education. The main argument running through the chapter attempts to intertwine these three elements which is: *that by developing a teacher education and training that is sensitive to cultural diversity in the context of global impact and change, education provision could become more relevant, adaptive, creative and forward looking as we enter a new millennium.*

Globalisation will be based on the author's view that it is a *process* which is essentially multifaceted and intimately related to free trade, technological innovation and information communication, demographic change linked to the development of global societies, socio-cultural, economic and ideological convergence (Thomas, 2003). Globalisation is primarily an *exogenous* process which means that ideas and information arising from outside a system have the potential to produce fundamental change to that system. But globalisation is not only an exogenous process, but one that can be harnessed to meet the needs of children's education and schooling, and therefore a nation's future citizenry. However, successful harnessing can only be achieved provided policy makers, teacher educators, teachers, and pupils are prepared to accept change, and are sufficiently open minded to adapt, initiate and implement new ideas in schools, colleges, as well as in their lives. In other words, there is a crucial *endogenous* aspect to the consequences of globalisation for education. The meaning of *endogenous* in the context of globalisation refers to forces within a system, which have the potential to counter exogenous influences, by adapting and enriching them further. Much of the endogenous nature of globalisation is closely related to the culture of a society. Therefore for global culture to merge successfully (which in essence means selectively), into existing cultural contexts, understanding merger of both on the part of educators is essential.

Cultural diversity is no longer a marginal issue linked with a few immigrant groups, and small numbers of ethnic minorities within a larger society. It has become an important issue in the provision of education, so much so, that societies have had to face the fact that educational provision may itself have to be diversified, in order to meet the very real challenge of globalisation and demographic consequences of that process. According to Corson (1998), post modernity has two distinct but conflicting features, on one hand a trend away from centralisation, mass production and consumerism which embrace national schools and state health services, and on the other hand, a development of flexible technologies and an emphasis on accountability, diversity of educational provision and more school autonomy. We need to add to Corson's perceptive analysis, also the impact and consequences for educational provision of globalisation as well. This gives a whole new and wider meaning to cultural diversity as a key factor in education policy decisions for many countries.

This means, that while cultural diversity needs to be addressed as an issue in educational planning, the need to equip students to survive in the ever competitive global market place has understandably become the priority, and consequently the special cultural needs of pupils are in danger of being ignored. Therefore, any society that recognises the need to address the issue of cultural diversity as part of a policy of education for diversity in a changing global context, must seek a consensus between the conflicting demands of postmodernism outlined above. Achieving this consensus means that education and schooling needs to be diversified, reflecting a culture sensitivity for both teachers and learners, as well as preparing children for the global 'internet' world of the new millennium.

The *notion of cultural diversity* is therefore one which not only embraces cultural traditions, language, religion and established social and societal mores, but the cultures of modernity, post-modernity and the recent subcultures which they have spawned eg new forms of industrial and commercial production, enhanced status of media empires, celebritism, the power and influence of internet communication systems. Very diverse cultures and subcultures that are emerging as these newer adjuncts to cultural diversity are being used across the global spectrum. Therefore, any consensus which educators are required to address, may need to consider their inclusion within a newer notion of cultural diversity. A key determinant in attaining the success of any consensus, depends on the way teachers will be trained, and the extent to which teacher educators are sufficiently prepared for the task. This raises the need for a different approach to teaching and teacher education reflecting cultural diversity and thence cultural sensitivity.

The author will focus principally on teacher education as one of several aspects to the wider debate about the impact of globalisation on educational provision in the future. However, some of the issues that pertain to the wider subject of education have common threads to changes in the way teachers are trained, particularly when examining the role of cultural diversity. Therefore, in the early section of the chapter some of these common threads will be teased out, as a background to the more germane discussion concerning teachers and their future training. The curriculum will be the main focus of the discussion relating to teacher education, but reference teacher development will also be made, as this area is closely linked to implementing a training curriculum.

The chapter will be structured around three questions these appear below.

- How does globalisation relate to cultural development and a notion of a *global culture?*
- What is the relationship between the notion of global culture, cultural diversity and educational provision?
- To what extent can teacher education accommodate cultural diversity arising from the impact of globalisation?

Globalisation and Cultural Development

In addressing the first of the three questions above, the reader will be provided with a backdrop to the main focus of the chapter, namely the ways in which understanding cultural diversity can become a meaningful part of the education and training of teachers, in a world that is rapidly changing as a result of the intense pace of globalisation. We will examine firstly the nature of globalisation and its dimensions, and then explore global culture both as a notion and as a factor in the process of cultural development.

(i) The nature of globalisation

Globalisation is not a new notion, it has been with us for many years albeit in less obtrusive and comprehensive guises. Michael Sadler, the well known British comparative educationist at the turn of the 20th century, noted that the economic and spiritual changes sweeping over the world at that time, were to be irresistible forces to which teachers needed to understand their inner significance, so that education would have to adapt to be a successful process, (Higginson, 1979; Watson, 2000). One can trace the start of global economic trends as far back as the days of the Romans, Phoenicians and subsequently the Silk Road from the far East during the middle ages. The British, Dutch, French, Portuguese and Spanish colonial influences also played their part in the history of globalisation, which was intensified in the mid 19th century as a result of the industrial revolution (Hallak, 2000).

Modernisation at the turn of the 20th century in the form of wider more efficient and effective forms of communication such as faster shipping, the laying down of telephone and cable systems, both national and international, and eventually air travel across continents, accelerated the globalisation process. In 1947 the General Agreement on Tariffs and Trade (GATT) was signed, with the hope that world trade could now be organised more effectively between nations on an agreed footing. As we reached the end of the 20th century, we see an even faster rate of globalisation taking place which has continued unabated into the 21st century, and which is likely to get even more intense and comprehensive.

Globalisation is therefore a truly global phenomenon already affecting the lives of millions of people. However, it is not only about more economic freedom, technological innovation and the spread of ideas, and greater interdependence between organisations (both unilateral and multilateral), but it is essentially about *people and their capacity to generate new ideas*. It is also about jobs, life styles, decisions about living and about the extent to which they think they are in control, and are controlled from outside their lives. Globalisation is essentially a behavioural process. It is about trying to shape ones destiny and about our destiny being shaped by others, the so called globalisers. Globalisation therefore. has a salient psycho-cultural basis to which we will return later in the chapter.

The author (Thomas, 2003), identifies nine dimensions and their components which reflect the nature and complexity of the process of globalisation. See Table 10.1 below.

The *economic dimension* includes the role of world stock markets, large corporate finance bodies, industrial conglomerates and loan aid agencies such as the World Bank and IMF. The *educational* dimension includes the development of human resources through formal and informal training, the role of further and higher education which act as sites for knowledge and skills training and the promotion of new ideas. The *environmental dimension* includes the use and depletion of energy resources, changing land use, and the exploitation of resources in the oceans of the world. The challenge of global warming and the removal of industrial wastes would also form part of this dimension. The *demographic dimension* includes the movement of peoples between countries, and across regions, brought about as a result of conflict and/or the search for better life styles. The *health dimension* is closely linked to human well being and the spread of good health practice to improve the quality of life of all populations. The *network dimension* is perhaps the most obvious one concerning globalisation with the recent and speedy developments in IT, increase use of computers at work and at home, and the dominance of global media that have instantaneous and constant radio/TV coverage for 24 hours a day.

The *political dimension* includes the power and influence of supra-regional bodies eg World bank, International Monetary Fund (IMF) to over ride and often determine national policy relating to economic, political and cultural development, giving rise to the doubts about the future of the nation state. The *socio-cultural*

Table 10.1   Nature of globalisation: key dimensions of globalisation and their components

Dimensions	Components
Economic (Free Trade)	Free trade, role of stock markets, Corporate Financial Institutions, Banking, Middle and small business enterprises, Aid Agencies.
Educational (Human Resource Development)	Changing patterns of training and education, emphasis on Knowledge. Acquisition, use and application, need to generate new ideas, promote scientific discovery.
Environmental (Ecological Change)	Global warming, national resources depletion, changing landscapes, discovery of new energy resources.
Demographic (Migration)	Economic migration, asylum seekers, refugee movements and political changes & pressures.
Health (Human well being)	Spread of diseases and infections. Awareness of good and bad health practices, Emphasis on suitable nutrition, and improving mental health, person isolation and alienation as negative outcomes.
Networks (Communication)	Mass media e.g. TV, newspapers, radio; personal computers, internet, telecommunication, transport.
Political (Power relationships)	Supra-regional Institutions. Regional groupings eg EU, ASEAN, OAU, OAS, UN, WB IMF and WTO Bilateral, National – Subnational/Local.
Socio-Cultural (Changing identities)	Global languages (international) versus local languages, religion, customs, traditions new cultures, cultural transference, cultural erosion.
War/Conflict (Events)	Effects of global and regional conflicts, rise of terrorism.

GLOBALISATION

KEY:

EU = European Union	UN = United Nations
ASEAN = Association of South East Asian Nations	WB = World Bank
OAU = Organisation of African Unity	IMF = International Monetary Fund
OAS = Organisation of American States	WTO = World Trade Organisation

dimension to globalisation involves changes to the role and place of national languages in national life, changing attitudes to cultural and religious beliefs and institutions, and an increase in cultural transference often accompanied in some societies by cultural erosion. The *war/conflict dimension* typifies, in recent years, the extent to which both regional and global conflict has become part of the wider globalisation process, affecting demographic composition through migration.

All nine dimensions, it could be argued, are related to various aspects of cultural diversity and educational provision, but the demographic, educational, and socio-cultural dimensions have particular resonance to the argument put forward earlier in the chapter.

The nature of globalisation outlined above has given rise to a number of consequences which have important implications for education, and teacher education in particular. Teachers will need to be trained in the years ahead in different cognate areas in order that they can meet the challenges of globalisation. One key cognate area of future training should reflect the socio-cultural dimension of globalisation. The need to have an understanding of changing cultural contexts by teachers poses a key dilemma for their training and education, insomuch that their training should reflect sensitivities to cultural diversity in school and society, while also meeting challenging global changes which will affect future education practice. In other words, teachers will need to appreciate that cultural diversity is a more dynamic, more fluid and a wider concept that hitherto. It could be argued that cultural diversity could embrace global culture, and therefore in the sub section that follows, an analysis will be made of what global culture is and how it relates to the notion of cultural diversity.

(ii) What is global culture and how extensive is it?

If culture is perceived as a set of encounters, Gearing (1979) with the potential for the transference of meaning through ideas, be they transient or more enduring (Thomas, 1992, 2003), taking place within and between generations of people over time, then *global culture* is already an existing notion. To the extent global culture is becoming part of everyday life, will depend on what particular elements of the global culture we are discussing eg the impact of the personal computer, increasing popularity of fast food such as McDonalds and sales of other brand products. Furthermore, it also depends on which part of the globe these influences are greatest? It is clear from an analysis of the growing amount of literature written on the subject of globalisation since the late 1980s, that globalisation has gathered enormous pace, although its impact is patchy in places and certainly its control is limited to a few rich economies (Green, 1997). However, the consequences of globalisation have contributed increasingly to a notion of a growing global culture (Thomas, 1997; Hallak, 2002). Let us briefly identify some of these consequences that may be instrumental in constituting a notion of global culture which appears to comprises of a number of sub cultural components.

A new culture of economics The advent of globalisation and its intensification in the latter part of the 20th century has meant that a culture of economic freedom has become the order of the day, and with it the opening up of markets world wide. Today, many countries in the Latin America, South Asia and the far East are active players in the conduct of world trade. Formerly, only goods and services were traded across national boundaries, but now the nature of trading has changed to include often large movements of skilled and unskilled labour, means of production, and the deregulation of stock markets, and greater internationalisation of banking and financial services. This can be perceived as the emergence of a new *economic culture* embracing much of the world.

Advent of a very pervasive communication culture   Perhaps one of the many spectacular outcomes of the technological revolution related to globalisation, has been the development of the internet through the use of personal computers (PCs). Not only have they facilitated the exchange of ideas between people from different parts of the world, when previously it took days, weeks even months for such ideas to be communicated, it now takes seconds. This is having an untold effect on the social, cultural as well as the economic aspects of all societies that are exposed to the global internet. For instance, a very noticeable effect is that a culture of *instantaneous personal exchange* (IEP) between users, is superseding longer generative periods of ideational transfer and consolidation, more typical of past cultural development. IEP is perhaps the most visible affect of globalisation, and one which is becoming increasingly widespread in the world of work.

Apart from the instantaneous effect of information technology, users can enter a world of greater choice and accessibility, can communicate at any time and with a whole host of people hitherto not possible.

Language dominance and cultural uniformity vs cultural diversity   The use of the English language as the principal means of most global communication, especially through the internet, has been seen by some as a valuable step in improving human understanding in a global society. In other words, modern day information systems have, through the use of English, brought about a certain *uniformity* amongst those who use the various systems across, and increasingly within national boundaries.

However, there is clearly a danger of the *uniformity* principle being allowed to override and take precedence over national considerations, such as the use of mother tongue languages and the conservation of cultural identities. Nevertheless, most international diplomacy, aviation, stock markets, research reporting in science and technology and many areas besides, rely on the use of English as the dominant means of communication. This signifies that many aspects of global culture are strongly bound up with English, which in turn is likely to play a key part in the future development of global culture and to cultural development in the longer run.

The culture of interdependency and a new polity   Perhaps the most noticeable trend as a result of globalisation, has been the increasing extent to which almost all nations of the world are becoming interdependent with one another. Hallak (2000) in fact thinks it is the '... main characteristic of globalisation ...'

Advances in IT have facilitated greater flows of capital between financial organisations both national and international. People around the globe are becoming more conscious than ever about political events in and around them, as has been the case in the worldwide reporting of the 1990 and 2003 Iraq wars.

There is greater consciousness of the scourge of HIV/AIDs, and its possible prevention as a result possibly of global networking and news coverage. Furthermore, there is an awareness of issues like global warming and its consequences for the future of the planet.

The almost uncontrollable pace of globalisation as discussed earlier in this paper, has meant that there is greater fluidity of all boundaries between organisations, the workplace, intra-national regions, nation states and even continents. While writers such as Fukuyama (1992) see these developments as having a positive effect on many peoples across the world, enhancing the spread of a culture of *global liberal democracy*, there are those those who see it as having the opposite effect (Watson, 2000). There is a feeling of being *overwhelmed* and nowhere more evident is this feeling felt, than in the perceived threat to national identity through the erosion of the nation state and global socio- cultural uniformity and standardisation.

Although the consequences of globalisation are patchy over different parts of the world, there are common trends which can be detected in the socio – cultural sphere that are rapidly producing cause for concern, adding to sentiments which question, and even oppose the rapidity is advancing its influence. Global culture affects the world of work and employment prospects, by replacing former practices with the introduction of new skills in banking, marketing, industry, farming and commerce. Such trends have lead to redeployment with retraining, or unemployment. A key issue here is the ability and readiness of people to adapt to new work requirements, in order that they can cope with rapid change in their work practices.

Global culture then may lead to a sense of inevitability, as mentioned earlier in the trend towards ever more standardisation and uniformity of peoples' day to day lives e.g. the consumption of fast foods and the craving for designer brands. Even the role of English as the dominant international language might be seen as contributing to an *over-universalising* influence responsible for the erosion of other languages and thereby the cultural contexts which they typify? This is perhaps a rather negative view of global culture. Might it not be better to view the cultural consequences of globalisation as a stage at which human cultural development can be enriched presenting us with opportunities to re-examine our ideas concerning cultural diversity, cultural universals, and particularly their place in educational provision for the 21st century? It is to the second question which examines this issue that we turn to next.

Global Culture, Cultural Diversity and Educational Provision

I have argued elsewhere (Thomas, 2002), that an educational process that purports to be sensitive to cultural influences begs the question, namely should it include all cultural influences, whether they be culture specific or culturally universal? In other words, how far can educators accept *cultural inclusivity* when it pertains to the theory and practice of education? The probable answer would be that a fair measure of cultural specificity eg cultural values, religion specifics, and much that is universally necessary would be required. For instance, it is clear that modern day school curricula need to address the comprehensive and instantaneous effects of the internet, and its impact on human information processing. This is certainly a key element of a so called global culture.

In other words, schooling must be sensitive to the age of information technology (ICT), and the new cultures that stem from it, alongside established values and subject areas such as humanities and aesthetics.

These new cultures are not only enveloping industry and the world of commerce, but are increasingly becoming part of schooling and home life as well. On the other hand, the new cultures should not be allowed to erode cultural traditions which provide security, continuity and richness to the life of a society (Thomas, 1994). This is particularly pertinent in an education system which aims to uphold cultural and moral values.

In today's global world, it is a clearly an advantage to have a certain amount of standardisation e.g. transport (especially for safe air travel), scientific measurement and financial services. However, it becomes more controversial and difficult to extend the uniformity principle to policies affecting political and socio-cultural concerns. The underlying concepts of desirability and societal acceptance will always be at the heart of any moves to select what globalisation has to offer in benefiting a society. The goal of balance will without doubt be of paramount importance in achieving a *modus vivendi* between the forces of globalisation and anti-globalisation, and it is here that education has a key role to play. Nevertheless, one cannot be over optimistic about the success of education in this role, as political and especially economic forces will always be dominant when it comes to controlling events, but this should not mean that educators should take a back seat. Before we pass on to the third question posed in this chapter, we need to delve into the wider issue of how globalisation relates to educational provision, discussing how global culture and cultural diversity fit into the relationship, and specifically to teacher education.

(i) Knowledge as the driving force of globalisation and education change

Globalisation is becoming a key force in controlling the world economy as we enter the second millennium, and one of the driving forces is the need for knowledge and information required to reorganise not only economic systems, but political, social and cultural institutions as well. According to Carnoy and Rhoten (2002), in their insightful analysis of the relationship between education change and globalisation, there has been an intertwining of global economics with international institutions that promote education change. While at the macro transnational level there are big changes happening to the economies and national political systems of many countries in the world, the impact of globalisation at the micro- local level, especially in classrooms, appears to be limited as yet.

One reason, is that globalisation is a fast process, and educational change is a slow one, in view of its long term goals and the lengthy gestation period measuring educational outcomes. It can be argued that education is more shaped by globalisation rather being a key agent in shaping the process. Nevertheless, in the longer term, education may be able to re-assess the impact of globalisation, identifying and hopefully slowing the pace of socio-cultural erosion and the marginalisation of cultural identity.

Therefore, a successful and meaningful relationship between globalisation and education will encompass the task of making educational institutions (eg schools, colleges and universities), ready to adapt to the forces of change brought about by globalisation. These forces operate less now then hitherto through nation states, as more and more international institutions controlling banking, financial services, trade, industry and the corporate decision making, eg stock markets, banks, corporate business make the key decisions. An ideological package for education includes, decentralisation, privatisation, client/consumer choice, accountability, assessment/certification and, flexible organisational structures, with national governments having a crucial but not inflexible stake in the future direction in education policy.

The crux of assessing the main relationship between globalisation and education is how the ideological package will affect what ultimately goes on in schools, and how knowledge which is relevant to schooling is passed down from the international (global) level to schools and colleges.

However, expectations of the consequences of globalisation and predictions for education change related to globalisation can end up in a state of mismatch resulting in unpredictable outcomes such as the changing roles of teachers with reference to knowledge selection and presentation. The mismatch is mainly due to future assumptions about globalisation not being made clear to education policy makers and politicians? For instance, will the pace of globalisation continue? Will nation states and local communities still have a key role and therefore control of what goes on in schools and society? And finally, will education provide society with a sound, rational and pragmatic assessment of globalisation, and its socio cultural affects on the future direction of human resource development? Unless these issues are resolved, mismatches will continue to be made between many of the stakeholders.

(ii) Globalisation parameters and their impact on education

The author has identified eight key parameters of globalisation that have, and continue to have, an impact on education and education change (Thomas, 2003). The eight parameters are identified as; Knowledge Impact, Political Policy, Economic Prioritisation, Changing Labour Market, Information Technology Education, International Comparisons, Socio-Cultural Impact and Demographic Changes For more details of the eight parameters the reader is directed to the author reference quoted above. For the purposes of the present chapter, *two* of the parameters have direct reference to the main argument stated in the introduction, these are Knowledge Impact (KI) and the Socio-cultural Impact (S-CI).

KI refers to how the users of new knowledge are able to process it, and convert into meaningful information for their daily lives. They also have to fit new knowledge and information into existing epistemologies and practice which will be more meaningful in future contexts.

The S-CI refers to the power of international networking and the effect it has on a marginalisation of cultural and national identity. There is a real concern in many societies about a loss of cultural values due to globalisation eg Malaysia, Thailand, Singapore. This is mainly perceived as a result of changing market values, effect of modernisation, (meaning Westernisation) on youth, typifying a new global culture which is perceived to threaten traditional values, religion and local culture. It presents educators with a new set of conflicts and issues, such as the rise of open society, attitudes to the rights of women and minorities, changing views on sexual orientation and the rise of individualism and personal freedoms. Teachers and their mentors such as school principals and teacher educators have their task cut out in order that a rational accommodation of these issues are achieved.

KI is perhaps the real driving force behind globalisation, and stems from the ideational power of humans to think creatively, and the ability to transform ideas into application and actions. However, the S-CI parameter is of particular importance for exploring the nature of cultural diversity, global culture and their roles in the future education and training of teachers.

The impact of these two parameters on education change will depend on how effectively they are seen to affect national and local levels of society. An analysis of these two parameters will prove to be of value *only* if they are seen to effect changes in education that benefit students, teachers and parents. Clearly, educators have a key role to play in relating how the two parameters influence future teacher education policy and practice.

It is to the third question which was posed earlier that we now turn, to examine how policy and practice relating specifically to teacher education could accommodate cultural diversity arising from the impact of globalisation, and the attendant dominance of global culture.

Making Teacher Education More in Tune with the Cultural Impact of Globalisation

Teachers who find difficulty in meeting the challenges of cultural diversity in school, and the ever increasing reality of the existence of a global culture, may find that they need skills and knowledge coupled with new patterns of training to reconcile the dilemma. The author has argued elsewhere (Thomas, 2002), that teacher education and training should be part of a wider process of a more Culture Sensitive Education (CSE), in which stakeholders such as pupils, head teachers, teacher educators, parents and the community need to be involved. Before examining more specifically what influences global impact in the guise of a global culture will have on teacher education, let us examine in a little more depth the relations between CSE, and teaching, learning and training.

(i) Global cultural impact and the role of CSE

The underlying philosophy of a CSE attempts to spell out at least three parameters, before it can be viewed as a sound and effective component within formal schooling. The first parameter of *Cultural inclusivity* raises an issue about the extent to which cultural diversity, and cultural uniformity need to be considered, when devising new forms and approaches to the development of a relevant training curriculum. The second parameter is *cultural sensitivity*, which entails not only being aware of a particular cultural institution, custom, cultural object or artefact eg an initiation icon, but also being aware of cultural values and attitudes. However, sensitivity in the context of which it used here, is more than just awareness. It is also about actively engaging people's feelings and attitudes, as well as customs and long standing institutions into the dynamics of education. Furthermore, cultural sensitivity is closely linked to cultural selectivity, as it would be necessary to select which is relevant and which is not. The third parameter namely, the nature of the *cultural dynamic* needs to be understood before either cultural selectivity or culture sensitivity can take place successfully. The view of culture referred to earlier in the chapter by Gearing (1979) and Thomas (1992), points out that durable cultural encounters (i.e. ideas), can to be passed from generation to generation through modes of communication such as language, thinking, dance and drawing, while more transient encounters become redundant quite soon. Therefore culture is not a static, but a dynamic process which results in a diverse mosaic of patterns and activities, in which cultural sensitivity and selected cultural mores and traditions can merge and interact within a total system.

The trans-national nature of the school has meant that both schooling and the school are becoming increasingly universalistic in nature, reflecting similar outcomes throughout the world. But this process takes place against a backdrop of existing cultural contexts which reflect intra-cultural specificity. Many of the cultural encounters which take place in school are both formative and durable, be they universal e.g. learning to count, read, write or culture specific eg studying local languages and customs. The teacher's future role would therefore be pivotal in acting as a cultural bridge between the polarities. To achieve this new role, a teacher education curriculum must reflect and if possible bridge this bipolarity, to supply the content and skills needed to produce teachers that are aware of important cultural sensitivities.

Therefore the three parameters discussed above are not only essential hallmarks of a culture sensitive process of education, but they also relate closely, to the development of a relevant *culture sensitive education* and training for teachers. Not only will the teacher need to be trained as an effective agent in the art of cultural transmission, but he or she will also need to have an education and training in pertinent cultural knowledges and skills, that form a natural and necessary background to understanding the cultural diversity of the children that are being taught.

The parameter of cultural sensitivity would occupy a salient place in the training of teachers, as it is part and parcel of the processes of teaching, learning and thinking which accompany the study of content and skills.

The highly socio-interactive nature of cultural sensitivity would also figure prominently during the practicum training, and in further training as part of in-service programmes. For this parameter to be successfully incorporated into the development of a culture sensitive teacher training, a knowledge about the values and beliefs of pupils, which are often intertwined within the cultural diversity of classrooms, would be desirable if not essential. A deeper understanding of the third parameter, namely that of the cultural dynamic, which entails both transient and durable encounters, would assist teacher educators to make their training more pragmatic, meaningful, flexible and reflective; four features essential for an effective culture sensitive training. A training curriculum which helps to emphasise these features would go some way in meeting the goal of a culture sensitive education and training. It is to the changing nature of the teacher education curriculum that we now turn.

(ii) The changing curriculum of teacher education

The curriculum of teacher education in the current global context is perhaps best viewed from the standpoint of identifying the needs of learners and teachers, as well as that of society at large. It is possible to distinguish between two components of need. The first category we will call *extrinsic*, and the second category *intrinsic*. *Extrinsic* needs are those which feature in all modern societies requiring a highly skilled and qualified work force. Meeting these needs usually targets the short to medium term span of a person's working life. Extrinsic needs are closely associated with the functioning of society and are to some extent the person's motivational regimen.

Intrinsic needs have an inner longer term personal dimension which is integral to person's development as a human being e.g. moral and spiritual development, love of learning, aesthetics. Both types of need are usually catered for during the schooling years and beyond, as they are not mutually exclusive. There is an overlap between the two components as training to meet extrinsic needs may have intrinsic side effects for the person. This means that teacher education and training requires a curriculum that is able to meet both categories. It is obvious that globalisation has made it more necessary than ever before, that we re-examine both types of need, and develop ways in which teachers can help bridge the global with the local context. The gap between the two is becoming greater in both economic and cultural terms, as new knowledge and practices are made available bringing with them changing value systems for whole of society.

Table 10.2 shows the main cognate components serving both extrinsic and intrinsic training needs. However, the table also shows a third component called ICT (Information Communication Technology), which although it stands as a component in its own right, also bridges the extrinsic and extrinsic cognate areas, providing a means to express and understand the two main cognate areas. The ICT component is in reality the manifestation of global culture, with its emphasis on communication theory and new skills. This ICT component will have has an increasingly dominant influence on the other two. ICT is essentially extrinsic being a necessary pragmatic requirement assisting teachers in executing their pedagogical skills. However, there is also an intrinsic side to the subject reflected in the development of a theoretical base linked to communications theory.

The KI and the S-CI will play an important part in changes to the training curriculum. Clearly, knowledge impact affects all three components of the training curriculum as it introduces new ideas and skills. The Socio-cultural impact will continue to have an eroding effect on most of the intrinsic areas listed, unless the training curriculum emphasises the cultural values which underline all seven areas identified under intrinsic needs in Table 10.2. If this can be accomplished, then cultural diversity has a good chance of being fostered successfully as part of teacher preparation, providing a sound basis for not only a Culture Sensitive Education (CSE), but for a Culture Sensitive Teacher Education (CSTE) as well (Thomas, 2002). However, the long term effectiveness and success of a CSTE, will depend on the opportunities which teachers will be given to develop all three training components. In the concluding section of this chapter, it is to the issue of teacher development that we now turn.

Table 10.2   The training curriculum: main cognate components including common ICT * support

COGNATE COMPONENTS – EXTRINSIC NEEDS	COGNATE COMPONENTS – INTRINSIC NEEDS	ICT
Language + Communication	Aesthetics + Music	ICT Theory
Mathematics	Craft	Computer Skills and Literacy
Science and Environmental Studies	Values Education	Networking
Business Studies	Cultural Studies	Learning Networks
Humanities	Global Issues	Graphics + Design
Education Theory + Practice	Citizenship	
Education Disciplines	Sport + Leisure	

* Information Communication Technology

(iii) Teacher development and the impact of globalisation

The notion of Life Long Teacher Education is not a new one but it is closely related to the notion and rationale of teacher development (Thomas, 1993). Many countries engage in versions of this notion through successful in-service programmes and professional upgrading, leading to the award of an advanced diploma and/or higher degree. However, the difference as we enter the 21st century is that the nature and pattern of career development needs to adapt to the changing global demands. The globalisation parameter of *Knowledge Impact (KI)* is already having a profound effect at all levels of education, and the ways knowledge and skills are being delivered.

Over the last decade or so, the teaching profession has experienced profound changes to it roles and status world wide, which have affected recruitment and morale amongst many of its members (Fischman, 2001). Teachers face competition in their own sphere of expertise, as they no longer hold a monopoly as the suppliers of information and basic skills. New ways of acquiring and processing knowledge, has meant that students can access knowledge for themselves, often at home on PCs or in cyber-cafes. There is also a growing trend that a new set of players, mainly from the private sector can also instruct and supply new knowledge and skills relevant to study purposes and the world of work. These players not only supplement teachers, they may even supplant them in the years ahead.

It is clear that the preparation of teachers has tended to lag behind developments in ICT, so much so, that in some countries eg UK and USA, children are better equipped than their teachers in accessing and processing information for their studies. Also older teachers tend be resistant to such changes and therefore are less prone to retrain. In the light of these changes, there is a need to revisit the ways in which teachers are prepared and furthermore, given support during their working life.

Table 10.3 provides a scenario, from which ideas about how professional development might be conceived, for preparing teachers to adapt successfully to new and challenging global contexts of the future. Table 10.3 shows two columns. The first identifies new roles and responsibilities for teachers and teacher educators. The second column suggests some key areas which could form a basis for teacher development and training, to cater for changing professional roles in the context of education change linked to globalisation. Items 1–6 in the first column characterise the type of role in which each individual teacher might require further training, according to his or her needs. Items 7 and 8 reflect more cooperative roles which teachers need to develop, items 9–12 emphasise social and cultural awareness roles in the context of the effects of ICT on teaching and learning. In many ways the contents of Table 10.3 mirrors the interplay between the exogenous and endogenous aspects of globalisation. Much of the influence of KI is associated with the exogenous determinants affecting education while the SCI is seen as a signal for educators to ensure that globalisation is suitably contained as part of endogenous response to the process.

The potentially eroding nature of S-CI may be overlooked in the rush to accommodate the KI. However it is precisely because of this danger, that programmes for meaningful teacher development need to safeguard and reinforce wherever possible, the best values of existing cultural contexts and cultural diversity. This is not to argue against the advent of global culture with all its dynamism and pragmatism. On the contrary, it is to allow teachers to benefit from new ideas through globalisation, but in which a sound balance is achieved between social and cultural foundations and global culture.

Table 10.3   Teacher* development for new roles and responsibilities in the context of globalisation

	NEW ROLES AND RESPONSIBILITIES	AREAS FOR EDUCATION AND FURTHER TRAINING
1	More Teacher Autonomy in Class.	• Emphasis on training in class management.
2	Use of more flexible Pedagogies.	• Training teachers in tutorial skills.
3	More effective classroom management.	• Critical Incident training for autonomous facilitatory roles.
4	Teacher as tutors and instructors.	• Developing more flexible pedagogical and assessment strategies.
5	Teacher as a partner with learner in assessment.	• Basic technical training for servicing.
6	Basic technical 'know-how' for servicing PC Hardware/software	
7	Cooperative Teaching with other teachers and with ICT experts.	• Group dynamics training for working teams with other teachers and other professionals eg ICT experts, private sector personnel.
8	Teachers as broker in information access, Selection and application.	
9	Awareness of Network Learning and Teaching.	Courses on
10	Culture Sensitive Teaching and Learning.	• Network Learning,
11	Social Responsibility of using ICT.	• Cultural Diversity and Globalisation,
12	Environmental and Global Cultural Awareness.	• Social and Religious Values in a Global World,
		• Environment Issues.

* includes Teacher Educators

Epilogue

Understanding the complex interplay between exogenous and endogenous influences, is at the heart of determining the extent to which globalisation can effect education change. McGinn (1997) in the mid 1990s, expressed doubts about the capacity of globalisation to permeate knowledge production and transmission, as far as schooling is concerned. To what extent is this true in 2003? It is certainly the case that classrooms in many countries have not been affected by globalisation, or if so, only superficially. Having ICT facilities in a school or in a classroom, does not necessarily mean that there have been fundamental changes to the curriculum and styles of teaching.

Similarly, even if some of the contents of the ideological package which were discussed earlier in the paper such as privatisation, accountability measures and certification, which characterise the effects of globalisation and are in place, there is some way to go before we can be assured of their successful outcomes for schooling.

However, the picture is not all doom and gloom. There is evidence accumulating form the USA and UK about the development of Virtual Training Centres (VTCs) which provide ICT back up, as well as being in possession of research publications, which teachers will find valuable for their teaching (Davis, 1999). In higher education, the effects of globalisation are being felt by lecturers having to come to terms with students being 'knowledge seekers' rather than being taught by traditional methods, such as lectures, seminars and even practicals (Pincas, 2002). The so called notion of *borderless higher education* is typified by specialist knowledge being provided by others eg internet websites, as well as at universities. Students also have more access to one another without the constraints of space and time. In Singapore, the budget for ICT has been more than doubled to S$2 millon for the use of computers in teaching and learning for and by students (Gopinathan and Sharpe, 2002). A similar story unfolds for teacher education in Japan and South Korea. Kim and Kim (2002) report from South Korea that the Master Plan of 1997 for the equipping all teacher preparation colleges with ICT support for each student, will be completed by 2003. In Malaysia, the advent of the SMART project in just under 90 schools country wide, and the growing numbers of school computer laboratories in primary and secondary schools, mean that teacher upgrading in ICT and related subjects is also underway.

From the standpoint of cultural diversity and teaching, Lee (2002) makes a salient point about the notion of interplay as far as Malaysian teacher education is concerned, when she describes the way global and local forces interact to produce a national response to global trends. There is a need for such national response in all societies, especially when they ensure that exogenous influences are appropriately balanced with endogenous ideas and practices. However, the best balance between global culture on one hand, and the local context on the other, can only be attained by effective and committed teachers. In that regard little has changed. in spite of the freneticism generated by the 21st century version of globalisation.

References

Carnoy, M. and Rhoten, D. (2002), 'What does Globalisation Mean for Educational Change? A Comparative Approach, 1–9', *Comparative Education Review*, vol. 46(1), pp. 1–9.

Corson, D. (1998), *Changing Education for Diversity*, Open University Press, Buckingham.

Davis, N. (1999), 'The Globalisation of Education Through Teacher Education with New Technologies: A View Informed by Research', *Educational Technology Review*, Autumn/Winter, pp. 8–11.

Fischman, G.E. (2001), 'Essay Review: Teachers, Globalisation and Hope: Beyond the Narrative of Redemption', *Comparative Education Review*, vol. 45(3), pp. 412–418.

Fukuyama, F. (1992), *The End of History and the Last Man*, Penguin, Harmondsworth.

Gearing, F. (1979), 'A reference model for a cultural theory of education and schooling', in F. Gearing and L. Sangree (eds), *Toward a Cultural Theory of Education and Schooling*, Mouton Press, The Hague.

Green, A. (1997), *Education, Globalisation and the Nation State*, Macmillan, London.

Gopinathan, S. and Sharpe, L. (2002), 'The teacher is the key: professionalism and the strategic state', in E. Thomas (ed), *Teacher Education: Dilemmas and Prospects*, World Yearbook of Education, Kogan Page, London, pp. 23–32.

Hallak, J. (2000), 'Globalisation and its Impact on Education', in T. Mebrahtu, M. Crossley and D. Johnson (eds), *Globalisation, Educational Transformation and Societies in Transition*, Symposium Books, Oxford, pp. 21–40.

Higginson, J.H. (ed) (1979), *Selections from Michael Sadler*, Dejall & Meyorre, Liverpool.

Kim, W.H. and Kim T. (2002), 'Globalisation and *dirigisme:* teacher education in South Korea', in E. Thomas (ed), *Teacher Education: Dilemmas and Prospects*, World Yearbook of Education, Kogan Page, London, pp. 33–44.

Lee, M.N.N. (2002), 'Educational Reforms in Malaysia: Global Challenge and National Response', in M.N.N Lee (ed), *Educational Change in Malaysia*, Monograph Series No: 3/2002, Universiti Sains Publication, Penang.

McGinn, N. (1997), 'The Impact of Globalisation on National Education Systems', *Prospects: Quarterly Review of Comparative Education*, vol. 28(1), pp. 41–54.

Pincas, A. (2002), 'Borderless Education: a new teaching model for United Kingdom higher education', in E. Thomas (ed), *Teacher Education: Dilemmas and Prospects, World Yearbook of Education*, Kogan Page, London, pp. 227–237.

Thomas, E. (1992), 'Schooling and the School as a Cross Cultural Context for Study', in S. Iwawaki, Y. Kashima and K. Leung (eds), *Innovations in Cross Cultural Psychology*, Swets & Zeitlinger, Amsterdam, pp. 425–441.

Thomas, E. (1993), 'The professional development and training of teacher educators', in E. Thomas, E. Sharma, M. Khanna and H. Jatoi (eds), *Policy and Practice in Initial Teacher Training, Commonwealth Secretariat*, Commonwealth Secretariat Publications, London, pp. 1–19.

Thomas, E. (1997), 'Developing a culture sensitive pedagogy: tackling a problem of melding "global culture" within existing cultural contexts', *International Journal of Educational Development*, vol. 17, pp. 13–26.

Thomas, E. (2002), 'Toward a culture-sensitive teacher education: the role of pedagogical models', in E. Thomas (ed), *Teacher Education: Dilemmas and Prospects*, World Yearbook of Education, Kogan Page, London, pp. 167–179.

Thomas, E. (2003), 'Strategies for Teacher Education and Training in the Context of Global Change – Plenary Paper given at the International Conference on Teaching and Teacher Education', *Islamic International University, Kuala Lumpur*, Malaysia September 16–18th.

Watson, K. (2000) 'Globalisation, Educational Reform and Language Policy in Transitional Societies', in T. Mebrahtu, M. Crossley and D. Johnson (eds.), *Globalisation, Educational Transformation and Societies in Transition*, Symposium Books, Oxford, pp. 41–67.

Chapter 11

Teachers, Globalisation and the Prospect for Self-Education

Les Tickle

In this chapter I have attempted to couple contrary, contemporary perspectives on education and teaching with educational ideas from Eastern philosophies, to provide what Clarke (1997) called 'ancient wisdoms adapted and applied to the present condition' – in this case the condition of globalisation. I want to argue that the interchange of ideas between Asian and Western thought offers an opportunity for the analysis and understanding of, and potential for a new response to the forces of globalisation which are evident in their reported impact on teachers' lives and work (e.g. Delors, 1996; Smyth et al, 2000). The chapter will weigh some of that evidence and those ideas with personal perspectives and experience in search of a positive, enabling, and educative response to what might otherwise be perceived as a pessimistic prospect for education in general and teacher education in particular.

A Personal and Political Perspective

The ideas in this chapter have a long history, yet they have a definitely topical relevance for today's climate of intense educational debate in the contemporary global environment. For teachers this is an environment that impacts on their lives and work in the form of performance management, the imposition of innovation, conflicting expectations, removal of professional authority, the denial of authentic intellectual experience, intensification of work, blame and lack of trust, doubt and uncertainty (Elliott, 1998; Smyth et al, 2000). The broader educational environment is manifest as international comparisons and competitiveness in educational standards, seismic shifts in curriculum ideology, and systemic disturbance in examination arrangements. These in turn are wrapped within the crosscurrents of interconnectedness between economic interests, new communication systems, military conflict, human migration and political movements.

Within that wrapper, the issue of what education is for, questions about how it should be organised and resourced, and debates about the role and power of teachers form an internal family of controversy. It is not always immediately evident that issues of education and the induction of the young are involved in that wider landscape of concerns. Yet the ecology of education is bound up with the world news on international relations and security. It resides in questions of cultural identity and allegiance to different faiths. The manufacture, trade, distribution and use of armaments, food, and energy on a global scale impacts directly but discretely on questions of what education and schooling are for, how they should function, and in whose interests. The same is true in relation to the destruction of and concern for the global environment; in the existence of monopolies on the production, pricing and sale of drugs and of information technology devices and software, and so on.

My interest in the educational ideas that I will explore in this chapter probably began in childhood with the realisation that self-induced learning would be more productive and satisfying than teachers' so-called teaching. Perhaps as a consequence, in preparing to become a teacher I was impressed by ideas such as Abraham Maslow's (1943, 1954) theory of human motivation; Carl Rogers' (1969) person-centred education; and Jerome Bruner's (1977) definition of educational excellence as the maximisation of individual potential. The educational aims and pedagogical principles that appealed most, broadly labelled as liberal and humanistic, placed the responsibility for learning primarily with the learner. They ascribed to the teacher a mentoring role as the adult partner in joint / collective intellectual enquiry. However, for me this was coupled with pragmatic politics that also countenanced didactic instruction to ensure that students should not be disadvantaged when they eventually had to function in a wage-earning economy. The combination of liberal/progressive and academic curricula (Goodson, 1983) offered intensely optimistic and idealistic perspectives on educating. The utilitarian/vocational curriculum (*ibid*) anchored that idealism in a grounded realism, disquiet, even dissatisfaction and dissent, in the knowledge that the job involved recreating a subservient underclass of waged labour. These co-habiting curricula created tensions and dilemmas about learners and learning which many teachers experienced in practice within the state education system in England, especially in post-Plowden primary education or as champions of non-selective (comprehensive) secondary education (Berlak and Berlak, 1981; Hargreaves, 1985). In more recent times the hope and the dilemmas have continued to feature in my work as a teacher educator (see Tickle, 1987a,b, 1994, 2000).

Comprehensive education and equality of opportunity were the banners under which I marched into teaching with a mission. But as a student of sociology alarm grew apace with research literature that demonstrated systemic structural disadvantage of some sections of the school population, and argued persuasively that the main political purpose of public school systems is the legitimation, not the elimination, of social inequalities (e.g. Salter and Tapper, 1981). Shockingly, according to this view, the unjust and unequal allocation of life chances, replicating educational and economic advantage of some over others, was precisely what we were employed to participate in. Equally disconcerting was (and is) the idea that this amounts also (albeit sometimes unwittingly) to participation in one of the means by which human beings are made subjects of social systems. The tensions and ambiguities in these juxtapositions of hope and despair has been addressed variously in the social sciences in terms of personal agency / social structures; determination / determinism; and congruence / conflict between individuals and their communities. Closer to the present topic, it has been seen in terms of student teachers' and newly qualified teachers' social strategies. These are said to range from *congruence*, where personal and institutional values coincide; to *compliance*, when they do as required despite personal preferences; and *redefinition*, when they resistance imposed requirements and re-create situations (and their ideas) in their own terms (Lacey, 1970, Zeichner and Tabachnick, 1985, Tickle, 1997).

That relationship and the place of reflexivity within it – the monitoring of our own conduct in the context of our social and material environments – is one of the most profound interests in the social sciences (see Giddens, 1991, Bryant and Jary, 2001). It is also a central issue in the Action Research movements among teachers and teacher educators (Carr and Kemmis, 1986; Hollingsworth, 1997). Its essence is conveyed nicely in the following:

> In all my texts and documents, there were, so far as I can tell, no moments of pure unfettered subjectivity; indeed the human subject itself began to seem remarkably unfree, the ideological product of the relations of power in a particular society (Greenblatt, 1980, p. 256, cited in Holstun, 2000, p. 64).

Such ideological (re)production puts schools at the interface between social structures and individual identities and sees teachers as instruments of ideology and culture. It does the same for teacher educators – as Smyth et al (*ibid*) put it: teacher educators produce the waged labour that in turn reproduces the waged labour! For some people then, schooling and its socialisation function provides a necessary stabilising process, while from a contrary, critical perspective education should be an essentially tranformative process for both individuals and their communities. The difference is that the former sees 'politics as something done *to* human subjects, or done in order to *create* them' (Holstun, 2000, p. 68 original emphasis). The latter 'encourages us to view politics as something done *by* human subjects in groups – a complex array of elective practices by which people can at times remake themselves and their own history' (*ibid*). The main tension for transformative educators comes between submitting to forces we'd rather resist and pursuing creative means for maximising our own and our students' involvement in our social futures. While we wrestle with the conflicts the denial of educational (and thus occupational and developmental) opportunities is evident all around us. It can be found in social class, ethnic, and gender divisions in my homeland. It exists in a socially and economically divided Europe. The financially impoverished nations of Asia, Africa, and South America exemplify it. And the disadvantaged indigenous communities of wealthier countries such as Canada, Australia and the USA provide further reminders.

From one perspective it might be thought that teachers are simply culpable. Certainly the rock band Pink Floyd's view of teachers engaged in processes of mind control presents that challenge. Their 1983 video track *The Wall* is haunting with its regimented ranks of goose-step-marching animated hammers accompanied by the lyrics:

> *We don't need no education;*
> *we don't need your thought control.*
> *Dark sarcasm in the classroom;*
> *teachers, leave them kids alone.*
> *Hey, teachers, leave them kids alone.*

Social commentary like this 'from below' can have considerable emotional impact on committed professionals. So can recognition that students must submit to meaningless curricula and restrictive assessment and testing regimes. That adds serious disquiet about the education on offer in schools. The clash of pessimistic voice and optimistic intent can be found in both academic analysis (research) and phenomenal experience (classroom practice). They are articulated in work such as Anne and Harold Berlak's *Dilemmas of Schooling* (Berlak and Berlak, 1981), and Michael Huberman's (1993) *The Lives of Teachers*. They also occur in Gramsci's concepts of *professional* and *organic* intellectuals (see Becker, 1996), and Paulo Freire's (1970, 1972) activist educators. The Berlaks showed thoughtful primary school teachers wrestling to reconcile conflicting interests that were embedded in the very purposes of schooling and their own educational ideals. Huberman showed teachers whose states of being ranged from deep demoralisation and disaffection to joy and satisfaction. Gramsci challengingly (and hopefully incorrectly) ascribed teachers to an intellectual underclass serving the interests of tradition and social stability through the repetitive and mindless transmission of stagnant knowledge. Freire (1972) on the other hand provides the hope that we might become activists engaged in the evolution of knowledge; interacting with society as well as with our students; struggling to change minds in public debate as well as classroom discourse; defending academic freedom and the voice of dissent, and fighting for decent standards of personal well-being and social justice (see Tickle, 2001).

This is not to suggest, then, that it is the fault of teachers that we might be an underclass trading unworthy goods, but it does raise awareness of our contrary, unstable and potentially damaging states of being. Recently the author (and ex-teacher) Phillip Pullman (2003) commenting on England's national curriculum for teaching the mother tongue summed up the situation like this:

(the Qualifications and Curriculum Authority) thinks that reading consists of using strategies to decode, selecting, retrieving, deducing, inferring, interpreting, identifying and commenting on the structure and organisation of texts, identifying and commenting on the writer's purposes and viewpoints, relating texts to the social, cultural and historical contexts. That's it. Nothing else. That's what it wants children of 11 to do when they read. It doesn't seem to know that reading can also be enjoyed because enjoyment doesn't feature in the list of things you have to do.

He went on to describe the requirements for writing, making lists of words, following a model paragraph, and then observed:

...day in, day out, hour after hour, this wretched system nags and pesters and buzzes at them, like a great bluebottle laden with pestilence. And then all the children have to do a test; and that's when things get worse.

Echoing Foucault's disciplinary regime of institutions, he described classrooms as like prison cells with teachers and pupils locked helplessly inside. But Pullman is not the only recent observer of this condition. Alternative education becomes more popular with parents who can afford it. Teachers' trade unions in England threaten to boycott national testing. Teacher retention there is said to be less than 50 per cent after five years in the job. Worldwide insufficient people want to enter the job in the first place, especially among the graduate workforce in richer nations. But how should we account for and understand such phenomena in what on the face of it should be a socially progressive and morally committed purposeful pastime for all humanity? More to the point, how should we respond?

Teacher Appraisal and Assessment

The national curriculum in England was devised and implemented during the second quarter of the last century. It is matter of record that at least in part this was a reaction to global economic forces like the oil crisis of 1973 and the stringent loan conditions imposed on the UK Government by the International Monetary Fund and World Bank. Control of public spending and centralised management of 'basic schooling' were seen as means of trying to ensure that Britain became economically competitive in the global marketplace, while also providing a solution to a 'crisis of expectations' among the population (Wallace and Tickle, 1983). It is not my purpose to enter into the broader policy analysis here, because it has already been done elsewhere. But I do want to note that such impressions as I have presented with their obvious tensions between educational hope and institutional disease were evident in the accompanying introduction of Teacher Appraisal in England in the mid-1980s. At that time the School of Education at UEA, Norwich hosted meetings of the national teacher appraisal steering group. The project report in one of the six pilot local education authorities, Suffolk, was published under the title *Those Bearing Torches,* in the sense of lighting the way towards an optimistic future for teacher development. In response, Marion Dadds from the Department of Education at Cambridge University published her evaluation of those same trials under the title *Those Being Tortured,* a reference to the actual experience of teachers being appraised.

After protracted disputes between government and employers on the one hand, and professional associations on the other, the independent Arbitration and Conciliation Service (ACAS) presented a system based on 'self-appraisal'. This could be interpreted as the appraisal of teaching by teachers themselves – a form of self-monitoring, which presumably could lead to self-dismissal from the job! For those of us concerned with the education of teachers, however, it provided space for a different interpretation based on the appraisal and development of the 'self' by teachers, involving personal development, or self-education. Here was an opening for Maslow's concept of the self-actualising teacher, for Rogers' person-centred professional development, for Bruner's maximisation of potential.

Maslow (1943, 1954) had articulated the idea of self-actualisation and made it well known among psychologists in the West. Carl Rogers (1969) explored its implications for education in his book *Freedom to Learn*. Bruner's (1977) *The Process of Education* placed the curiosity and imagination of teachers at the heart of the educational enterprise. Maslow later (1973) applied his ideas to teaching in a now obscure article entitled '*What Is a Taostic Teacher*'. Central to the principle of Taoistic teaching is a view of 'great hope for and trust in personal potential, the wisdom of self-choice, and a tendency to self-actualize' (Maslow, 1973, p. 150). The pedagogical implications are explicit: trusting learners, avoiding manipulation or indoctrination or shaping learners into some pre-determined form, in favour of uncovering potential and reaching 'the fullest height that the human species can stand up to or that the particular individual can come to' (ibid, p. 153). This presumes a concept of the educator who can be entrusted with responsibility to evolve consciousness, on the basis of their own achievements and continuing intellectual engagement. The implication for educators is put like this:

> the best helpers of other people are the most highly evolved, healthiest, strongest, most fully developed people. Therefore, if you want to help others ... clearly one part of your job is to become a better person (Maslow, 1973, p. 153).

Bruner, Rogers and Maslow claimed that personal growth is achieved by simultaneously helping others to grow, through an interactive and reflexive process in which the educator, too, has essential self-actualising needs and potentials. While these are capable of being nourished by the educational process, they can also be thwarted by bureaucratic and structural ones. As Maslow put it long before the intensification of accountability in schools and quality control of teacher performance:

> As Taoistic trust develops in the educational enterprise, there would be more leeway given to teachers, less regard for centralisation, fewer orders coming from the rule book (ibid, p. 156).

With these sentiments in mind the idea of self-appraisal was adopted in my own in-service courses for teachers, who were invited to investigate deeply personal issues that were relevant to their lives – matters of personal substance. They were also supported in researching, examining, understanding, and developing their professional and pedagogical practice – matters of concern in the classroom and the school. In doing so, the teachers pursued a wide range of imaginative, complex and delicate self-generated, self-defined, and self-managed projects (see Tickle, 1999, 2001). For example, a young female teacher experiencing sexual harassment from colleagues and pupils alike sought to understand *their* problem, and to help them become better educated. A gay teacher who felt vulnerable lest his sexuality should become known, and thus was not participating fully in school life, sought to understand and overcome his vulnerability in order to contribute more fully to his community in the way he believed he should. An art teacher, frustrated that real art was excluded from his own life and his pupils' experiences, established an experimental studio in the classroom where he practised his own work during lesson time as a role model for student activity. Many such projects emerged, coupled with evidence of surprise, and delight, on the part of teachers who participated in these courses (see Tickle, 2001).

However, as I have already indicated, the dominant national and international climate of teaching and schooling has increasingly pursued a 'skills' orientation with a tightly managed curriculum, associated mechanistic testing, and both national and international league tables of results. Teacher education has followed suit, fostering the normative pursuit of technical competence and classroom routine, in an international search for 'standards', to the detriment of the teacher as a person (Lipka and Brinthaupt, 1999). The award and confirmation of Qualified Teacher Status (QTS) in England is based firmly on a system of teacher assessment under managerial control of specified, technical performance criteria with little mention of personal development (Tickle, 2000, 2001). The classroom is seen here as a place of performance by teachers, rather than a place of learning for teachers.

The Present Condition

I want to argue that the kind of continuous self-education advocated by Maslow is especially necessary in the light of contemporary adverse conditions affecting the teaching profession across the world. For the moment I have simply called this condition 'globalisation', a word that has come to represent the particularly harsh environment that currently affects schools and classrooms. It is an environment of uncertainty, tension, risk, and paradox (Delors, 1996), of 'change forces' as Michael Fullan (1993, 1999) called them. It is characterised in the wider world beyond schooling by what Giddens (1991) sees as the cross-currents of social, political, economic, military, and symbolic aspects of human endeavours. In addition to the characteristics cited earlier, some commentators (for example Elliott, 1998; Stronach et al, 2002) have noted that the consequences for education include phenomena such as:

- the penetration of market forces into public sector social policy and provisions, resulting in changes in funding mechanisms, management structures and practices, and competition for clients and resources;
- competing conceptions of curriculum and pedagogy, experienced as contradictions and ambiguities by teachers;
- the treatment of knowledge primarily as an exchange commodity acquired and traded in the market economy of schooling and employment;
- rapid technological innovations, increased momentum in the knowledge explosion, and a focus on 'new output' performances of students.

I have previously argued, following Smyth and Shacklock (1998) and Smyth et al

(2000) that the sum result implies the delivery of bureaucratically defined curricula by people low in the chain of command. In these circumstances teachers become disaffected from their labour and alienated from what is unsatisfying and meaningless work devoid of opportunities for creative self-expression. What is more it leaves little room for personal agency, for curriculum 'voice', or for engagement in *praxis*, the life-blood of contributory, collective, social well-being. The condition is said to leave teachers bewildered and demoralised as they cope with conflicts, contradictions, and crises in schools, becoming de-skilled and de-professionalised in the process (Huberman, 1993). Stronach et al (2002) sound a little less pessimistic. Observing disorder in the struggle and contest that is the contemporary site of teachers' professional identities, they focus on:

> A crisis of non-identity, frequently expressed as an uncertainty and uneasiness about identity, role boundaries and client relationships (which depict) dynamic and ambivalent aspects of situated performance (and teachers engaged in) mobilizing a complex of occasional identifications in response to shifting contexts (p. 117).

Or, perhaps, expressing the right to sell their labour in other circumstances, leaving the profession in droves or not entering it in the first place. Or participating in National Union of Teachers ballots to disengage from setting Standard Attainment Tests for 7, 11 and 14 year olds. Or continuing to be locked in and disgruntled by newly imposed punitive exit rules applied through the teachers pension scheme, which now exerts a five per cent *reduction* in pension for each year of premature retirement.

These consequence of the present condition have coincided with movements among curriculum policy makers and reformers as far afield as Hong Kong (HKEC, 1999), Australia (NSWDET, 1998), Namibia (MEC, 1993), and England (TTA, 1999) at least in the rhetoric of school based curriculum development, teacher self-actualisation, and teaching as a research-based profession. But around that rhetoric the impact of globalisation continues, while behind the rhetoric there is a need to understand what self-education means for teachers. My own re-conceptualisation of the teacher as organic intellectual educator was a move towards that (Tickle, 1991). But to achieve it we would need to ensure that several central elements, or counter-conditions, are present in relation to our work and lives, including:

- an open discourse and development of understanding about the purposes of education;
- a desire to educate teachers as an intellectual resource and social force;
- the will to define and appreciate the profession according to educational criteria.

Each of these presumes that we want as teachers to make a difference to the course of events in society through the medium of education, making a difference for ourselves and our students. That presumption is not at all clear in the world at large, since those elements appear to have been lost in the face of the contemporary adverse conditions. But I believe they are worth striving for. However, that striving will depend on us satisfying the need to understand our relationship with learning and with the processes of professional self-education.

On the face of it, then, the condition of globalisation conspires against processes of teacher *education* and professional dignity, leaving teachers with crises in schools and little space to develop in person (Lipka and Brinthoupt, 1999). Yet as Elliott (1998) points out in sentiments reminiscent of Giddens' reflexive citizenry, it also presents opportunities to respond with imagination. Here I want to propose that the imagination can be found in pre-modern cultural traditions. I will draw upon Clarke's (1997) notion of 'ancientwisdoms that can be adapted and applied to the present condition'. This is a search for a contemporary, constructive response to the effects of globalisation upon teachers, to be found in issues of self-identity, individual action, and communal well being in ancient scriptures. Indeed thanks to Clarke's study of hermeneutic encounters between Asian and Western thought, I want to celebrate and enjoy the possibility of a neat irony. It is that in the face of globalisation's immediate and recent impact on teachers and students in schools, the constructive response can be found in an equally global but long-standing interaction between ideas of educational interest and importance.

Teachers as Self-actualising Individuals

This is difficult mission to imagine in the current contexts of bureaucratisation, enforced curricula, accountability, quality audits, inspections, performance pay, and that violence which is being done to the individual identities of teachers and pupils alike. Bryant and Jary (2001, p. 126) measure the mission thus:

> Maybe Giddens is at times ... too sanguine on the potential for individual agency and people power and too inattentive to the structural constraints of modern global capital.

But it has to be imagined to realise a radical transformation of teachers' work. The human failings of mistrust; simplistic views of teaching; and the surrender to technical performance criteria would be the first targets for those who commend the possibility of finding a counterpoint position. In these terms, the current curricula characteristics are anti-educational and require action in the promotion of alternatives. At the core of that action is the aim to maintain an intrinsic interest in learning and in lifelong development of the self among those who are the professional educators, towards, as Maslow put it:

> learning to be and become a human being, and a particular human being. It is the learning that accompanies the profound personal experiences in our lives ... the unique instances, not the results of drill and repetition ... (educational) moments ... very poignant combinations of the emotional and the cognitive which leave insights that remain forever. In such experiences we discover who we are, what we are, and what we might become (Maslow, 1973, p. 159).

Thus he argued:

If teachers are going to be able to open their pupils to peak experiences, they must first learn to recognise them and to nurture them in their own lives (ibid, p. 163).

The sense of it can be gained from Rogers (1983, p. 145) description of some of the characteristics of the self-actualised person:

- Not necessarily adjusted to his culture;
- Not a conformist;
- Not necessarily happy with his situation;

But:

- At any time in any culture living constructively;
- Continuing to be him/ herself;
- Creatively adapting and surviving under changing conditions;

Radically, this brings the possibility of new and positive meaning to words like disillusioned, disaffected, uncooperative, subversive. Such characteristics might result from reactions to unacceptable conditions and lead to the independent career-long learning that some of us continue to crave on behalf of our profession (Smyth et al, 2000, Stronach et al, 2002, Tickle, 2000, Woods, 2002). The assumption is that the self-actualisation of teachers is essential for the well being of the education service and the future of an educated society. For example, in the Hong Kong Education Commission's (1999) *Blueprint for Education in the 21st Century* self-actualisation is a key concept. The Learning Age, a slogan used by UK policy makers, includes the desire for a citizenry equipped with the capacity for life-long and life-wide self-education, producing adaptable, flexible, versatile, courageous, imaginative, problem-solving citizen-learners (Woods ibid).

Of course, these particular characteristics are neither universal nor fixed in time. As Bruner (1985) said, decisions have to be made at a personal and local level as well as nationally and internationally about 'what a learner should be in order to assure that a society of a particularly valued kind could be safeguarded.' He pointed out that those decisions are made according to value judgements about how the mind should be cultivated and to what end. But his argument is that whatever those decisions are, they must apply first and foremost to educators themselves, in order that they can in turn be manifested towards and transmitted to students. They should not simply be applied to, but generated by, teachers. And it seems that certain qualities of mind appeal to the concept of the self-actualising teacher. For example, for Woods' (2002, p. 74) such teachers would enjoy the magic, thrill, excitement, enthusiasm, joy, and accomplishment of their work. They will also be charismatic, self-confident, independent, inventive / creative, innovative / ingenious. They will have ownership and control of their circumstances and decisions; engage in work that is relevant and meaningful in educational terms; and be capable of orchestrating role conflict and dilemma resolution (Woods, 2002, pp. 75–77). In short, they will engage in *praxis*.

The Teacher's Self

These (or whatever is valued, in Bruner's sense) can be viewed as individual 'self-characteristics', what it is that is to be actualised by the person who is fulfilling the role of the teacher. But there is a common imprint in ideas about an *educational self* that is concerned with the growth of the capacity to learn continuously, as an essential element in the deployment of personal responsibility (Gadamer, 2001, Cleary and Hogan, 2001). The common imprint is one that includes self-motivation, self-confidence and self-learning developed, to use Gadamer's term, in conversation with others and with one's circumstances. The place of a conscious reflexive self working in a dialectical relationship (conversation) with others, with events, and with the environment is a central component of Taoist, Ch'an Buddhist, and neo-Confucian traditions. In this view, the content of consciousness is experience, the sum of information that enters the mind and is interpreted by it (though the self may not be aware of the process in the normal sense of being aware, or being self-conscious, equivalent to intuitive action and tacit knowledge). Constantly aspiring to move oneself forward constitutes a process by which the self is built and rebuilt through interaction with others and through a reflexive capacity applied to the self. This is the theoretical basis of Symbolic Interactionism (Cooley, 1902, Mead, 1934) which sought to understand the process of social / self construction. It is the reflexive self that renders us capable of interpreting, judging, analysing and evaluating circumstances, the expectations which others ascribe to us, and the meanings which we place on our experiences of the world, i.e. our own perceptions, interpretations, conceptions, knowledge, actions, beliefs, values.

It thus provides a mechanism of self-interaction, a capacity to address, respond to, and re-address our values, beliefs and perspectives. It gives us the capacity to plan and organize action *with regard to ourselves* as well as towards our circumstances as we perceive them. Through this process it is possible to engage with experience in ways which involve self-consciously forming and guiding conduct, or guiding and forming the values and beliefs that lie behind that conduct towards ourselves, others, and situations. Action in this perspective is constructed through reflexive capability, as distinct from some behaviour which might be driven by instinct, or by instantaneous and overriding powers of emotion, or by indoctrination, or coercian, or prescriptions of what we should do and what we should be imposed by powerful others. It is thoughtful, ethical, participative and intelligent action. McLean (1999, p. 58) articulates the case in relation to schoolteachers like this:

> Images of self-as-person and self-as-teacher are critical to the process of becoming a teacher because they constitute the personal context in which new information will be interpreted, and are the stuff of which a teaching persona is created ...

The worth of different kinds of self-image in helping to author personal and professional development becomes a crucial factor in this process, as McLean points out, arguing that some images do not help teachers imagine themselves coping with ambiguities, or negotiating conflicting demands, or managing dilemmas (McLean, 1999, p. 58). Or in some cases perhaps they do not see themselves as managing events and experiences that contribute to the creative re-construction of themselves. Yet:

> experienced people are those who have learned from events in their lives and have learned because they were aware of their fallibility. That is, they have learned because they were open to the possible refutation of their beliefs and prejudices and could therefore revise or supplement them in a productive way (Warnke, 1987, p. 157).

The orientation offered by Taoist, Buddhist and neo-Confucian concepts of the self and of knowing invite us to look closely at what Eisner (1979) called ineffable knowledge and experience. Against the odds of rational positivism's grip on Western educational research and on curriculum policy, teacher performance and pupil assessment, such radical and dissenting voices continue to be heard. Dadds (1996) has raised the tone of passionate teaching. Hargreaves (2002) has mapped the emotional geographies of it. Neufeld and Kompf (2002) want the seductiveness of a rational science of teaching to be overthrown by theories of professional knowledge which directly confront 'the body's passions, not to mention those passions' relationship to the teaching and learning process.' The experimental project of a science of teaching cannot be fulfilled, they say, because it is doomed by its 'desire to somehow grasp and control the flux of experience' (ibid, p. 52). Here there is an internal paradox: the challenge is to overcome the self in order to cultivate one's true self, and ensure that the essentialist outer world of supposedly objective knowledge and existentialist inner extreme are both confronted. That can only be achieved, they argue, through one's own striving, in ways that renounce the outer circumstances that impede development and by cleaning house through the 'exhumation' of personal bias.

A Response to Globalisation

If Gramsci *was* correct in ascribing teachers to the dead weight of tradition and the ossification of knowledge, this concept of the passionate self-educating teacher would indeed create a culture shock for the profession. If he was *not*, the shock waves should be felt from below by those who seek to control the minds of teachers. In short, to return to Holstun (2000), politics should be something done by teachers from within their classrooms , rather than something done to them from without. Gramsci's challenge raises the question: do we have a profession made up of organic intellectual educators, or must we create one for the well being of society? A further question is: can, and if so where can, the individual imagination play a significant part in re-creating that external world, as well as one's own internal world?

I want to make a further visit to the ideas of Anthony Giddens (1991) and the work of J.J. Clarke (1997) in order to find some answers to those questions. Anthony Giddens's work is a gem in the current array of ideas. His self-reflexive citizen, though subject to 'disembedding and disempowering forces that threaten the self' also has 'equally strong tendencies to re-embedding and re-empowerment' so that s/he can 'shape and redirect personal and social events' (Bryant and Jary, 2001, p. 116). Rather than the alienated, repressed, fragmented, or spoilt identities that post-modernists report, Giddens's late moderns are potentially at least part of a new response to the impact of both local and global inequalities and obstacles to progress (ibid, p. 121).

One example of this response is Hutton's (1999) analysis of ways in which self-awareness means that people no longer simply accept their condition and their circumstances. Hutton cites 'the mushrooming of black and grey economies as evidence of such trends. Neither Giddens nor Hutton overlook the evidence that suggests some forces of globalisation continue to outrun the powers of new responses, or that shows events are patchy; but they offer hope of social participation in processes of transformation. And their analyses alert us to the need to bear in mind the characteristics of an environment where that is possible – characteristics in which uncertainty and risk are endemic, and change is inevitable. What appeals here is the idea that the intellectual economy – the accumulation of intellectual wealth and well being among professional educators – might need to be based on a mushrooming of a black and grey knowledge economy. This idea is so nicely disrespectful of the dominant agenda of school effectiveness regimes, prescribed curricula, and normative testing, and so potentially subversive of the official currency, that I shall follow the idea up on some other occasion, elsewhere.

For the moment I want to hold on to the idea of praxis: educational engagement is the practical pursuit of what is good, bonding the discernment of right ends with deliberation about the right means of bringing them about (Carr and Kemmis, 1986, Elliott, 1991). That is, learning is not just about understanding why the world is as it seems but also about the space in which we envisage how it could be different and carrying out actions to make it so. In this vein Wang Yang-ming's (1472–1529) co-existing worlds of objective study and intuitive knowledge are reconciled in his unity of knowledge and practice, in which to know and not to act is the same as not knowing. Wang regarded separation of the two as leading to the undesirable consequence of theory being unrelated to practice and of people knowing what should be done but failing to act. This concept of praxis is said to have had widespread influence in reform movements in China up until the present time, one example of which was Mao Tse-tung's contention (in *On Practice*) that theory and practice must go together to both acquire knowledge and to change reality (Chai and Chai, 1973, p. 155).

From a different countenance Buddhist tradition also reminds us that we constantly experience a changing self, as well as facing the inevitability of changing circumstances. This has the implication that individuals must learn to live with psychological as well as social change, for that is the nature of a reality:

> Reflection on the simple fundamental facts of our experience brings immediate recognition of constant change. ... the characteristic thing about phenomena is their dynamism. ... everything is indeed in a state of transformation. In each moment the future becomes present and the present past (Wilhelm, 1960, p. 18).

Here the accent is on keeping within the flow of change. Influence is achieved through a knowledge of the laws of change, which enable actions to be introduced into its flow rather than against it, and by recognising the moment for intervening. Ch'an Buddhism also emphasises wisdom and the ability to handle critical situations in practical application, with both mind and external environment in constant activity (Chai and Chai, 1973, p. 115). In keeping with the Chinese love of paradox, the one thing that is unchanging is change itself and mental activity is in union with mental stillness:

> In this point of view, which accords the responsible person an influence on the course of things, change ceases to be an insidious, intangible snare and becomes an organic order corresponding to man's nature (Wilhelm, 1970, p. 22).

The questions then are about where the sources of change are located, and who or what controls the process of change. This is the imponderable: whether and to what extent teachers can operate in a managed environment or as environmental managers. Clarke (1997, p. 214) takes up the discussion about different concepts of self and self-development and the notion of the 'radical impermanence' that Buddhism teaches, by placing *becoming* above being.

In summarising the consequent emphasis on transience and the value of the seemingly insignificant, on 'emptying out' as a path to wisdom rather than constructing and confirming identity, Clarke is keen to point out that this does not deny the existence of a conscious self, but it changes our view of it. It is a view that allows for, even encourages, de-construction and radical reflexiveness. It appears as a personal, releasing, form of *becoming*. Giddens it seems, like the neo-Confucian Wang Yang-ming, prefers the idea of life-politics rather than emancipatory politics (Bryant and Jary, 2001, p. 116) but my intuition is that they go hand in hand.

The central tenet of Ch'an teaching and the reflexivity crucial to Wang's neo-Confucian principles and practices has questioning of social issues and the transformation of personal perceptions as both purposeful and nicely disrespectful. As Wang put it:

> If words are examined in the mind and found to be wrong, although they have come from the mouth of Confucius, I dare not accept them as correct. How much less those from people inferior to Confucius! If words are examined in the mind and found to be correct, although they have come from the mouth of ordinary people, I dare not regard them as wrong. How much less those of Confucius! (cited in De Bary, 1970, p. 155).

With regard to school teachers in modern times, Stronach *et al* (2002, p. 30) round up as many optimistic indicators as we can muster (as) the only hope of a politics that is *for* professionalism as well as about professionalism'. Their ground for optimism lies partly in what they see as an irresolvable, imminent and necessary conflict between workers required to perform within externally imposed conditions to meet prescribed targets, and educators entrusted to live with risk and creativity in pursuit of educational excellence. This gives us the task of creating new identities, of 're-storying' our selves in and against the school effectiveness culture, centralised national curricula, and the globalising tendencies of the present time. They argue that if that culture does not self-destruct because it is so evidently anti-educational, then it is certainly 'easily mocked' and 'vulnerable' (p. 131). The task of exploiting that vulnerability will require us to follow Gadamer's (2001) demand that we take responsibility for building the capacity to self-educate. Gadamer, too, found inspiration in ideas emanating from south and east Asia (Magee, 1997) that offered hope of a constructive, global response to the present threats of a different kind of globalising tendency.

References

Bary, W.T. de (ed), (1970), *Self and Society in Ming Thought*, Columbia University Press, New York.

Becker, C. (1996), 'The Artist as Public Intellectual', in H.A. Giroux and P. Shannon (eds), *Education and Cultural Studies*, Routledge, London.

Berlak, A. and Berlak, H. (1981), *Dilemmas of Schooling*, Methuen, London.

Bernstein, B. (1996), *Pedagogy, Symbolic Control and Identity: research, theory, critique,* Taylor and Francis, London.

Britzman, D.P. (1991), *Practice makes perfect: a critical study of learning to teach*, State University of New York Press, Albany.

Bruner, J. (1977), *The Process of Education*, Harvard University Press, Cambridge, Massachusetts.

Bruner, J. (1985), 'Models of the learner', *Educational Researcher*, June/July, pp. 5–8.

Bryant, G.A. and Jary, D. (2001), *The Contemporary Giddens: Social theory in a Globalizing Age*, Palgrave, London.

Carr, W. and Kemmis, S. (1986), *Becoming Critical: Knowing Through Action Research*, Falmer Press, Lewes.

Chai, C. and Chai, W. (1973), *Confucianism.* Woodbury, Barrons Educational Series, New York.

Clarke, J.J. (1998), *Oriental Enlightenment*, Routledge, London.

Cleary, J. and Hogan, P. (2001), 'The Reciprocal Character of Self-Education: Introductory Comments on Hans-Georg Gadamer's address Education is Self-Education', *Journal of Philosophy of Education*, vol. 35(4), pp. 519–527.

Cooley, C. (1902), *Human Nature and the Social Order, 1983 edition*, Transaction Books, New Brunswick, New Jersey.

Dadds, M. (1995), *Passionate Enquiry and School Development*, Falmer, London.

Delors, J. (1996), 'Learning the Treasures Within: Report to UNESCO of the International Commission on Education for the Twenty First Century', UNESCO, Paris.

Eisner, E. (1979), *The Educational Imagination*, Macmillan, London.

Elliott, J. (1991), *Action Research for Educational Change*, Open University Press, Milton Keynes.

Elliott, J. (1998), *The Curriculum Experiment*, Open University Press, Buckingham.

Freire, P. (1970), *Pedagogy of the Oppressed*, Penguin, Harmondsworth.

Freire, P. (1972), *Cultural Action for Freedom*, Penguin, Harmondsworth.

Fullan, M. (1993), *Change Forces: Probing the Depths of Educational Reform*, Falmer Press, London.

Fullan, M. (1999), *Change Forces: the sequel*, Falmer Press, London.

Gadamer, H.G. (2001), 'Education is Self-Education', *Journal of Philosophy of Education*, vol. 35(4), pp. 529–538.

Gethin, R. (1998), *The Foundations of Buddhism*, Oxford University Press, Oxford.

Giddens, A. (1991), *Modernity and Self-Identity*, Polity Press, Cambridge.

Goodson, I. (1982), *School Subject and Curriculum Change*, London, Croom Helm.

Hargreaves, A. (2002), 'Teaching in a box: emotional geographies of teaching', in C. Sugrue and C. Day (eds), *Developing Teachers and Teaching Practice*, Falmer Press, London.

Hollingsworth, S. (ed) (1997), *International Action Research: A Casebook for Educational Reform*, Falmer, London.

Holstun, Y. (2000), *Ehuds Dagger: Class Struggle in the English Revolution*, London, Verso.

Hong Kong Education Commission (HKEC) (1999a), 'Education Blueprint for the 21st Century', Education Commission of the Hong Kong S.A.R, Hong Kong.

Huberman, M. (1993), *The Lives of Teaches*, Cassell, London.

Hutton, W. (1999), 'Up, Up and A Way', *The Observer*, 21st November.

Lacey, C. (1977) ,*The Socialisation of Teachers*, Methuen, London.

Lipka, R.P. and Brinthaupt, T.M. (eds) (1999), *The Role of Self in Teacher Development*, State University of New York Press, Albany.

Lipka, R.P. and Brinthaupt, T.M. (1999), 'Balancing the personal and professional development of teachers', in R.P. Lipka and T.M.Brinthaupt (eds), *The Role of Self in Teacher Development*, State University of New York Press, Albany.

Lortie, D. (1975), *Schoolteacher*, University of Chicago Press, Chicago.

Magee, B. (1997), *Confessions of a Philosopher*, Phoenix, London.

Maslow A.H. (1943), 'A theory of human motivation', *Psychological Review* vol. 50, pp. 370–396.

Maslow, A.H. (1954), *Motivation and Personality*, Harper and Row, New York.

Maslow A.H. (1973), 'What is a Taoistic Teacher?', in L.J. Rubin (ed), 1973, *Facts and Feelings in the Classroom*, Ward Lock, London.

McLean, S.V. (1999), 'Becoming a teacher: the person in the process', in R.P. Lipka and T.M. Brinthaupt (eds), *The Role of Self in Teacher Development*, State University of New York Press, Albany.

Mead, G.H. (1934), *Mind, Self and Society*, University of Chicago Press, Chicago.

Neufeld, J. and Kompf, M. (2002), 'Educational research and teacher development: from ivory tower to tower of Babel', in C. Sugrue and C. Day (eds), *Developing Teachers and Teaching Practice*, Falmer Press, London.

Pink Floyd (1983), *The Wall,* Channel 5, London.

Rogers, C. (1969), *Freedom to Learn*, Charles Merrill, Columbus.

Salter, B. and Tapper, T. (1981), *Education, Politics and the State*, Grant McIntyre, London.

Smyth, J. and Shacklock, G. (1998), *Re-Making Teaching*, Routledge, London.

Smyth, J. et al (2000), *Teachers' Work in a Globalizing Economy*, Falmer Press, London.

Spretnak, C. (1991), *States of Grace: The Recovery of Meaning in the Postmodern Age*, Harper Collins, San Francisco.

Stronach, I., Corbin, B., McNamara, O., Stark, S. and Warne, T. (2002), 'Towards an uncertain politics of professionalism: teacher and nurse identities in flux', *Journal of Education Policy*, vol. 17(1), pp. 109–138.

Teacher Training Agency (TTA) (1999), *Teaching As A Research Based Profession*, Teacher Training Agency, London.

Tickle, L. (1987a), *Learning Teaching, Teaching Teaching*, Falmer Press, Lewes.

Tickle, L. (1993), 'The Wish of Odysseus: new teachers receptiveness to mentoring', in D. McIntyre, H. Hagger and M. Wilkin (eds), *Mentoring*, Kogan Page, London.

Tickle, L. (1994), *The Induction of New Teachers: reflective professional practice*, Cassell,

London.

Tickle, L. (1999), 'Teacher Self-Appraisal and Appraisal of Self', in R.P. Lipka and T.M. Brinthaupt (eds), *The Role of Self in Teacher Development*, State University of New York Press, Albany.

Tickle, L. (2000), 'Teacher probation resurrected: England 1999–2000', *Journal of Education Policy*, vol. 15(6), pp. 701–713.

Tickle, L. (2001a), *Teacher Induction: The Way Ahead*, Open University Press, Buckingham.

Tickle, L. (2001b), 'Professional Qualities and Teacher Induction', *Journal of In-Service Education*, vol. 27(1), pp. 51–64.

Tickle, L. (2001c), 'The Organic Intellectual Educator', *Cambridge Journal of Education*, vol. 31(2), pp. 159–178.

Wallace, G. and Tickle, L. (1983), 'Middle Schools: the heart of schools in crisis', *British Journal of Sociology of Education*, vol. 4(3), pp. 223–240.

Warnke, G. (1987), *Gadamer: hermeneutics, tradition and reason*, Polity Press, Cambridge.

Wilhelm, H. (1960), *Change*, Princeton University Press, New Jersey.

Woods, P. (2002), 'Teaching and learning in the new millennium', in C. Sugrue and C. Day (eds), *Developing Teachers and Teaching Practice: International research perspectives*, Routledge/Falmer, London.

Zeichner, K.M. and Tabachnick, B.R. (1985), 'The development of teacher perspectives: social strategies and institutional control in the socialisation of beginning teachers'. *Journal of Education for Teaching*, vol. 11(1), pp. 1–25.

Chapter 12

Concluding Remarks

Cedric Cullingford

The history of globalisation has been one of technological change, mostly comparatively recent, and colonisation in one form or another, from Genghis Khan to the Scramble for Africa in the later nineteenth century. The idea of cultural and financial imperialism is not new but is often treated as if it were, forgetting the complex notions of difference and the isolation of communities, and ignoring the slowness of change.

One of the well trodden clichés of our time is the speed of change, usually invoked in order to cajole people into changing their skills or their lifestyles. Change is a concept used to batter people around the head, as if it could excuse the need for every new policy. That there are rapid changes in some matters, mostly technological, is not to be doubted but the assumptions of change in other matters, mostly cultural and personal, can also blind people to others' points of view. What changes in information on the internet does not necessarily make any deeper changes in the hearts and minds of the individuals who have access to it, let alone those who do not. It is an unchanging human phenomenon to assume threat what is disseminated is received, that what is taught is learned and that what is said is understood. An examination of the unending history of the world would soon dissipate such simplistic notions of change. The irony is that at a time of greater optimism, when there was genuine hope for the constantly improving future, the phrase that was often banded about was 'Plus ça change....' implying that all is essentially unaffected. In our age of anxiety, of fear, of a sense of risk, let alone the threat of climate change and terrorism, it is interesting to not how often the idea of change is embraced as an assumed good.

The awareness of the 'shock' of differences has to be tempered by the realisation both of continuities and of differences; the promotion of change has not only a distinctly political tone but is also a result of a narrow, peculiarly capitalistic western point of view. One only needs to revisit the 'eternal' Rome to experience a strong sense of continuity. In the place of notion of great and sudden historical change – suddenly there were barbarians, of all was plunged into dark ages – we see the constant adaptations of the existing order, the recycling of usable elements, so eloquently visible in all the ancient Roman columns that are a natural part of the later buildings. Cultures are rarely obliterated and the notion that they are is a comparatively recent one. In the past old buildings, temples of monasteries would have been plundered for their stone, in a type of recycling. Nowadays we would not dream of disturbing the past in such a way; it would be left intact, or restored. It would also need to be restored as a result of the more recent phenomenon of bombing and rebuilding with all the ironic respect for the obliterated respect for the past.

The visible parts of the past remind us both of unchanging values and the ways in which at deeper levels, cultures remain slow to adapt to instant new phenomena. This book includes a celebration of the complexities of culture, of the fact that beyond fashion there are values and attitudes embedded in the familiar; and that to everyone the familiar will be different. The chapters all look at the neglected human dimension of change, of immunity form external influences, on the quiet assertion of local and community rights. Even the most ancient technology of communication, language, has all kinds of pitfalls in understanding because of the local interpretation of the same words.

This book, taking the point of view of people rather than abstractions, challenges some of the assumptions associated with the international scene. It challenges some notions of domination, of 'McDonaldisation' as it is sometimes called, on to the domination of the market forces of the 'developed' world. But the chapters also crucially challenge some to the educational ideas within the systems of the west, with the notions of skills rather than self-awareness, with the idea of learning as a process of acquisition rather than a social phenomenon.

Perhaps the very term 'globalisation' is an odd one. The globe seems both so neat and so complete. The idea of 'planetisation' gives more of a sense of the compactness of the world in is larger context, and of the vulnerability in its isolation. All the parts of the planet, from the environment to the dignity of people depend on each other. Sometimes, as in the ignoring of international treaties, of the exploitation of cheap manual labour, it does not seem like this; yet this is the most famous and most apparent aspect of what is understood in planetisation.

Whatever the terms used there are large ideas that need to be understood more intimately and the cliché replaced by something better. Like 'sustainability' the overall notion can be misused on all kinds of way. What appears to be a given understanding can turn out to be a very parochial (if loud) point of view. Only when understandings are developed form the accumulation of individual' points of view will we really be able to achieve collective understanding. This makes 'culture' such a difficult term and this book adds to the riches of interpretation! Culture involves a whole host of understandings as places, from individuals to groups, form homes to neighbourhoods, form natural regions to conglomerates.

One of the problems that confront understanding is the very existence of one type of attempt to come to grips with complexity. Some of the insights are actually displaced by being problematised. Real issues are displaced by the formation of academic 'disciplines'. Cultural questions are divided into different and exclusive discourses. A great deal of damage has been done in the name of subject disciplines, where the control of the language, and the domination of the network has meant specialisms can be created in a way that demands exclusiveness and clear boundaries. Notions that need to be dealt with more openly can suffer in this intellectual narrowness; intense cleverness devoted to the isolation of understanding.

Taking real cases and hearing the voices of people help us to go beyond the narrow exclusiveness and help us question some of the policy assumptions. The promotion of the idea of change and the need for it is part of the hysteria that surrounds constant changes in policy as if legal agreements or mission statements themselves made a difference. What an examination of cultural planitisation does is to make people inspect their own systems and their own assumptions.

There are international movements that seem to suggest a more integrated world. The United Nations symbolises such hope. For some time after the Second World War it had a high reputation. Nowadays it is ignored and despised, not considered valuable by the great powers and seen to fail in the small ones, as in Rwanda. Such large bodies should suggest a kind of future; but such a vision has no present credibility. The same could be said in international monetary agreements; especially when one considers the actual state of Africa. On the other hand we have the small isolated communities like those still undiscovered, where unchanging ways of life continue.

Thus us the world constituted in cultures large and small, some so grandiose we hardly think of them as cultures, and others so obviously a style of living which is unique we forget their isolation.

This book should add to the richer part of the debate; of what it is actually like for individuals. It should also challenge some received notions and comfort us in the way in which people visiting other countries retain a sense of self, a desire for practicality and a respect for the kindness, the tolerance and the humour of the people they encounter.

Name Index

Subject Index